ghtseeing

English	French	Pronunciation
here is __?	Où est ___?	oo ay __
dge	le pont	luh poh^n
stle	le château	luh sha
hedral	la cathédrale	lah kat-dRahı
urch	l'église (f)	lay-gleez
rden	le jardin	luh zhahR-dæ^n
useum	le musée	luh mew^p-zay
lace	le palais	luh pah-lay
rk	le parc	luh pahRk
uare	la place	lah plahs
ket	le billet	luh bee-yay
r two	pour deux	pooR duh
urist info	l'office du	luh-fees dew^p too-Rees-muh
ffice	tourisme	
wn center	le centre ville	luh sah^n-tRuh veel

ays and Times

English	French	Pronunciation
onday	lundi	læ^n-dee
uesday	mardi	mahR-dee
ednesday	mercredi	mehR-kRuh-dee
ursday	jeudi	zhuh-dee
iday	vendredi	vah^n-dRuh-dee
turday	samedi	sahm-dee
nday	dimanche	dee-mah^{n}sh
inute	la minute	lah mee-new^{p}t
ur	l'heure (f)	luhR
ek	la semaine	lah suh-mehn
onth	le mois	luh mwah

odging

English	French	Pronunciation
hotel	un hôtel	æ^n (n)uh-tehl
&B	une chambre d'hôte	ew^n shah^n-bRuh doht
eservation	une réservation	ew^n Ray-zehR-vah-syoh^n
oom	une chambre	ew^n shah^n-bRuh
o you have ooms vailable?	Avez-vous des chambres libres?	ah-vay-voo day shah^n-bRuh lee-bRuh?
ow much is ?	C'est combien?	say koh^n-byæ^n?
double oom	une chambre à deux personnes	ew^n shah^n-bRuh ah duh pehR-suhn
ingle room	une chambre à une personne	ew^n shah^n-bRuh ah ew^n pehR-suhn
th shower	avec douche	ah-vehk doosh
th toilet	avec toilettes	ah-vehk twah-leht
r one night	pour une nuit	pooR ew^n nwee
r __ nights	pour _ nuits	pooR __ nwee
om ... to	de ... à	duh ... ah

English	French	Pronunciation
for __.		
Do you have?	Avez-vous_.	ʁay voo _?
Where is ___?	Où est ___?	oo ay ___?
Where are __?	Où sont __?	oo soh^n ___?
Do you accept credit cards?	Acceptez-vous des cartes de crédit?	ahk-sehp-tay voo day kahRt duh kRay-dee?
this (noun)	ceci	suh-see
that (noun)	cela	suh-lah
cash register	la caisse	lah kehs
That's all.	C'est tout.	say too
a receipt	un reçu	æ^n Ruh-sew^p
I'm just looking.	Je regarde seulement.	zhuh Ruh-gahRd suhl-mah^n
sale items	les soldes	lay suhld
open	ouvert	oo-vehR
closed	fermé	fehR-may
a tobacconist shop	un tabac	æ^n tah-bah
a bookstore	une librairie	ew^n lee-bReh-Ree
a market	un marché	æ^n mahR-shay
a supermarket	un supermarché	æ^n sew^p-pehR-mahR-shay
a department store	un grand magasin	æ^n grah^n mah-gah-zæ^n
a bakery	une boulangerie	ew^n boo-lah^n-zhRee
a pastry shop	une pâtisserie	ew^n pah-tees-Ree
a pharmacy	une pharmacie	ew^n fahR-mah-see
a perfume shop	une parfumerie	ew^n pahR-few^{p}m-Ree

Colors

English	French	Pronunciation
beige	beige	behzh
black	noir	nwahR
blue	bleu	bluh
brown	marron	mah-Roh^n
gray	gris	gRee
green	vert	vehR
pink	rose	Rohz
purple	violet	vyuh-leh
red	rouge	roozh
white	blanc	blah^n
yellow	jaune	zhohn
dark ___	___ foncé	___ foh^n-say
light ___	___ clair	___ klehR

French Survival Guide
The Language and Culture You Need to Travel with Confidence in France

Elizabeth Bingham, Ph.D.

World Prospect Press
Waverly, Iowa

Publisher's Note

This book is designed to help prepare travelers for their trips abroad. Its purpose is to educate and entertain. It is sold with the understanding that the publisher and author are not giving legal or financial advice. The author and World Prospect Press shall have neither liability nor responsibility to any person or entity with respect to any loss or damage caused, or alleged to be caused, directly or indirectly, by the information contained in this book.

If you do not wish to be bound by the above, you may return this book to the publisher for a full refund.

Copyright ©2014 by Elizabeth R. Bingham

World Prospect Press
P.O. Box 253
Waverly, IA 50677
www.worldprospect.com

First Edition
10 9 8 7 6 5 4 3 2 1

Publisher's Cataloging-in-Publication
(Provided by Quality Books, Inc.)

Bingham, Elizabeth.
    French survival guide : the language and culture you
need to travel with confidence in France / Elizabeth
Bingham, Ph. D. -- First edition.
    pages cm
    Text in English and French.
    Includes index.
    Includes French-English, English-French dictionaries.
    LCCN 2014938511
    ISBN 978-0-9703734-5-8

1. French language--Conversation and phrase books--
English. 2. France--Description and travel.
I. Title.

PC2121.B56 2014   448.3'421
                         QBI14-600073

Table of Contents

Acknowledgments

This book is the result of much research and numerous trips abroad. It was influenced by the experiences and observations of many others, to whom I owe a great debt. I would like to thank in particular my various travel companions, who put up with both my ignorances and my insistence that we do things the French way, when I knew what that was. So, many thanks to Elaina Toenjes, Bruce Toenjes, Jay Toenjes, and Rachel Toenjes Zander, to Emily Bingham, and to Micki Reints. They greatly enlivened and enhanced my trips to France.

Special thanks to Linda Bingham, for exploring Canadian-French culture with me, to David Zelle for sharing his insights as a visitor to France, and to blues guitarist Craig Erickson, for reminding me what writers do and spurring me to finish this project—although he is certainly not aware of it!

I gratefully remember my dear grandmother, Beverly Moffitt, for accompanying me on my first trip to France, when we bumbled our way through many meals and some public transportation hiccups, but had a fabulous time regardless.

I am deeply indebted to Jeanine Black and Elizabeth Zwanziger, Ph.D., for their superb editing and proofreading skills. This book benefited immeasurably from their deep cultural and linguistic knowledge and their sometimes sharp pens. Any errors, inaccuracies, or flabby sentences that remain are entirely my own responsibility.

As always, I owe deep thanks to my husband, who makes all my travel, writing, and publishing possible. I am especially grateful for his technical help, without which this book would probably be in longhand. My hero!

About the Author

Elizabeth Bingham loves to travel and loves to teach. She combines these passions in her *Survival Guide* series, in which she prepares travelers for the language and culture they will experience abroad.

As an avid traveler, Dr. Bingham knows how useful even a little cultural knowledge and language ability are. She, too, has been in an unfamiliar country, bewildered by the foreign culture and unable to communicate. Her *Survival Guides* grew out of her desire to help others avoid that situation, to help them know what to expect, what to do, and what to say when they visit a different country. She has found that even minimal preparation can make a world of difference in the enjoyment and rewards of a trip abroad.

Bingham has a Ph.D. in Applied Linguistics/Foreign Language Education from the University of Texas at Austin. She has taught writing and German at the university level. In addition to extensive European travel, she has lived in Germany and Austria, teaching English and conducting research there. Since 1999, she has lived in northeast Iowa, promoting foreign language and culture through teaching and writing.

Dr. Bingham can be reached through World Prospect Press by e-mail at bingham@worldprospect.com or at P.O. Box 253, Waverly, IA 50677.

Introduction

Have you ever traveled in a country where you don't know the language? Maybe you're a little afraid of what might happen if you do. Will you get hopelessly lost? Will you not have a clue how to book a room, buy a ticket, or read a schedule? Will you order something horrible to eat because you don't know any better? And perhaps the biggest fear of all, will you make an absolute fool of yourself because you don't know any of the local customs? This is a pretty grim scenario. Almost enough to keep a would-be traveler at home. But it doesn't have to be that way!

There is a world of difference between being in a foreign country knowing nothing of the language and being in the country knowing a little of it. The first experience is confusing, frustrating, and frequently misleading. (I write as one who accidently ordered two lunches for myself at the same time during my first visit to Italy, when I could not communicate beyond *yes, no, hello,* and *excuse me.*)

The second experience, with just a little knowledge of the language, brims with understanding and communication by comparison. Instead of skittering along the surface of a foreign culture, you are able to dip into it, understand some of it, and participate in it. Traveling becomes a rich, heady adventure. You don't just look at museums and visit churches; you participate in the day-to-day culture of a country and its people.

Surprisingly, you don't have to devote months of time and effort to reap the benefits of a foreign language. At the start, you get enormous returns for your efforts. Every little bit helps, no matter how advanced you are, but the gains are even greater at the beginning. Going from zero language knowledge to a little bit is a giant leap in ability.

You may think you don't need to know anything about a foreign language to travel in Europe, because everyone speaks English. I hate to disillusion you, but that's not exactly true. Yes, most young people now study English, and yes, people involved in tourism usually speak at least some English, but many, many people are uncomfortable with English or simply don't know it at all. This is particularly true off the beaten path, in areas that aren't inundated with tourists, and with middle-aged and older people. Granted, you *can* get by with English and gestures, but that approach can be very frustrating. Plus, with such a language handicap, you'll learn about and experience a lot less of the country.

It may be especially tempting not to bother learning a new language if you will be with a guided tour group. Don't be lulled into overlooking *some* language preparation! People respond so warmly to attempts to use their language. Besides, common courtesy dictates that you should at least be able to say things like "Excuse me" and "Thank you" in a way that people in your host country will understand.

Learning a foreign language really involves learning a foreign culture, too. What good does it do to know the right words and phrases if you don't know the right time to use them? This *Survival Guide*, like any other good introduction to a foreign language, includes pertinent cultural information. Knowing about culture is important for linguistic reasons, but also so you can fit in better, avoid offending people, and appreciate what the locals are doing. Knowing some of the culture *and* some of the language allows you to communicate more completely and have a deeper, more satisfying experience in a foreign country. And even better, the cultural information is painless to learn. As social creatures, we like to learn about how people are like and different from ourselves.

Ideally, we would all learn a foreign language and culture before traveling abroad. You may even have bought audio language lessons or thought about enrolling in a course with that noble purpose in mind. Realistically, though, most of us already lead full lives, and making time for language study is not a top priority. What usually happens is that time quickly runs out, and suddenly it's a mere week before departure (or maybe we're even on the flight overseas!) before we get serious about tackling the language of the country we are about to visit. That's the reality this *Survival Guide* is designed to meet. It provides the most important language and cultural information to people with limited time to learn it.

You will learn the basics here: travel vocabulary, very basic grammar, everyday cultural information. All you need to add later is a small dictionary or phrasebook (for extra vocabulary) and at least one sightseeing guide, and you're good to go. Armed with these resources and a little training beforehand, your visit is sure to be a success. You can be a confident, savvy foreign traveler, communicating with the locals, participating in daily life, and experiencing the culture firsthand.

Please, let me know how both your studies and your trip turn out. I would like to know what worked for you and how I can make this book better for others. You can reach me care of World Prospect Press, P.O. Box 253, Waverly, IA 50677 or via email at bingham@worldprospect.com.

I wish you good luck, successful studies, and happy travels!

Elizabeth

Disclaimer

French language and French culture can vary greatly from place to place and among different people in the same place. Regional, generational, and socioeconomic variations remain strong to this day. While the language and culture tips offered in this book represent common usage and practices, they do not cover all the variation of speech and customs one may experience in France. Rest assured that you can communicate with others using the material you learn from this book, even though people may pronounce words differently, have entirely different words for things, or have different local customs. All French speakers can understand "standard" French, even if that's not what they speak themselves, and you should not offend anyone if you follow the customs discussed in these pages.

1   Greetings and Introductions

Bienvenue!

Welcome to *French Survival Guide*, the down-to-earth, bare-bones introduction to French that aims to make your trip abroad as smooth and enjoyable as possible with minimal preparation. In a perfect world, all travelers would have time to take a few courses in the language of the country they are going to visit. Unfortunately, that's a reality for very few of us. Time is precious, and most language courses are long, because—let's face it—languages are complicated. That's where this *Survival Guide* comes in. It's an information-packed mini-course that concentrates on preparing you to travel in France or other French-speaking countries in the shortest time possible. How does *French Survival Guide* accomplish this?

- It cuts out unnecessary vocabulary and grammar, focusing on what is most useful to you as a traveler.
- It includes important aspects of culture that you may encounter.
- It gives you lots of opportunity to practice with built-in exercises.
- It provides study tips, so you can use your preparation time most efficiently.
- It tells you what you can safely skip, if you are short on time.

This *Survival Guide* won't make you fluent in French. It's not magic. But it will help you communicate in the French language and culture. It will prepare you for what to expect as a traveler and how to deal with it, what to say and when to say it. As with any other skill, learning a foreign language does require some effort, and you get out of it what you put into it. That doesn't need to scare you off, though. Realistically, most travelers don't need to know that much of a foreign language to benefit from it. So, do what you can and enjoy your growing ability to communicate in French!

Absolute bare-bones French

Even if you acquire nothing else in French, do learn to say the following phrases. You will communicate on a very basic level and will earn good will for using some of the local language.

yes	oui	*wee*
no	non	*noh*[n]
please	s'il vous plaît	*see voo play*
thank you	merci	*mehR-see*
excuse me	excusez-moi	*ehks-kew*[p]*-zay mwah*

Study tip: Practice speaking the language as much as you can. Read aloud as you go through vocabulary lists and work on written exercises. Every bit of practice helps. When you have completed a lesson, go through it again, practicing how to say things. Try to imagine yourself in the situations described and see what you can remember to say. Try to find someone to practice *with*.

Study tip: What can you cut if you are pressed for time? The exercises, grammar tips, and any vocabulary sections that you know you won't need (such as renting a car). At the very least learn greetings, manners, and some numbers, along with the simple but very useful words listed above. The culture notes are interesting and worth reading, even if you are short on time.

Culture note—Paris versus the country

Although Paris sits in the north-central part of France, it is the undisputed center of the country—culturally, politically, economically. Around one-fifth of the country's population lives in and around the capital, including an even higher percentage of young adults. French cities in general claim about three-quarters of the country's population. That leaves the countryside sparsely populated and comparatively elderly.

While each of the many regions of France has its distinct personality, in general the pace of country life is slower and the people may be more relaxed and openly friendly than in the city.

Importance of pronunciation: While you can let a lot of grammar slide and still communicate perfectly well, you need a reasonably close pronunciation of words or people won't know what you are trying to say. A reasonable goal at this level is to be understandable, not to sound like a native speaker. Because French is notoriously difficult for beginners to pronounce (and I include myself in this group), I recommend that you look over the pronunciation guide below before continuing to the first vocabulary section. Once you become familiar with how the sounds of French match up with the spellings, you will at least have a fighting chance of pronouncing written words.

Pronunciation guide

The pronunciation guide below is just that—a guide—and is not intended to cover all possible pronunciations of letters or letter combinations. It provides somewhat simplified, close approximations of the sounds of French. The explanations below should enable you to pronounce the words in this book well enough to be understood and to take a good stab at new words you encounter in French.

Read the following tables across like this: "The French letters *a, à,* and *â* are pronounced like the English sound in *father* and can be found in the words *ça* and *pâté*." American English pronunciation is used in the English examples. Try not to move your lips and tongue much when you make the vowel sounds. French vowels are "purer" than American ones. That is, vowels in French don't start with one sound and end with another, as American vowels (dipthongs) often do. (For example, "I" starts with an "ah" sound and ends in an "ee" sound.)

Vowels

French	English	Example
a, à, â	ah (f<u>a</u>ther)	ç<u>a</u> [*sah*], p<u>â</u>té [*pah-tay*]
é, -er[1], -ez[1], -et[1]	ay (l<u>a</u>te)	ét<u>é</u> [*ay-tay*], parl<u>ez</u> [*pahR-lay*]

---

[1] at the end of a word

è, ê, e	eh (l<u>e</u>t)	s<u>e</u>pt [*seht*], être [*eh-tRuh*]
eu, œu, e[2]	uh (th<u>e</u>)	p<u>eu</u> [*puh*], <u>œu</u>f [*uhf*], j<u>e</u> [*zhuh*]
e[3]	ay (d<u>ay</u>)	l<u>es</u> [*lay*], d<u>es</u> [*day*], c'<u>es</u>t [*say*]
i, î, y	ee (b<u>ee</u>)	<u>î</u>le [*eel*], qu<u>i</u> [*kee*], f<u>i</u>lle [*feey*]
o, ô, au, eau	oh (t<u>o</u>ne)	<u>au</u> [*oh*], h<u>ô</u>tel [*oh-tehl*], b<u>eau</u> [*boh*]
o[4]	uh (d<u>uh</u>)	<u>o</u>range [*uh-Rah^nzh*], <u>o</u>bjet [*uhb-zhay*], car<u>o</u>tte [*kah-Ruht*]
ou, où, oû	oo (t<u>oo</u>th)	<u>où</u> [*oo*], n<u>ou</u>veau [*noo-voh*]
oy, oi	wah (w<u>a</u>tch)	v<u>oy</u>age [*vwah-yahzh*], m<u>oi</u> [*mwah*]
u, û	ew° (d<u>ew</u>)[5]	<u>u</u>ne [*ew°n*], br<u>û</u>lé [*bRew°-lay*]

Semiconsonants

The following combinations of letters produce sounds that are similar to the sounds of the letters *y* and *w* in English.

i + ll *or* vowel + il	y (<u>y</u>et)	f<u>i</u>lle [*feey*], sol<u>ei</u>l [*suh-lay*]
u + i *or* ou + i	wee (bet<u>wee</u>n)	s<u>ui</u>s [*swee*], h<u>ui</u>t [*weet*] <u>oui</u> [*wee*], L<u>oui</u>s [*lwee*]

New sounds

Some French sounds are not found in English, so we can't just look at English examples to figure out how to say them.

<u>French</u>	<u>Pronunciation</u>	<u>Examples</u>
u or û	ew° (dew)[5]	<u>u</u>ne [*ew°n*], br<u>û</u>lé [*bRew°-lay*]
r	R	<u>r</u>ue [*Rew°*], <u>r</u>ouge [*Roozh*], s<u>û</u>r [*sew°R*]

To produce the *ew°* sound, say "ee," as in t<u>ee</u>th, hold the sound steady and round your lips. Do you hear the sound change? Now say "ee" a few times with your lips rounded from the start. It's similar to the sound in the English word *dew*. I add a raised little ° in the pronunciation to remind you to round your lips.

---

[2] sometimes

[3] sometimes, especially when followed by *s*

[4] when the syllable ends in a consonant sound

[5] round your lips

Because the French R is so different from the English *r*, its production must be explained. First, forget your flat, broad American *r*. You will not need it in French. The French R is produced at the back of the mouth, a little farther back than where you make the *k* sound. Just pull your tongue a little away from the back of your mouth so air can get through. If you try this, you should get a raspy, gargly sound. If you can gargle, you can pronounce the French R. In reality, the R almost always gets glossed over and smoothed out some, but it's still not an American *r*.

If you can't make the French *r*, at least substitute a softer, British-like *r* (think *muth-uh* for "mother"). The American *r* is probably the loudest, most obvious marker of an American accent, and it doesn't sound the least bit natural in other languages, so do try to back off when you say an *r* in French. To remind you to make your *r* differently than in English, the pronunciation symbol in this book is a small capital R.

Nasal vowels—When a vowel (a, e, i, o, or u) is followed by a single *n* or *m* in the same syllable, the vowel sound needs to come through the mouth *and* the nose. This nasalized sound is indicated in this book by a raised ^{n} after the vowel. Whenever you see this symbol, think of directing the vowel right before it up through your nose. You will not pronounce the *n* itself, as we would in English. Don't worry about sounding nasal—you're *supposed* to. So put on your best Pepé Le Pew accent and give it a try.

pardon [*pahR-doh^n*]	cent [*sah^n*]
pension [*pah^n-syoh^n*]	dans [*dah^n*]
oignon [*uh-nyoh^n*]	orange [*uh-Rah^{n}zh*]

In order to approximate the major nasal vowel sounds, it is necessary to introduce another pronunciation symbol: æ (called an ash), pronounced like the *a* in "ash" or "jack."

æ sounds like the *a* in "a̲sh" or "ja̲ck"

The nasalized version of this sound is like the second *a* in ban<u>a</u>na and will be transcribed in this book as æ^n. You will see this sound in words that have a nasalized *u* or *i*, such as *parfum* and *cinq*.

un [æ^n]   bien [*byæ^n*]
lundi [*læ^n-dee*]   loin [*lwæ^n*]
parfum [*pahR-fæ^n*]   cinq [*sæ^{n}k*]

If the *n* or *m* is followed by a vowel, the vowel before the *n* or *m* is not nasal. Contrast the following pairs:

un [æ^n] / une [*ew^{o}n*]
bonjour [*boh^n-zhuhR*] / bon appétit [*buh (n)ah-pay-tee*]
fin [*fæ^n*] / fine [*feen*]
cancer [*kah^n-sehR*] / caniche [*kah-neesh*]

Consonants

Most consonants are pronounced in French similarly to how we say them in English. There are some important differences, though.

First, final consonants are usually silent, except for C, R, F, and L, which are usually pronounced. (The common reminder is to think of the English word "careful": CaReFuL.) For example, you do not pronounce the final consonant on words like *chocolat* [*shuh-kuh-lah*], trois [*tRwah*] and *chercher* [*shehR-shay*]. But wait! *Chercher* ends in *r.* Should we pronounce that final *r*? Er-verbs in infinitive form are a notable exception to this "*r* as a final consonant" guideline; *parler, arriver,* etc.—those endings are pronounced *ay* despite ending in *r.*

Second, if the word ends in an *e,* then the consonant directly preceding it <u>is</u> pronounced. Consider the following pairs:

court [*kooR*] / courte [*kooRt*]
droit [*dRwah*] / droite [*dRwaht*]
grand [*gRah^n*] / grande [*gRah^{n}d*]
gris [*gRee*] / grise [*gReez*]

Third, when they are in certain combinations, a number of consonants in French are pronounced differently than we would expect.

ch	sh	chocolat [*shuh-kuh-lah*], chercher [*shehR-shay*]
gn	ny[6]	oignon [*uh-nyoh^n*], lignée [*lee-nyay*]
th	t	the [tay], maths [maht]

There are other surprises, as well, as you will see below. These
different pronunciations include the following:

ç	s	ça, [*sah*], garçon [*gahR-soh^n*]
c (before e, i, y)	s	centre [*sah^n-tRuh*], cinq [*sæ^{n}k*]
c (before a, o, u)	k	carte [*kahRt*], complet [*koh^n-play*]
g (before e, i, y)	zh[7]	gentil [*zhah^n-teey*], gilet [*zhee-lay*]
g (before a, o, u)	g	galerie [*gahl-Ree*], gorge [*guhRzh*]
h	silent	hôtel [*oh-tehl*], habiter [*ah-bee-tay*]
j	zh[7]	je [*zhuh*], jour [*zhooR*]
qu or final q	k	qui [*kee*], cinq [*sæ^{n}k*]
s between vowels	z	musée [*mew^o-zay*], résidence [*Ray-zee-dah^{n}s*]

[6] as in canyon
[7] as in pleasure

Reducing the final syllable
If the final syllable of a word is weak (ends in the schwa sound,
"uh"), there's a tendency in French to just drop it. Therefore, the
word for book, for example, *livre*, can be pronounced fully—*lee-
vRuh*—or, more commonly, chopped off to *leev*, with just a hint,
perhaps, of an *r* on the end. You have no doubt heard the famous
museum, the Louvre, pronounced this way [*loov*].

Stress

In French, syllables are stressed pretty evenly, with a tiny punch on the last syllable of a word, if it's not a weak syllable (such as the final syllable in *livre* is). In general, try not to make any syllables louder than others. More advanced instruction will discuss nuanced rules about stress, but keeping stress even is a good rule of thumb for beginners.

Liaison

As explained above, when a word ends in a consonant, that consonant is usually not pronounced (for example, *beaucoup*—*boh-koo*). This is especially true for a final *s*, *t*, or *x*. However, if the next word starts with a vowel and the words are spoken fluently, one leading into the next, then the consonant sound often *does* carry over to the start of the next word, linking them together in speech.

For example, the plural form *mes* ("my") is pronounced *may* on its own or in front of a consonant. The word for friends, *amis*, is pronounced *ah-mee*. But if you want to say "my friends" in French, and you're not separating the words distinctly (as learners often do), then this phrase is pronounced *may zah-mee*.

This linking of word sounds is called *liaison*. Liaison will be marked in this book by parentheses around the sound that carries over from the previous word: *may (z)ah-mee*. Remember that the parentheses show that the sound is used only when linked to the following word. The consonant would not be pronounced when saying the second word in isolation. Note that the letters *s* and *x* are pronounced as a *z* sound in liaison, as we saw with *mes amis*.

Elision

In certain situations in French—one word ends in a vowel and the next word begins with a vowel or vowel sound—the final vowel of the first word drops out and is replaced with an apostrophe. This is called *elision*. For example, *le hôtel* becomes *l'hôtel* and is pronounced *loh-tehl*. "I have" is *je ai*, shortened to *j'ai*, pronounced *zhay*.

Elision occurs specifically when using two-letter pronouns that end in *e* (such as *je*), as well as the singular definite articles *le* and *la* ("the") or the word *si* ("if").

Exercise 1.1

Choose the correct pronunciation for each word or phrase.

1. parle   a) *pahR-lay*   b) *pahR*   c) *pahRl*

2. arrivez   a) *ah-Ree-vay*   b) *ah-Ree-vehz*   c) *ah-Reev*

3. d'accord   a) *duh ah-kuhR*   b) *dah-kuhR*   c) *duh-kaRd*

4. petit œuf   a) *puh-tee uh*   b) *puh-tee uhf*   c) *puh-tee (t)uhf*

5. peut-être   a) *puh-eht*   b) *puh-eh-tRuh*   c) *puh-teh-tRuh*

6. aujourd'hui   a) *oh-zhooR-hoo*   b) *oh-zhooR-hwee*   c) *oh-zhooR-dwee*

7. le soir   a) *luh swahR*   b) *lay soh-eeR*   c) *lee swee*

8. voici   a) *voy-see*   b) *vwah-see*   c) *voh-ee-see*

9. un hôtel   a) *uhn hoh-tehl*   b) *$æ^n$ oh-tehl*   c) *$æ^n$ (n)oh-tehl*

10. C'est ici.   a) *say (t)ee-see*   b) *sawt ee-see*   c) *say (t)ee-kee*

Answers: 1) c (The *e* on the end means you pronounce the *l*.), 2) a (*-ez* on the end is pronounced *ay*.), 3) b (Because of elision, the first *d* carries over to the *a*; the *d* on the end is not pronounced.), 4) c (The *t* on the end carries over when the next word starts with a vowel sound. The *f* on the end is pronounced—CaReFuL.), 5) c (The first *t* carries over, and the *e* on the end means you should pronounce the *r*.), 6) c (The *h* is not spoken, and because of elision, the *d* carries over.), 7) a, 8) b (*oi* is usually pronounced *wah*.), 9) c (The *n* is nasalized in *un*, the *h* is not pronounced, and the *n* carries over in liaison.), 10) a (*e* is not pronounced *aw*, the *t* carries over in liaison, and *c* is pronounced *s* before *i*.)

Culture note—Proper greetings

The standard greeting during the day in France is *Bonjour*, and in the evening (after about 6 p.m.) it's *Bonsoir*. Greetings are usually followed by *madame*, *monsieur*, or *mademoiselle* (or something equivalent, such as the first name, if you are on a first-name basis). So, when you enter your hotel and the male reception worker says, *"Bonjour, madame/monsieur,"* you should reply, *"Bonjour, monsieur."* People who know each other well may use the more informal greeting of *Salut* [sah-lew^o].

If you are greeting someone you know, they may ask you, *ça va?* (How's it going?). You are expected to answer *ça va* (Fine). You may notice that when French people greet each other, they are comfortable standing much more closely to each other (about a foot apart) than Americans are.

Reality check: If you are afraid that you must be semi-fluent in French to travel to France or another French-speaking country, don't be. You can get by in many tourist spots with no French whatsoever. Most workers in the tourist industry know at least some English. On the other hand, if you think there's no real need to learn any French, realize that not all French people can (or will) speak English, and many of those who do may know only minimal English, even in highly touristed areas. Knowing a little French can make your life much easier in France. In addition, you can earn good will when you try to use French.

Greetings

A good place to start when learning a new language is with greetings. If you can greet people properly, they are likely to think you are well-mannered and will think better of you, even if you can't say anything else in their language.

Hello	Bonjour	boh^n-zhooR
Hi (informal)	Salut	sah-lew^o
Good evening	Bonsoir	boh^n-swahR

Culture note—Kiss or shake hands?

Greetings between French people (although not generally with tourists) often involve kisses or handshakes, as do departures. The French handshake seems impersonal compared to an American one: a quick shake of hands (one "pump"), fleeting eye contact, and that's it. No deep, extended eye contact, no lingering hand clasp. That would be too personal, an invasion of privacy. If you are greeting people in a group, socially or for business, greet everyone, including the handshake (or, less frequently, a kiss), whether you know everyone or not. That's the rule: greetings for all. This includes any children or relatives present. Note that whoever has the higher social rank (older, female) should initiate the handshake.

What about the kiss greeting? *La bise* [*lah bees*] is indelibly tied with our image of French greetings. The double kiss is common between women and between women and men, both for greeting and departing. (Men kissing men is reserved for family.) Usually you touch right cheeks first, kissing the air, then switch to the left cheeks. *La bise* is never a single kiss in France; it can extend to three or even four pecks, but the double kiss is most common. If you find yourself in a kissing situation (unlikely), follow the lead of the French person.

Introductions

One of the joys of travel is meeting new people. Learn how to introduce yourself and ask others their names.

(Lit.) How do you call yourself?	Comment vous appelez-vous?	kuh -mah^n voo (z)ah-play voo?
I call myself ___.	Je m'appelle ___.	zhuh mah-pehl ___
Pleased to meet you.	Enchanté.	ah^n-shah^n-tay
And you?	Et vous?	ay voo?
How are you?	Comment allez-vous?	kuh-mah^n (t)ah-lay voo?
(I'm) very well, thanks.	Très bien, merci.	tRay byæ^n, mehR-see
How's everything?	Ça va?[8]	sah vah?
Everything's fine.	(Oui), ça va.	(wee), sah vah

[8] Informal. Generally not used with someone you would address as *vous*.

Culture note—Formality

The French language, like many others, preserves a distinction in formality that the English language has long since dropped. There is a formal way to address people, the *vous* [*voo*] form, as well as an informal way, the *tu* [*too*] form. French speakers usually address people they don't know well or whom they know in formal contexts with the formal *vous* form. Addressing someone with the wrong level of formality could cause offense, particularly if you are too informal. Forget your native informality: Do not address adults with *tu* before you have been invited to. Because travelers interact primarily—if not exclusively—with strangers, this guide focuses on the *vous* form.

Do note, however, that family members, intimate friends, and young people use the *tu* form with each other. Thus, if you visit French relatives, they may use the *tu* form with you, even though you may never have met them before.

Study tip: Do the exercises if you have time to. If you don't have time, skip them. They help, but you can get by with oral practice.

Exercise 1.2

Can you get through a French introduction without looking at the answers? How do you say the following in French?

1. My name is ____.

2. What's your name?

3. How are you?

4. Fine, thanks.

Answers: 1) Je m'appelle _____. 2) Comment vous appelez-vous? 3) Comment allez-vous?/Ça va? (informal) 4) Très bien, merci./(Oui), Ça va, merci.

Culture note—Titles

French people use titles more often than Americans do, as you will quickly notice with the ubiquitous *madame, monsieur,* and *mademoiselle.* The term *mademoiselle* is used for girls or young women. If a woman is old enough that she could be married, it's safer to use *madame,* even if you don't know her marital status. (In fact, in French legal documents, all adult women are now referred to as *madame,* to parallel the use of *monsieur.*) You should avoid adding someone's family name to the title when speaking to that person, because that could be perceived as overly familiar. As with the use of *tu,* do not address adults by their first names unless you have been invited to do so.

Culture note—The gracious guest

The French do not often invite new acquaintances (or even old friends, for that matter) into their homes. City apartments are usually very small, and privacy is vigilantly guarded. It's an honor if you are invited to someone's home. Dinner invitations are usually for 8 p.m. You should not arrive early, but slightly late is all right, such as 10-15 minutes late for a meal. For a traditional, somewhat formal visit, consider the following tips. Dress up for dinner and bring a small gift for your hosts, such as flowers or high-quality candy, but nothing large or extravagant. (Don't bring wine, or you may be implying that your hosts' wines are inadequate.) Quality is more important than quantity. Feel free to accept whatever drink is offered, but don't request something different. Do your best to be polite (not nosy or noisy) and sociable (willing to participate in discussions). Should you be invited for drinks (an *apéritif*), often including appetizers (*canapés*) or snacks (*amuse-gueles* or *amuse-bouches*), expect to stay about an hour. Afterwards, make sure to send your hosts a note of thanks.

A word about grammar

Knowing a little bit of grammar can make using a language easier, because you can see some of the language's underlying system, the order, the rules for how things work. This book presents small "bites" of grammar throughout. If you find them interesting or useful, great! Follow the rules and make your French more grammatically accurate. If you find grammar to be boring or confusing, skip the grammar sections. Grammatical correctness is the frosting on the foreign language cake. It makes things "look" nice, "taste" a little sweeter, but the main component of communication (the "cake," so to speak) is vocabulary. Ideally you will learn vocabulary and grammar hand in hand, but if you have limited time and have to choose between grammar and vocabulary, definitely concentrate on vocabulary. You'll get a lot more bang for your buck there.

Grammar—Verb endings (present tense)

Type of verb: -er

parl<u>er</u> [*pahR-lay*] (to speak), cherch<u>er</u> [*shehR-shay*] (to look for), arriv<u>er</u> [*ah-Ree-vay*] (to arrive)

Subject	Verb ending	Example
je/j' (I)	-e	je parl<u>e</u> [*zhuh pahRl*]
		je cherch<u>e</u> [*zhuh shehRsh*]
		j'arriv<u>e</u> [*zhah-Reev*]
vous (you)	-ez	vous parl<u>ez</u> [*voo pahR-lay*]
		vous cherch<u>ez</u> [*voo shehR-shay*]
		vous arriv<u>ez</u> [*voo (z)ah-Ree-vay*]

Type of verb: -ir

fin<u>ir</u> [*fee-neeR*] (to finish), chois<u>ir</u> [*shwah-zeeR*] (to choose), réuss<u>ir</u> à [*Ray-ew^o-seeR ah*] (to succeed in)

Subject	Verb ending	Example
je/j' (I)	-is	je fin<u>is</u> [*zhuh fee-nee*]
		je chois<u>is</u> [*zhuh shwah-zee*]
		je réuss<u>is</u> [*zhuh Ray-ew^o-see*]
vous (you)	-issez	vous fin<u>issez</u> [*voo fee-nee-say*]
		vous chois<u>issez</u> [*voo shwah-zee-say*]
		vous réuss<u>issez</u> [*voo Ray-ew^o-see-say*]

Type of verb: -re

vend<u>re</u> [*vah^n-dRuh*] (to sell), attend<u>re</u> [*ah-tah^n-dRuh*] (to wait [for]), répond<u>re</u> [*Ray-poh^n-dRuh*] (to answer)

<u>Subject</u>	<u>Verb ending</u>	<u>Example</u>
je/j' (I)	-s	je vend<u>s</u> [*zhuh vah^n*]
		j'attend<u>s</u> [*zhah-tah^n*]
		je répond<u>s</u> [*zhuh Ray-poh^n*]
vous (you)	-ez	vous vend<u>ez</u> [*voo vah^n-day*]
		vous attend<u>ez</u> [*voo (z)ah-tah^n-day*]
		vous répond<u>ez</u> [*voo Ray-poh^n-day*]

Verbs are usually listed in language books and dictionaries in the *infinitive* form. The infinitive form is the basic form of the verb, the form it is in before we start changing it to reflect who or what is doing the action. Changing the verb like this is called *inflecting* or *conjugating* the verb. In English, the infinitive form of a verb uses the word *to* followed by the verb, for example, *to be*. That is why English translations of French verbs are usually listed as "*to* ___," to indicate that the verbs are in their basic, infinitive form.

When we *inflect* the verb, we change it to show who or what is doing the action. The English verb forms *is*, *am*, and *are* are all inflected forms of the verb *to be*. In English (or whatever your native language is) you automatically know how to inflect the verb for person (*I* versus *you* versus *she*) and for number (singular or plural). Even though the inflection is automatic, it still follows rules of the language that you internalized at a very early age and don't have to think about. When we learn a foreign language, most of us have to think about the rules, at least until we get enough experience that they become automatic, too. Here are the rules for inflecting most French verbs (shown in the tables above).

The verb in infinitive form consists of two parts, the stem and an ending of *-er*, *-ir*, or *-re*. For example, here are some verbs that you will see in this book, with a hyphen added to separate the stem from the ending: *parl-er* (to speak), *arriv-er* (to arrive), *fin-ir* (to finish), *chois-ir* (to choose), *vend-re* (to sell), *attend-re* (to wait [for]). With most verbs, you start with the stem of the verb, for example *parl-*, and add an ending to it that goes with (or "agrees") with the subject. In French, there are different endings for "you" and "I" forms of the verbs, and those endings also vary according to the verb family, that is, whether the infinitive verb ends in *-er*, *-ir*, or *-re*.

Let's start with a verb from the largest verb family (*-er* endings) and see how this works. With the verb *parler* (to speak) and most other *-er* verbs, if you want to talk about yourself, you add the ending *-e* to the verb stem: *je parle* [zhuh pahRl] (I speak). If you are talking directly to someone (usually using a question or command), you use the *vous* form. With an *-er* verb, the *vous* ending is *-ez*. So "You speak" is *vous parlez* [voo pahR-lay], or, more likely, "Do you speak?", which is the more familiar *Parlez-vous?* [pahR-lay voo?].

With verbs ending in *-ir*, such as *choisir* (to choose), the *je*-ending for these verbs is *-is* and the *vous*-ending is *-issez*. Thus, *I choose/I'm choosing* is *je choisis* [zhuh shwah-zee] and *you choose/you're choosing* is *vous choisissez* [voo shwah-zee-say]. Notice that French does not use different forms for "am choosing" and just plain "choose" (as well as an emphatic form, "I do choose"). (This is the case for all verbs in French. Just use the regular present tense verb form to tell that someone is in the process of doing something. In English, we have to learn the "progressive" form for this. Isn't it nice when French is simpler?)

The last verb class is those ending in *-re*. The I-ending is *-s* and the you-ending is again *-ez*. If we start with the verb *attendre* (to wait), we remove the *-re* infinitive ending and add the *-s* or *-ez* to inflect for *I* and *you*. So *I'm waiting* is *j'attends* [zhah-tah^n] and *you're waiting* is *vous attendez* [voo (z)ah-tah^n-day].

Reality check: This focus on "kind of verb" and different endings can be a little overwhelming at first. If you don't want to mess with verb formation rules yet, you can get by just fine by learning the forms that are presented in the vocabulary lists and not worrying about how they were derived.

Grammar—Verb endings (present tense)—Summary

Subject	-er verbs	-ir verbs	-re verbs
je (I)	-e	-is	-s
vous (you)	-ez	-issez	-ez

Exercise 1.3

Practice inflecting the regular verbs below. *Regular* means that the verbs follow the rules as explained above.

1. aider [*eh-day*] (*to help*)

    I help/you help

2. marcher [*mahR-shay*] (*to walk*)

    I'm walking/Are you walking?

3. regretter [*Ruh-gRay-tay*] (*to regret*)

    I regret/you regret

4. danser [*dah^n-say*] (*to dance*)

    I dance/you dance

5. habiter [*ah-bee-tay*] (*to live [in]*)

    I live/you live

6. attendre [*ah-tah^n-dRuh*] (*to wait for*)

    I wait for/you wait for

7. descendre [*day-sah^n-dRuh*] (*to descend/go down/get off [bus, train]*)

    I'm getting off [the bus]/Are you getting off [the bus]?

8. chérir [*shay-ReeR*] (*to cherish*)

    I cherish/you cherish

9. voyager [*vwah-yah-zhay*] (*to travel*)

    I'm traveling/Are you traveling?

10. travailler [tRah-vah-yay] (*to work*)

   I work/you work

11. recommander [Ruh-kuh-mah^n-day] (*to recommend*)

   I recommend/Do you recommend?

12. avertir [ah-vehR-teeR] (*to warn*)

   I'm warning/you're warning

Anwers: 1) j'aide/vous aidez, 2) je marche/vous marchez? or marchez-vous?, 3) je regrette/vous regrettez, 4) je danse/vous dansez, 5) j'habite/vous habitez, 6) j'attends /vous attendez, 7) je descends/vous descendez? or descendez-vous?, 8) je chéris/vous chérissez, 9) je voyage/vous voyagez? or voyagez-vous?, 10) je travaille/vous travaillez, 11) je recommande/vous recommandez? or recommandez-vous?, 12) j'avertis/vous avertissez

Culture note—Gestures

Gestures are important in France and can convey worlds of meaning without words. Most people have seen at least a caricature of a French person kissing the tips of his fingers to indicate that something is delicious or otherwise worthy of approval. (This extends to attractive women, by the way.) And surely we are aware of the insult when someone extends his right arm and then smacks it with his left hand, bending the arm at the elbow (the French equivalent of the middle finger). You may not be aware, however, that "drilling" your finger into your temple means that someone is crazy. Or that an extremely common gesture, pouty lips accompanied by a "poof" sound, means "it's nothing." If a person wears the same pout but exhales more strongly, it can signal exasperation.

If a French person is fed up with something, she pulls her hand across her forehead. Shrugging the shoulders can mean something is ridiculous, and stroking the cheek or jaw with the back of a hand indicates boredom. You may have the impression that it's normal to snap your fingers to get your waiter's attention, but that act is considered very rude and condescending. The OK symbol (thumb and index finger forming a circle) is OK in France, and used with puckered lips it means excellent. Thumbs up and thumbs down mean the same as in the U.S.

Culture note—French privacy

An early warning to Americans visiting France—*They live by different social rules there.* Traditional French social rules are no better or worse than ours, but they are wildly at odds with what Americans are used to, and the sooner you learn the differences, the sooner you can adjust your expectations and the better experience you will have among French people.

Paramount among French social rules is understanding the French concept of privacy. Traditionally, the French build a mental wall around their homes, family, and friends. That is their private life, where they are loving, friendly, warm and amusing. What exists outside that wall (and that includes work, other French people, and tourists) is public life. Public life calls for detachment, for personal reservation, for dignity. Connecting with outsiders, through chit-chat or even eye contact, is too personal and a violation of privacy. That warmth and connection are properly reserved for one's intimates, not strangers on the street or in the shops. There are exceptions to this emphasis on privacy, of course, but do not expect the French to follow American rules on social openness.

Grammar—Irregular verbs

Just when you thought verbs were confusing enough, along comes a large group of *irregular* verbs that don't follow the usual rules. Many of the most common verbs are irregular. For example, one big exception to the verb inflection rules is the verb *to be*, which is highly irregular in all western European languages, including English. In French, the infinitive form of *to be* is *être* [eh-tRuh] which looks like a regular *-re* verb, but the inflected forms are *je suis* [zhuh swee] and *vous êtes* [voo (z)eht]. You have to memorize irregular forms. Here are some very common irregular verbs.

to be
être [eh-tRuh]
je suis [zhuh swee] (I am)
vous êtes [voo (z)eht] (you are)

to have
avoir [ahv-wahR]
j'ai* [zhay] (I have)
vous avez [voo (z)ah-vay]
(you have)

*je is contracted to j' when it is in front of a vowel or most hs.

to do/to make
faire [fehR]
je fais [zhuh feh] (I make)
vous faites [voo feht] (you make)

to go
aller [ah-lay]
je vais [zhuh veh] (I go)
vous allez [voo (z)ah-lay] (you go)

to come
venir [vuh-neeR])
je viens [zhuh vyæⁿ] (I come)
vous venez [voo vuh-nay] (you come)

to see
voir [vwahR]
je vois [zhuh vwah] (I see)
vous voyez [voo vwah-yay] (you see)

Culture note—Watch those teeth and eyes!

Because of an intense sense of privacy, most French people do not smile much if they are not among their intimates. It does not mean they are mean, unfriendly, or don't like you. It just means there is nothing in particular to smile about most of the time. With this mindset, then, they can be understandably suspicious of people who smile for no apparent reason, even wondering whether there's something wrong with them. And French people certainly don't walk down the street greeting strangers with a smile and a hello. That's invading the privacy of others. Even making eye contact on the street can be an invasion of privacy.

So what should the culturally savvy visitor remember in France? To avoid sending the wrong message: 1) Don't walk down the street smiling at everyone. Try to curb those facial muscles from their reflexive pull. 2) Don't greet strangers in public (unless they are service personnel, serving you, and then remember to use a title). 3) Don't make eye contact with strangers (unless they are serving you, and then keep the eye contact brief).

Should you find yourself in a friendly, informal setting where people *do* greet you, smile at you, and make eye contact, reciprocating will be an easy adjustment for most Americans.

Origins

While less likely in privacy-loving France than elsewhere, it's possible that people may ask where you are from. You may want to recognize the following questions and know how to answer them.

from	de/d'*	*duh*
where	où	*oo*
where from?	d'où	*doo*
to come	venir	*vuh-neeʀ*
Where do you come from?	D'où venez-vous?	*doo vuh-nay voo?*
Where are you from?	D'où êtes-vous?	*doo eht voo?*
I come ___.	Je viens ___.	*zhuh vyæ^n ___.*
I am ___.	Je suis ___.	*zhuh swee ___.*
from the U.S.	des Ètats-Unis	*day (z)ay-tah (z)ew^o-nee*
from Canada	du Canada	*dew^o kah-nah-dah*
from England	d'Angleterre	*dah^n-gluh-tehʀ*
from Australia	d'Australie	*doh-stʀah-lee*
And you?	Et vous?	*ay voo?*

*form varies, depending on what follows it

Culture note—Stereotypes of Americans

Just as Americans have stereotypes of the French, the French have stereotypes of Americans. In the French mind, many Americans are loud, naive, unsophisticated, sloppy, and over-interested in money, both the making and the spending of it. They brag, dress carelessly, without much style, and do not have strong family ties. Although pleasantly enthusiastic, they are superficial and not very interesting. As much as we Americans might not care for this critique, I know that I, at least, must plead guilty to much of it.

Directional phrases

It's ___.	C'est ___.	*say ___*
north (of)	au nord (de)	*oh nohʀ (duh)*
south (of)	au sud (de)	*oh sewᵒd (duh)*
east (of)	à l'est (de)	*ah lehst (duh)*
west (of)	à l'ouest (de)	*ah lwehst (duh)*
close (to)	près de	*pʀeh duh*

Exercise 1.4

Practice asking and telling about origin.

1. Ask someone where she is from.

2. Tell where you are from.

Answers: 1) D'où venez-vous/êtes-vous? 2) Je viens/suis ___.

Culture note—Origins

Unless you live in a large and well-known city (Chicago, New York, Los Angeles) or in a well-known state (New York, Florida, California), many people won't recognize the place name or know where it is. To give them an idea, tell where your home is in relation to a place people might know. Don't be surprised, however, if you get nothing more than a vague nod in response. The United States is a large country, and an intimate knowledge of U.S. geography is sometimes limited abroad.

Leave-taking

Just as you will want to greet people, you will want to say goodbye.

goodbye	au revoir	*oh ʀuh-vwahʀ*
'bye	salut	*sah-lewᵒ*
see you soon	à bientôt	*ah byæⁿ-toh*

Culture note—Departure

When you leave people, including workers in a restaurant or shop, it's good manners to say goodbye and try to use a title, mirroring what you said when you arrived: *Au revoir, madame! Au revoir, monsieur! Merci, madame!* Another common phrase to depart with is *Bonne journée* [buhn zhooR-nay] ("Have a good day") or *Bonne soirée* [buhn swah-Ray] ("Have a good evening"). The correct response is *merci*, with a title. Informal ways to say goodbye include *salut* or *ciao* (so long, see you).

When departing from friends and colleagues, most people kiss cheeks or shake hands again. As when greeting, they go through the whole procedure with everyone present. This is unlikely to affect you as a tourist, however.

Manners

It always pays to be polite when you are traveling in a foreign country. Learning how to say *please*, *thank you*, and *excuse me* should be a top priority.

please	s'il vous plaît	*see voo play*
thank you (very much)	merci (beaucoup)	*mehR-see (boh-koo)*
you're welcome	il n'y a pas de quoi *or* de rien	*eel nyah pah duh kwah* *duh Ryæⁿ*
excuse me	excusez-moi	*ehks-kewᵒ-zay mwah*
sorry	pardon	*pahR-dohⁿ*

Culture note—Etiquette

Savoir-faire means knowing how to behave in all situations, and, historically, it has been the key to fitting in and enjoying life in France. The French expect everyone—including visitors and children—to act correctly at all times. While this may be a fading ideal, what has traditionally constituted good manners in France? The list can (and does) fill books, but here's a start.

Well-mannered French people include a title when greeting people (although this is often overlooked in tourist situations). They say *merci* and *pardon* a lot. Men open doors for women and stand when one enters the room for the first time. They also let a woman enter and exit an elevator first. French people respect the privacy and space of others. They keep to themselves and do not smile at strangers. They assume others are watching them at all times, and they act and dress accordingly. They have excellent posture and control over their bodies, voices, and facial expressions. They do not speak loudly and do not talk with their hands in their pockets (highly offensive).

They generally wear nice clothing—classy and tasteful—and have well-coiffed hair that probably is not curled, straightened, gelled, or sprayed. They eschew public personal hygiene, such as combing hair or applying make-up in public. They live according to France's social hierarchy and do not mix social levels as readily as Americans do. According to traditional French social rules, when among strangers, it is well-mannered to be reserved and dignified and, if someone is not following society's rules, visibly cold, distant, or put out.

Being polite in France means following the social rules and respecting others; it does *not* mean being overtly friendly. Is it any wonder that Americans are sometimes bewildered and offended by French behavior, and vice versa? What constitutes good behavior in one country often translates as bad behavior in the other. For most Americans, visiting France calls for a complete resetting of what is considered "appropriate behavior."

Exercise 1.5
What might you say in each of these situations?

1. Someone thanks you.

2. You want someone's attention.

3. You're making a request.

4. Someone has given you something.

5. You bump into someone.

A. S'il vous plaît.

B. Merci.

C. Pardon.

D. Excusez-moi.

E. Il n'y a pas de quoi./De rien.

Answers: 1) E, 2) D, 3) A, 4) B, 5) C

Useful Expressions

yes	oui	*wee*
no	non	*noh^n*
maybe	peut-être	*puh-teh-tRuh*
OK	d'accord	*dah-kuhR*
and	et	*ay*
or	ou	*oo*
but	mais	*may*
Just a moment.	Un moment.	*æ^n muh-mah^n*
Right away.	tout de suite	*toot sweet*
I understand.	Je comprends.	*zhuh koh^n-pRah^n*
I don't understand.	Je ne comprends pas.	*zhuh nuh koh^n-pRah^n pah*
I'm sorry.	Je regrette.	*zhuh Ruh-gReht*
Can you ___?	Pouvez-vous ___?	*poo-vay voo ___?*
to repeat	répéter	*Ray-pay-tay*
Can you repeat?	Pouvez-vous répéter?	*poo-vay voo Ray-pay-tay?*
to speak	parler	*pahR-lay*
slowly	lentement	*lah^{n}t-mah^n*
Can you speak slowly?	Pouvez-vous parler lentement?	*poo-vay voo pahR-lay lah^{n}t-mah$^{n?}$*
more	plus	*plew^o*
More slowly, please?	Plus lentement, s'il vous plaît?	*plew^o lah^{n}t-mah^n, see voo play?*
More loudly?	Plus fort?	*plew^o fuhR?*

Exercise 1.6

Write what you would say in each of these situations.

1. Someone is speaking too quickly.

2. You would like something repeated.

3. Someone is speaking too softly.

4. You don't understand.

5. You need a few seconds to complete something.

Answers: 1) Pouvez-vous parler lentement? *or* Plus lentement, s'il vous plaît. 2) Pouvez-vous répéter, s'il vous plaît? 3) (Pouvez-vous parler) plus fort, s'il vous plaît? 4) (Je regrette.) Je ne comprends pas. 5) Un moment, s'il vous plaît.

Culture note—Small-talk taboos

Should you be in a situation where you would actually converse with French people (unlikely for most of us tourists, but it *could* happen), a few pointers are in order. Certain topics should be avoided with people you don't know well. Don't ask about occupations, income, or age. Those are all considered too personal to discuss in France. In fact, you should avoid discussing personal lives as much as possible. Avoid talking about family, politics, religion, health, or how much something cost.

Better topics are sports, history (but not French wars), and the arts. Food is often a good topic, along with wine and restaurants. One sure way to make a good impression and mark yourself as a good conversationalist is to be interested in other people's opinions.

Whatever you discuss, try to do so in a way that amuses, entertains, or surprises your listeners. Be quick, brief, and witty, if possible. The worst thing you can do when talking to others is to bore them. French speakers like drama, action, even conflict in their discussions, so don't be offended if people interrupt you, contradict you, or abruptly change the subject. They are just trying to keep things lively. Do avoid using slang, though, as it could strike people as vulgar.

Make sure you remain modest. It is very ill-mannered to boast. Don't monopolize the conversation. That would be dull and inconsiderate. And as you talk to people, keep your hands out of your pockets. That's considered rude.

Whatever you talk about, don't do it too loudly. Loud voices violate the privacy of nearby people. French people may occasionally speak loudly among themselves, but they usually try not to, and to them a loud tourist really stands out in a negative way.

Culture note—How not to look like an American tourist

It's unlikely that you will blend so well into French society that no one will identify you as a foreigner, but you can minimize the fact that you are an American tourist.

Why does it matter? For one thing, people appreciate it when visitors care enough to learn about their customs and try to fit in. You may get a warmer reception from locals if you make an effort to conform to French cultural standards. Another reason is that people who are obviously tourists are sitting ducks for petty criminals, who abound in certain urban areas. The more American you look, the more you will appear to be easy pickings. A third reason to care is that U.S. foreign policy sometimes leads to anti-American sentiment abroad. No one is likely to say or do anything to you, but why draw attention to yourself?

If you follow these easy guidelines, you will stand out much less as an American in France:

—Don't wear white tennis or running shoes
—Don't wear a ball cap
—Don't wear baggy blue jeans, shorts, or a track suit
—Don't wear loud colors or patterns
—Don't wear a fanny pack
—Don't talk loudly, inside or out
—Don't chew gum in public (very ill-mannered)
—Don't wear a lot of make-up
—Don't hang a camera around your neck
—*Do* attempt to use French (but ditch the American *r*)

Culture note—The blame game

If there is a problem on your visit to France—the wrong food delivered in a busy restaurant, for example—French social rules dictate that you shouldn't directly blame other people, even if they are clearly at fault. If something goes wrong, focus on finding a solution to the problem together, not on assigning blame. (That just makes people defensive, causes them to lose face, and makes *you* look bad.)

Culture note—The Gallic lover

The French are famously interested in and open about sexual matters. Many love to flirt. Extramarital affairs are generally more accepted (for men or women) and less likely to break up a stable, supportive family unit than in the U.S. Prostitution is relatively common. In some circles, sex is a favorite topic of conversation. And, oh, how the men love to look.

Polly Platt discusses in her book, *French or Foe*, what she calls "The Look," that admiring sweep from head to toe, a visual caress. "The Look" is supposed to be an affirmation of female attractiveness in France (whether you like it or not). The best response is simply to look away and do your best not to take offense. Be careful not to make eye contact with the "Look-er," or to smile at him, or you could be inviting him to the next level of intimacy. And women do not give men "The Look." That's an open invitation for a pick-up.

2 Lodging

Numbers (0-10)

Numbers are among the most useful vocabulary items you will learn in a foreign language. Learning all the numbers at once can be an overwhelming task, so this book breaks numbers into five different lessons. Start at the beginning and learn to count from zero to ten.

0	zéro	*zay-Roh*
1	un	*æ^n*
2	deux	*duh*
3	trois	*tRwah*
4	quatre	*kah-tRuh*
5	cinq	*sæ^{n}k*
6	six	*sees*
7	sept	*seht*
8	huit	*weet*
9	neuf	*nuhf*
10	dix	*dees*

Culture note—Handwritten numbers

French numbers can be a little confusing when written by hand. *Ones* have a swoop leading up to them, so they often look like *sevens* or an upside-down V to American eyes. French people don't confuse them with *sevens*, though, because a *seven* in France has a little bar crossing its stem. You will encounter handwritten numbers on bills, on some price tags, and on restaurant specials that are listed on blackboards.

Exercise 2.1
After practicing the numbers to yourself, translate the following into French.

1. zero

2. six

3. one

4. seven

5. two

6. eight

7. three

8. nine

9. four

10. ten

11. five

1) zéro [zay-ʀoh], 2) six [sees], 3) un [æⁿ], 4) sept [sehf], 5) deux [duh], 6) huit [weef], 7) trois [tʀwah], 8) neuf [nuhf], 9) quatre [kah-tʀuh], 10) dix [dees], 11) cinq [sæⁿk]

Culture note—Counting on fingers

When the French count on their fingers, they start with their thumbs. Thus, a count of *one* is indicated by sticking one thumb out. *Two* is the thumb and forefinger, etc. *Six* is all five fingers on one hand and the thumb on the other hand. It's useful to know this before ordering something at a bar or bakery or anywhere else you might indicate number by holding up fingers. For example, in a crowded bakery, you could accidentally double your order if you hold your index finger up, American style, to order one baguette. When the worker sees that you have the index finger up, she could assume that the thumb is out, too, and give you two baguettes.

Exercise 2.2

Practice some simple math.

1. quatre plus (*plewᵖs*) trois =

2. cinq moins (*mwæⁿ*) trois =

3. six plus quatre =

4. neuf et zéro =

5. huit moins un moins sept =

6. six moins cinq =

7. un plus trois =

8. dix moins quatre =

9. neuf moins six =

10. cinq et trois =

11. quatre plus un =

Answers: 1) sept [*seht*], 2) deux [*duh*], 3) dix [*dees*], 4) neuf [*nuhf*], 5) zéro [*zay-Roh*], 6) un [*æ^n*], 7) quatre [*kah-tRuh*], 8) six [*sees*], 9) trois [*tRwah*], 10) huit [*weet*], 11) cinq [*sæ^{n}k*]

Grammar—Gender of nouns

<u>Masculine</u>	<u>Feminine</u>
livre [*lee-vRuh*] (book)	carte [*kahRt*] (map)
lit [*lee*] (bed)	chambre [*shah^n-bRuh*] (room)
hôtel [*oh-tehl*] (hotel)	heure [*uhR*] (hour)

In French, all nouns have a gender. Every noun is either masculine or feminine. This is an example of *grammatical gender*, where gender has everything to do with grammar and less to do with natural or biological sex. While nouns for people and animals usually follow natural gender (nouns for males are masculine, and nouns for females are feminine), things are less clear for nouns that don't refer to people or animals. For example, in French, a book is masculine (*livre*), but a map is feminine (*carte*). A hotel is masculine (*hôtel*), but a room is feminine (*chambre*). There's no generic, sexless "it," in French; *everything* has a sex (gender), regardless of how mundane and sexless it appears.

It's a good idea to learn the gender of a noun along with the noun itself. That's why vocabulary listings in course books and dictionaries include an indication of the noun's gender: *le* or *m* for masculine, and *la* or *f* for feminine. The bad news is that grammatical gender can be hard to keep straight. The good news is that using the wrong gender with a noun will hardly ever keep people from understanding you.

Grammar—Definite articles, singular

before a . . .	Masculine *the*	Feminine *the*
consonant	le livre [*luh lee-vRuh*] (the book) le lit [*luh lee*] (the bed)	la carte [*lah kahRt*] (the map) la chambre [*lah shah^n-bRuh*] (the room)
vowel or most *h*s	l'oncle [*loh^{n}kl*] (the uncle) l'hôtel [*loh-tehl*] (the hotel)	l'heure [*luhR*] (the hour) l'école [*lay-kuhl*] (the school)

As you may know, the word *the* is called a *definite article*, because it usually refers to some definite noun—*the* bed, *the* book, *the* map. There are multiple forms of the definite article in French, based on the gender of the noun and the beginning letter of the noun. If a noun is masculine, *the* must also be masculine. It should also "fit" with the first letter of the noun. For example, if the noun begins with a consonant, the masculine form of *the* is *le* (as in *le livre*, the book). If the masculine noun begins with a vowel or an *h*, then *the* is usually shortened to *l'* (as in *l'hôtel*, the hotel).

If a feminine noun begins with a consonant, *the* is expressed as *la* (as in *la chambre*, the room). If a feminine noun begins with a vowel, then *the* is shortened to *l'* (as in *l'heure*, the hour). Remember, you should try to learn the gender of the noun when you learn the noun itself.

Exercise 2.3
Supply the correct form of *the* for the following nouns. The gender of the noun is indicated after the word itself by *m* (for masculine) or *f* (for feminine).

1. chaise [*shehz*] (chair, *f*)

2. lumière [*lew^o-myehR*] (light, *f*)

3. passeport [*pahs-puhR*] (passport, *m*)

4. table [*tah-bluh*] (table, *f*)

5. étudiant [ay-tew^p-dyah^n] (male student, *m*)

6. ascenseur [ah-sah^n-suhR] (elevator, *m*)

7. entrée [ah^n-tRay] (entrance, *f*)

8. porte [puhRt] (door, *f*)

9. réservation [Ray-zehR-vah-syoh^n] (reservation, *f*)

10. sucre [sew^p-kRuh] (sugar, *m*)

11. boisson [bwah-soh^n] (drink, *f*)

12. journal [zhooR-nahl] (newspaper, *m*)

Answers: 1. la, 2. la, 3. le, 4. la, 5. l', 6. l', 7. l', 8. la, 9. la, 10. le, 11. la, 12. le

Culture note—Energy conservation

French energy costs are astronomical by U.S. standards. Consequently, the French are much more energy conscious than most Americans. One way they conserve energy is to use timed lights or motion-sensitive lights in stairwells and hallways. If lights don't come on automatically, look for a glowing orange button on the wall and push it for light. It will turn off after a set time. In general, try to conserve resources in France. Your hosts will appreciate your efforts, and you will have the satisfaction of knowing that you are not one of those "wasteful Americans."

Culture note—Oh là là!

Oh là là is a familiar French expression of surprise or indignation. Usually heard as "oo la la" (as in c<u>oo</u>l) in the United States, the French pronunciation is "<u>oh</u> la la" (as in t<u>o</u>ne). The greater the excitement or indignation, the more "las" that may be tacked on to the exclamation. I know I have heard an *oh* followed by at least four *là*s on the streets in Paris. *Oh là là!*

On a similar (if less likely) note, I once heard a very grateful woman thanking the man who had helped her: *Merci beaucoup-coup-coup-coup-coup!*

Concrete Vocabulary

Practice identifying things around you. You can certainly get by without this vocabulary, but it's easy to practice at home, and it's quite possible that you might use some of these words at a hotel or restaurant or on a train.

What is that?	Qu'est-ce que c'est?	*kehs-kuh say?*
It's ___.	C'est ___.	*say ___*
Where is ___?	Où est ___?	*oo ay ___?*
Here is ___.	Voici ___.	*vwah-see ___*
There is ___.	Voilà ___.	*vwah-lah ___*
room	le salle	*luh sahl*
bedroom	la chambre	*lah shah^n-bruh*
floor (of room)	le plancher	*luh plah^n-shay*
floor (of building)	l'étage (m)	*lay-tahzh*
chair	la chaise	*lah shehz*
table	la table	*lah tah-bluh*
pen	le stylo	*luh stee-loh*
wall	le mur	*luh mew^{o}R*
door	la porte	*lah puhRt*
ceiling	le plafond	*luh plah-foh^n*
lamp	la lampe	*lah lah^{n}p*
light	la lumière	*lah lew^o-myehR*
window	la fenêtre	*lah fuh-neh-tRuh*
book	le livre	*luh lee-vRuh*
paper	le papier	*luh pah-pyay*

Exercise 2.4

Ask yourself "Where is ___?" and answer "Here is ___." For example, ask yourself, "Où est la fenêtre?" Gesture to the window and answer yourself, "Voici la fenêtre." Repeat until the words and phrases feel comfortable.

Days of the Week

Monday	lundi	*læ^n-dee*
Tuesday	mardi	*mahR-dee*
Wednesday	mercredi	*mehR-kRuh-dee*
Thursday	jeudi	*zhuh-dee*
Friday	vendredi	*vah^n-dRuh-dee*
Saturday	samedi	*sahm-dee*
Sunday	dimanche	*dee-mah^{n}sh*
week	la semaine	*lah suh-mehn*
weekend	la fin de semaine	*lah fæ^n duh suh-mehn*
	le week-end	*luh week-ehnd*
today	aujourd'hui	*oh-zhooR-dwee*
tonight	ce soir	*suh swahR*
tomorrow	demain	*duh-mæ^n*
day after tomorrow	après-demain	*ah-pReh-duh-mæ^n*
yesterday	hier	*yehR*
day before yesterday	avant-hier	*ah-vah^n-tyehR*
was	était	*ay tay*
What day is today?	Quel jour sommes-nous?	*kehl zhooR suhm noo?*
What's today's date?	Quelle est la date d'aujourd-hui	*kehl ay lah daht doh-zhooR-dwee?*
Today is __.	C'est ___.	*say ___.*
when?	quand?	*kah^n?*
morning	le matin	*luh mah-tæ^n*
afternoon	l'après-midi (m)	*lah-pReh mee-dee*
evening	le soir	*luh swahR*
night	la nuit	*lah nwee*
Thursday evening	jeudi soir	*zhuh-dee swahR*
Saturday morning	samedi matin	*sahm-dee mah-tæ^n*
Sunday afternoon	dimanche après-midi	*dee-mah^{n}sh ah-pReh mee-dee*

Culture note—Le week-end

French weekends are for socializing, not for work. Hordes of city dwellers flee to the country, clogging highways and roads. Weekends are also the busiest times at tourist destinations, so you may want to plan your own activities accordingly.

Exercise 2.5
Match the day of the week with the correct activity or description.

1. jeudi, ??, samedi	A. mercredi
2. commence (begins) la fin de semaine	B. dimanche
3. au milieu (middle) de la semaine	C. vendredi
4. conclut (concludes) la fin de semaine	D. lundi
5. commence la semaine	E. samedi

Answers: 1) C, 2) E, 3) A, 4) B, 5) D

Exercise 2.6
"Today is Monday." Knowing that, can you identify which day should fit each term? For example, if today is Monday, then "tomorrow" is Tuesday.

1. aujourd'hui

2. demain

3. après-demain

4. hier

5. fin de semaine

Answers: 1) lundi, 2) mardi, 3) mercredi, 4) dimanche, 5) samedi et dimanche

Culture note—Calendar weeks

French calendars show the week starting on Monday, not Sunday. The entire weekend is at the end of the week. The difference in calendars can cause confusion, so take a good look when you refer to one.

Months

January	janvier	*zhah^n-vyay*
February	février	*fay-vRee-yay*
March	mars	*mahRs*
April	avril	*ah-vReel*
May	mai	*may*
June	juin	*zhwæ^n*
July	juillet	*zhwee-yeh*
August	août	*oot or oo*
September	septembre	*sehp-tah^n-bRuh*
October	octobre	*uhk-tuh-bRuh*
November	novembre	*noh-vah^n-bRuh*
December	décembre	*day-sah^n-bRuh*

Exercise 2.7

Provide the month in which the holiday or activity takes place.
Use *en* for *in*. *En quel mois se célébre* ___?

1. Noël

2. Pâques (Easter)

3. la fête des mères

4. la fête des pères

5. la Saint-Valentin

6. "Thanksgiving"

7. la fête de l'Indépendance aux Ètas-Unis (Independence Day
   in U.S.)

8. la fête du travail aux Ètas-Unis (Labor Day in U.S.)

9. l'anniversaire de MLK, Jr.

10. "Halloween"

Answers: 1) en décembre, 2) en mars/en avril, 3) en mai, 4) en juin, 5) en
février, 6) en novembre, 7) en juillet, 8) en septembre, 9) en janvier, 10) en
octobre

Culture note—The August exodus

Many French people take their vacation in August, resulting in cities that are empty of locals and overrun by tourists. This is not all bad, however, as "tourist rules" take over, and everything from behavior to dress becomes more relaxed. You may well feel more comfortable in France during August than any other time of the year. If you are looking for the "authentic" French experience, however, August is probably not the time for it.

Culture note—Written dates

Dates in France are written from the smallest unit to the largest, that is, day-month-year. Christmas Day would be written as 25.12. It's especially important to remember the correct order when the date happens to be 12 or smaller. While Americans might figure out that 19.7. on a schedule indicates July 19 (as there is no 19th month), we might easily forget and read 8.7. as Aug. 7 rather than July 8.

Grammar—Definite/indefinite articles, singular

Masculine before a. . .	Definite article (the)	Indefinite article (a/an)
consonant	le lit [*luh lee*] (the bed)	un lit [$æ^n$ *lee*] (a bed)
vowel and most *h*s	l'hôtel [*loh-tehl*] (the hotel)	un hôtel [$æ^n$ *(n)oh-tehl*] (a hotel)

Feminine before a. . .	Definite article (the)	Indefinite article (a/an)
consonant	la chambre [*lah shah^n-bRuh*] (the room)	une chambre [*ew^{o}n shah^n-bRuh*] (a room)
vowel and most *h*s	l'école [*lay-kuhl*] (the school)	une école [*ew^{o}n ay-kuhl*] (a school)

You read before what a *definite article* is: a form of *the*, used to refer to a specific (or *definite*) noun, for example, *le* livre (*the* book). A different kind of article is an *indefinite article*, a form of *a* or *an*. We use an indefinite article when we aren't referring to a specific noun, but any noun of a certain type, for example, *a* book, instead of *the* book. Consider the difference in the following suggestions:

"Let's go to a movie tonight."

"Let's go to the movie tonight."

Do you see the difference? The first sentence suggests seeing *a* movie (any would do), while the second sentence suggests a particular movie, *the* movie.

As in English, French uses different words for *a* and *the*. As we already know, *the* is either *le* or *l'* for masculine nouns, and either *la* or *l'* for feminine nouns, depending on what letter the noun starts with. There are only two options for *a*. For masculine nouns, the indefinite article (*a*) is *un* [æ^n]. For feminine nouns, use *une* [ew^{o}n].

Culture note—Lodging

A hotel (*un hôtel*) can span a wide range of luxury in France, from very basic one-star accommodations to ultra-luxurious five-star properties. For most visitors, a three-star hotel is perfectly adequate, or two stars, if you are more budget-minded and don't mind more basic accommodations. First-class hotels are often overpriced. Hotels generally do not include breakfast in their prices, although you can usually buy breakfast on top of your room fee. Clarify this before making a reservation, if it is important to you. Hotel breakfasts are often expensive, but the convenience may be worth it.

If you prefer to stay in B&Bs, you want to find *chambre d'hôtes* [shah^n-bʀuh dohf], which are run by Gîtes de France (www.gites-de-france.com). A B&B will include a hearty breakfast and often the possibility of joining the family for other meals.

An *auberge* [oh-behʀzh] is a modest country inn, usually found off the beaten path. A *pension* [pahⁿ-syohⁿ] is like a rooming house, where guests pay for a room and some or all meals. A *gîte* [zheet] is a private residence that is rented to visitors. *Gîtes* can range from simple to luxurious, from city apartments to country estates.

Exercise 2.8
Concrete vocabulary review

Test yourself again. Practice asking and answering questions using the concrete vocabulary from earlier in this lesson (p. 46). Try to decide whether you would use *the* or *a* if you were speaking English, and then use the French version of that article.

| What's that? | Qu'est-ce que c'est? | *kehs-kuh say?* |
| It's ___. | C'est ___. | *say ___* |

For example, you might look at a chair and ask yourself, "Qu'est-ce que c'est?" and then answer, "C'est une chaise." Or point at the floor: "Qu'est-ce que c'est?" Answer: "C'est le plancher." Try to identify ten different things.

Exercise: 2.9
Can you say the following in French? Pay attention to the article: use *a* or *the* as indicated.

1. the bedroom
2. a table
3. a pen
4. a book
5. the window
6. the ceiling
7. the door
8. a lamp
9. a chair
10. the floor (of room)

Answers: 1) la chambre, 2) une table, 3) un stylo, 4) un livre, 5) la fenêtre, 6) la plafond, 7) la porte, 8) une lampe, 9) une chaise, 10) le plancher

Lodging

If you are arranging your own lodging, you should be familiar
with the vocabulary in this section. Even if your lodging will be
arranged for you, you will find some of these words and phrases
useful.

where?	où?	*oo?*
Where is ___?	Où est ___?	*oo ay ___?*
Here is ___.	Voici ___.	*vwah-see ___*
a hotel	un hôtel	*æ^n (n)oh-tehl*
a guesthouse	une pension	*ew^{o}n pah^n-syoh^n*
Is it far?	C'est loin?	*say lwæ^n?*
It's ___.	C'est ___.	*say ___*
here	ici	*ee-see**
there	là	*lah*
to the right	à droite	*ah dRwaht*
to the left	à gauche	*ah gohsh*
straight ahead	tout droit	*too dRwah*
on the corner	au coin	*oh kwæ^n*
around the corner	après le coin	*ah-pReh luh kwæ^n*
in the direction of ___	en direction de ___	*ah^n dee-Rehk-syoh^n duh ___*
nearby	tout près	*too pReh*
to/of here	d'ici	*dee-see*
north of here	au nord d'ici	*oh nuhR dee-see*
close to here	près d'ici	*pReh dee-see*
a long way	loin	*lwæ^n*
Go ___.	Allez ___.	*ah-lay ___*
Go down ___.	Descendez ___.	*day-sah^n-day ___*
Take ___.	Prenez ___.	*pRuh^n-nay ___*
Cross ___.	Traversez ___.	*tRah-vehR-say ___*
then	ensuite	*ah^n-sweet*

* Remember: If you use *C'est* followed by *ici* or another
phrase that starts with a vowel, the *t* at the end of *est* carries
over to the next word and is pronounced—*C'est ici* [*say (t)ee-
see*], for example.

Culture note—Tipping

It is polite to tip anyone who performs a service for you, including those you don't see. If you stay more than a couple of days in a hotel, you should leave a modest tip for the chambermaid on your pillow or the night table, say €1.50 per day. If the bellhop carries your bags or calls a cab for you, a tip of €.75 to €1.50 is in order.

Museum or tour guides typically receive €1 to €3 after a guided tour. Tour bus drivers get about €1.50 after an outing. As discussed more in Chapter Three, in restaurants the tip is almost always included in listed prices. If you see the words *Pourboire Interdit,* that means that tipping is forbidden.

Travel tip: If you will be in France during the high season or a holiday, you should reserve your lodging as early as possible, especially in tourist centers. Even if you need lodging in a non-peak period, you can rest more easily by reserving a room in advance. You can also find special deals on hotel Web sites that you may not learn about if you book a room on the spot in France.

You can frequently make reservations via fax or email or on the hotel's booking site. Details about accommodations and contact information can be found in travel guide books or by searching the Web. TripAdvisor.com, for example, is a useful resource. Or you could, of course, turn to a travel agent for help.

Can you ___?	Pouvez-vous ___?	*poo-vay-voo ___?*
to recommend	recommander	*Ruh-kuh-mah^n-day*
Can you recommend ___?	Pouvez-vous recommander ___?	*poo-vay-voo Ruh-kuh-mah^n-day ___?*
a hotel	un hôtel	*æ^n (n)oh-tehl*
reservation	la réservation	*lah Ray-zehR-vah-syoh^n*
I have ___.	J'ai ___.	*zhay ___*

I have a reservation.	J'ai une réservation.	*zhay ew^{o}n Ray-zehR-vah-syoh^n*
I am ___.	Je suis ___.	*zhuh swee ___*
My name is ___.	Je m'appelle ___.	*zhuh mah-pehl ___*
I don't have ___.	Je n'ai pas de ___.	*zhuh nay pah duh ___*
I don't have a reservation.	Je n'ai pas de réservation.	*zhuh nay pah duh Ray-zehR-vah-syoh^n*
Do you have ___?	Avez-vous ___?	*ah-vay-voo ___?*
a room	une chambre	*ew^{o}n shah^n-bRuh*
available rooms	des chambres libres	*day shah^n-bRuh lee-bRuh*
Do you have rooms available?	Avez-vous des chambres libres?	*ah-vay-voo day shah^{n}m-bRuh lee-bRuh?*
for tonight	pour ce soir	*pooR suh swahR*
certainly	bien sûr	*byæ^n sew^{o}R*
I'm sorry.	Je regrette.	*zhuh Ruh-gReht*
full	complet	*koh^h-play*
The hotel is full.	L'hôtel est complet.	*loh-tehl ay koh^h-play*
I would like ___.	Je voudrais ___.	*zhuh voo-dRay ___*
I would like a room.	Je voudrais une chambre.	*zhuh voo-dRay (z)ew^{o}n shah^n-bRuh*
a room with two beds	une chambre à deux lits	*(z)ew^{o}n shah^n-bRuh ah duh lee*
a single room	une chambre pour une personne	*(z)ew^{o}n shah^n-bRuh pooR ew^{o}n pehR-suhn*
for ___ people	pour ___ personnes	*poor ___ pehR-suhn*
with ___	avec	*ah-vehk*
without ___	sans	*sah^n*
twin bed	un lit à une place / un petit lit	*æ^n lee ah ew^{o}n plahs / æ^n puh-tee lee*
double bed	un lit à deux places / un grand lit	*æ^n lee ah duh plahs / æ^n grah^n lee*
an extra bed	un lit supplémentaire	*æ^n lee sew^o-play-mah^n-tehR*
shower	douche (f)	*doosh*

bathroom (private)	salle de bains (privée)	*sahl duh bæ^n (pRee-vay)*
toilet	toilette	*twah-leht*
Does it have ___?	Il y a ___?	*eel yah ___?*
a television	une télévision	*ew^{o}n tay-lay-vee-zyoh^n*
a hair dryer	un sèche-cheveux	*æ^n sehsh-shuh-vuh*
air conditioning	la climatisation	*lah klee-mah-tee-zah-syoh^n*
Is there ___?/Are there___?	Il y a ___?	*eel yah ___?*
Is there an elevator?	Il y a un ascenseur?	*eel yah æ^n (n)ah-sah^n-suhR?*
On what floor is it? (Literally, Is it on what floor?)	C'est à quel étage?	*say (t)ah kehl ay-tahzh?*
for one night	pour une nuit	*pooR ew^{o}n nwee*
for ___ nights	pour ___ nuits	*pooR ___ nwee*
I'd like a room for two people for three nights, with bathroom, please.	Je voudrais une chambre pour deux personnes pour trois nuits, avec salle de bains, s'il vous plaît.	*zhuh voo-dRay (z)ew^{o}n shah^n-bRuh pooR duh pehR-suhn pooR tRwah nwee, ah-vehk sahl duh bæ^n, see voo play.*
until	à	*ah*
key	la clé	*lah klay*

Culture note—Keys

Your hotel door may not lock automatically behind you. You may need to lock the door with the key. Also, in some places, you must plug the key or some other device into a slot in order to have power in your room. If you can't turn on the lights, look for someplace by the door to plug your key in. The slot could be head-high and look like a light switch, so check out all possibilities.

Exercise 2.10

Place the following in the correct order to make two conversations.

A. J'ai une réservation. _____

B. Bonjour, madame! _____

C. Pour deux nuits? _____

D. Oui, à lundi. _____

E. Bonjour, monsieur. Je m'appelle Mary Black. _____

F. Bien. C'est la chambre 9. Voici la clé. _____

Answers: 1) B, 2) E, 3) A, 4) C, 5) D, 6) F

A. Pouvez-vous recommander un hôtel près d'ici? _____

B. Bonsoir, madame! Avez-vous des chambres libres? _____

C. Je regrette, l'hôtel est complet. _____

D. Oui, l'Hôtel Montréal est après le coin. _____

E. Oui, pour quatre nuits. _____

F. Bonsoir, monsieur. Pour ce soir? _____

G. Merci, madame! Au revoir! _____

Answers: 1) B, 2) F, 3) E, 4) C, 5) A, 6) D, 7) G

from . . . to	de . . . à	duh . . . ah
from Monday	de lundi	duh læ^n-dee
to Thursday	à jeudi	ah zhuh-dee
how much?	combien?	koh^n-byæ^n?
How much is it?	C'est combien?	say koh^n-byæ^n?
Can you write it down for me?	Pouvez-vous me l'écrire?	poo-vay voo muh lay-kReeR?
everything	tout	too
included	compris	koh^n-pree
Everything is included?	Tout est compris?	too (t)ay koh^n-pRee?

Is ___ included?	___ est compris?	___ ay koh^n-pRee?
breakfast	le petit déjeuner	luh puh-tee day-zhuh-nay
sales tax (VAT)	la TVA	lah tay vay ah

Culture note—Amenities

Your hotel may provide different amenities than you would expect in American lodging. If your hotel is very small or budget-minded, you may need to use a bathroom and shower down the hall, which you might share with other guests. While you should receive towels to use (unless the room is very low-budget), you probably won't get a wash cloth, shampoo, or lotion. Your hotel will probably provide soap and perhaps a hair dryer, but ask first if these are important to you and you are staying in budget accommodations. Your bathroom might include a bidet, for private washings, either as a separate fixture or as part of the toilet.

Many old buildings don't have an elevator, or the elevator may be out of order, and hotel reception desks are sometimes located on the second or third floor. Your room may be even higher. Be prepared to climb. (Yet another reason to pack light!) Not all lodging includes air conditioning in the summer. Ask, if this is important to you. (*Il y a la climatisation?*) [*eel yah lah klee-mah-tee-zah-syoh^n*] Don't ask for air conditioning in winter months, even if it seems warm to you.

May I ___?	Puis-je ___?	pweezh ___?
to see	voir	vwahR
May I see the room?	Puis-je voir la chambre?	pweezh vwahR lah shah^n-bRuh?
Fine.	Bien.	byæ^n
OK	d'accord	dah kuhR
to take	prendre	pRah^n-dRuh
I'll take it.	Je la prends.*	zhuh lah pRah^n
No, I won't take it.	Non, je ne la prends pas.*	noh^n, zhuh nuh lah pRah^n pah

* **Grammar note:** The direct object *it* is expressed above as *la* (Je la prends) because it refers to *la chambre* (feminine) (shortened to *l'* before a verb beginning with a vowel). When the direct object *it* refers to a masculine noun, such as *le livre*, then it is expressed as *le* (or *l'* before a vowel).

too	trop	*tRoh*
It's too ___.	Elle** est trop ___.	*ehl ay tRoh ___*
expensive	chère**	*shehR*
small	petite**	*puh-teet*
noisy	bruyante**	*bRwee-yah^{n}t*
dirty	sale	*sahl*

** **Grammar note:** The adjectives listed above have all been inflected to go with the word *room* in French. (*Elle* is the feminine subject pronoun replacing *la chambre* here.) For example, *expensive* is expressed above as *chère* (ending in *-e*) because it refers to *la chambre* (feminine). If we were talking about an expensive book (*le livre*—masculine), it would be *cher*, without the *-e*. See p. 92 for more about adjective endings.

Do you have something ___?	Avez-vous quelque chose ___?	*ah-vay voo kehl-kuh shohz ___?*
less expensive	de moins cher	*duh mwæ^n shehR*
bigger	de plus grand	*duh plew^o gRah^n*
quieter	de plus calme	*duh plew^o kahlm*
better	de meilleur	*duh may-yuhR*
to have	avoir	*ah-vwahR*
May I have ___?	Puis-je avoir ___?	*pweezh ah-vwahR ___?*
a receipt	un reçu	*æ^n Ruh-sew^o*
the key	la clé	*lah klay*

Culture note—Street noise

French cities are noisy. If quiet is important to you, ask for a room away from the street (*une chambre qui ne donne pas sur la rue*). If you don't mind a little noise, you can sit at your window and watch French life bustle, roar, and clatter by.

Exercise 2.11

Translate into French.

1. Where is the *Hôtel Québec*, please?

2. Excuse me. Can you recommend a guesthouse?

3. Do you have rooms available?

4. I would like a double room with a bathroom for one night.

5. I would like a single room with a shower for three nights, from Sunday to Wednesday.

6. How much is it?

7. How much is a double room?

8. Is breakfast included?

9. How much is it without breakfast?

10. I'll take it (= *chambre*).

11. It (= *chambre*) is too expensive.

12. Do you have something less expensive?

13. I would like a receipt, please.

14. Where is the key?

Answers: 1) Où est l'Hôtel Québec, s'il vous plaît? 2) Excusez-moi. Pouvez-vous recommander une pension? 3) Avez-vous des chambres libres? 4) Je voudrais une chambre à deux personnes avec salle de bains pour une nuit. 5) Je voudrais une chambre à une personne avec douche pour trois nuits, de dimanche à mercredi. 6) C'est combien? 7) C'est combien une chambre à deux personnes? 8) Le petit déjeuner est compris? 9) C'est combien sans le petit déjeuner? 10) Je la prends. 11) Elle est trop chère. 12) Avez-vous quelque chose de moins cher? 13) Je voudrais un reçu, s'il vous plaît. 14) Où est la clé?

Grammar note: The phrase *Il y a* ___ [*eel yah* ___] means both *There is* ___ and *There are* ___ and comes in very handy as a question when you want to ask about the presence of things. Just use rising intonation, and a statement with *il y a* becomes a question. For example, when reserving a room, you may want to ask *Il y a une télévision?* (*Is there a television?*). After spending the day seeing sights, you may want to ask on your return, *Il y a des messages pour moi?* (*Are there any messages for me?*). You can use the phrase in any context, for example, *Il y a une table pour quatre?* (*Is there a table for four?*) and *Il y a une station de métro près d'ici?* (*Is there a metro station near here?*). You can also form a question by flipping things around to get *Y a-t-il* ___? [*ee ah-teel* ___?], but there's no problem sticking with *Il y a*, as long as you make it *sound* like a question.

Some location phrases you may want to use along with *Il y a* ___? include the following:

in the room	dans la chambre	dah^n lah shah^n-bʀuh
in the hotel	à l'hôtel	ah loh-tehl
near here	près d'ici	pʀeh dee-see

Important words

where?	où?	oo?
here	ici	ee-see
there	là	lah
which?	quel(s)/quelle(s)	kehl/kehl
that (an object)	cela/ça	suh-lah/sah
who?	qui?	kee?
when?	quand?	kah^n?
since when?	depuis quand?	duh-pwee kah^n?
for how long?	depuis combien de temps?	duh-pwee koh^n-byæ^n duh tah^n?
how far away?	à quelle distance?	ah kehl dees-tah^{n}s?
why?	pourquoi?	pooʀ-kwah?
how?	comment?	koh-mah^n?
how much/many?	combien?	koh^n-byæ^n?

Culture note—Floor numbers

A cause of much confusion: The system for numbering floors differs in Europe and the United States. A European first floor is an American second floor, etc. Here's a short table to help.

United States	France
first floor	*le rez-de-chaussée* [luh Ray-duh-shoh-say] (ground floor)
second floor	*le premier étage* [luh pRuh-myeh (R)ay-tahzh] (first floor)
third floor	*le deuxième étage* [luh duh-zyehm ay-tahzh] (second floor)
fourth floor	*le troisième étage* [luh tRwah-zyehm ay-tahzh] (third floor)

Just remember to add *one* to whatever French floor number you are given, and you'll get to the right floor.

3   Restaurants and Food

Numbers (11-20)

Time to tackle more numbers. First, review the numbers zero through ten (p. 41).

Now take a look at eleven through twenty. Practice saying them out loud.

11	onze	*oh^{n}z*
12	douze	*dooz*
13	treize	*tRehz*
14	quatorze	*kah-tuhRz*
15	quinze	*kæ^{n}z*
16	seize	*sehz*
17	dix-sept	*dees-seht*
18	dix-huit	*dee-(z)weet*
19	dix-neuf	*dees-nuhf*
20	vingt	*væ^n*

Exercise 3.1
Translate the following numbers into French. Try not to look at the list above.

1. eleven
2. sixteen
3. twelve
4. seventeen
5. thirteen

6. eighteen
7. fourteen
8. nineteen
9. fifteen
10. twenty

Answers: 1) onze, 2) seize, 3) douze, 4) dix-sept, 5) treize, 6) dix-huit, 7) quatorze, 8) dix-neuf, 9) quinze, 10) vingt

Exercise 3.2

Try some more math.

1. douze plus cinq =

2. dix-huit plus deux =

3. sept plus six =

4. dix-neuf moins trois =

5. dix plus un =

6. onze plus huit =

7.   dix-sept moins deux =

8. seize moins quatre =

9. neuf plus neuf =

10. huit plus six =

Answers: 1) dix-sept, 2) vingt, 3) treize, 4) seize, 5) onze, 6) dix-neuf, 7) quinze, 8) douze, 9) dix-huit, 10) quatorze

Culture note—French food

Traditionally, the French are absolutely fanatical about their food. French *gastronomie* is considered by many to be the finest in the world, sophisticated and pleasing. For many, food is one of life's greatest pleasures and should be planned, discussed, and enjoyed with the greatest leisure and discrimination possible.

Ideally, ingredients are purchased as close to the time of use as possible. Each dish is lovingly prepared. All nuances are evaluated and commented on. Nothing should be hurried—not the shopping, not the cooking, certainly not the eating. Traditional meals routinely last a couple of hours. They may include many courses, but generally offer small servings. Everything is planned out to complement everything else, for the diner's greatest enjoyment. The primary rule is to take your time. Don't order in a hurry. Don't eat in a hurry. You insult the food and the chef if you do.

Realistically, that time-consuming approach to food doesn't fit with all modern lifestyles, and French freezers contain convenience foods, just as American ones do. The ideal, however, remains the painstaking, meticulous meal preparation and the discriminating enjoyment of eating it. To better understand the French obsession with food, read the popular book *French Women Don't Get Fat*, by Mireille Guiliano. It provides a fascinating window into the French mindset about food and the body.

Food

Food is an integral part of any culture, with so many variations that we could easily have a series of books just on French cuisine. Here is a summary of the most common or important food words, to give you a taste of what to expect.

Reality check: Because there are so many food words, it's hard to learn them all. Don't worry about memorizing lists of food, if you are short on time. There is not really any need to. A quick look in the back of this book will show whether you are about to order rice (*riz*) or sweetbreads (gland meats) (*ris*). It makes sense to learn a few basic words for drinks you like and for basic foods you know you like (beef, chicken, potatoes), but don't waste precious study time on vocabulary that you will have time to look up when you need it. You will be better off concentrating on key phrases and cultural information, so you will feel comfortable entering a restaurant, ordering, eating, and paying.

Culture note—Posted prices

French eating establishments post their menus with prices where they can be read from outside. If prices aren't listed, that means the restaurant is expensive. Don't be put off by a short menu, including one handwritten on a blackboard. That indicates that the selection of freshest ingredients determines what will be offered. Do make sure you stick to the foods on the menu. It's a *faux pas* to ask for something that is not listed.

Where is ___?	Où est ___?	oo ay ___?
to recommend	recommander	Ruh-kuh-mah^n-day
Can you ___?	Pouvez-vous ___?	poo-vay voo ___?
Can you recommend ___?	Pouvez-vous recommander ___?	poo-vay voo Ruh-kuh-mah^n-day ___?
a good restaurant	un bon restaurant	æ^n boh^n Rehs-toh-Rah^n
with classic French cooking	de haute cuisine	duh oht kwee-zeen
with traditional, country food	de cuisine bourgeoise	duh kwee-zeen booR-zhwahz
with regional food	de cuisine régionale	duh kwee-zeen Ray-zhyoh-nahl
Is it very expensive?	C'est très cher?	say tRay shehR?

Culture note—Getting along with your waiter

Your waiter is a vital link in the dining experience. You want to establish a good rapport with him from the start. Despite his sometimes frosty appearance, greet him with a *Bonjour, monsieur*, a smile, and brief eye contact when he brings you the menu. That's the first step. Feel free to ask your waiter for assistance or additional information about the dishes. He is a professional and wants to share his expertise. I found the phrase *Pouvez-vous recommander_____?* (Can you recommend ___?) to be invaluable in both securing guidance and genuinely flattering my waiter, which led to warmer service.

Avoid requesting changes to a dish, or you may offend by implying you know better than the chef how the dish should be prepared. If you want dessert, you will usually order it at the end of the meal.

To get your waiter's attention, try to catch his eye and call *Monsieur!* or *s'il vous plaît*. Do not snap your fingers, clap your hands, or call *Garçon!*, which means, "Boy!" All are insulting practices and may result in poor service.

In the bustle of a full French restaurant, the waiter will probably be very busy during the meal. Don't get upset if he brings you the wrong dish. Kindly remind him what you ordered. Remember: Do not blame him. That would be poor form in France and would make *you* look bad. Focus on the fix, instead.

Culture note—Greetings in restaurants

It is polite to greet the service people in a restaurant with a *Bonjour!* or *Bonsoir!* when you enter. When you leave, tell your waiter *au revoir* and *merci* to be polite. If don't, you may be considered cold or stuck-up. Don't forget to add the appropriate title.

Culture note—Days of service

When reading to see when an establishment is open, look for the following terms: *tlj* is short for *tout les jours* ("all the days" = daily), *sauf* means except, and it will be followed by an abbreviation of the days the business is closed.

Culture note—Traditional Sunday dinner

A weekday lunch is often a two-hour affair, typically including several courses. Sunday dinner expands on the already expansive lunch. Sunday dinner is the most important family meal of the week. It is an extended, leisurely affair, often culminating in a nap or a walk. Expect to spend the whole afternoon if you are invited to participate.

Travel tips: A full restaurant usually shows where the locals eat and is a good bet in an unfamiliar town. A quick, reliable restaurant meal is *steak frites* [stehk fReef] (steak and French fries). For a rare (really rare!) steak, order it *saignant* [sehn-yah^n], medium-rare is *à point* [ah pwæ^n], and well-done is *bien cuit* [byæ^n kwee]. *Bien cuit* can range from a perfect American medium-rare to tough-as-shoe-leather overcooked. Unless you can't stand a pink center, *à point* may be the safer choice.

Places to Eat

The following list of terms will help you decide where you want to eat. Make a habit of checking out the posted menu (usually right outside the entrance) when choosing a place to eat.

le café	A community living room. Drink coffee, sit, talk, read. Grab a between-meal bite. Stay as long as you want. Different prices depending on where you eat/drink. Cheapest at bar. If seated at a set table, you are expected to order a meal (not just a sandwich).
la brasserie	Wider food selection, usually serving all day. If you sit in the dining area, you should order a hot meal. A bit more upscale, possibly larger than a café. May order a single course. Often specializes in a type of food, e.g., Alsatian. Often a good beer selection.
le bar	Small, for quick drinks, often standing. Economical.
le bar à vin	Café atmosphere, specializes in wine.
le salon de thé	A frilly, upscale café that usually has take-away specialties such as elegant pastries and canapés. Serves salads and other light fare. Can be small and informal.
le bistro	A simple, down-to-earth restaurant. Reasonable prices. Can be modern.
la crêperie	A restaurant specializing in crêpes, sweet or savory. (A *galette* is a savory crêpe usually made with buckwheat flour.)
le restaurant	Ranges from small family-run inns to the most elegant eating establishments. Expect to order several courses and wine.

Culture note—Le café-tabac

A particular kind of *café* is the *café-tabac* (immortalized in the movie *Amélie*). In addition to food and drink, a *café-tabac* also sells tobacco products, phone cards, lottery tickets, transportation tickets, maps, gum, postcards, stamps, newspapers, and magazines.

Culture note—Café bustle

In a full *café*, don't expect a warm welcome from the workers. They are too busy serving everyone. The waiter may place a slip of paper under your plate with your order information. You generally call the waiter when you are ready to pay and leave, but if you are sitting outside, you might be asked to pay first.

Culture note—To sit or not to sit

In a *café*—or anyplace that has a standing bar *and* tables with chairs—you must decide whether you want to stand at the bar or pay considerably more to sit down or pay even more to sit outside. Price should not be your only consideration. If time is of the essence, toss back your *express* at the bar and rush back out. If you are taking a break, though, it is well worth the cost to sit down and relax, especially at an outdoor café. As travel writer Rick Steves advises, don't think of it as paying an exorbitant price to eat or drink. Think of it as renting a prime piece of real estate. You may sit as long as you like, watching French life stream by.

Realize that restaurant seating in France is much closer than Americans are used to. Tables in general are small, and you are expected to take one that is no larger than your party requires. In other words, don't sit at a table for four if you are a party of two and a smaller table is available. It's also possible that your waiter or waitress will move you or your party at some point to accommodate a larger group. Unlike in other European countries, you should not sit at a stranger's table, even if the *café* is full.

Meals

A full French meal can easily have more than a half-dozen courses, usually including a starter (soup, fish, or special salad), a main dish, green salad, cheeses, dessert or fruit. It may have coffee or tea at the end. The following descriptions may help you nativigate your way through an elaborate meal.

le petit déjeuner (breakfast)
Breakfast is usually served from 7 to 10. A hotel breakfast is usually coffee (either *café au lait* or *express*), tea or hot chocolate, bread or croissants, butter, jam, yogurt, and possibly fruit. French people typically eat a very light breakfast.

le déjeuner (lunch)
Lunch is generally available from around 12 or 12:30 to 2 or 3. This is traditionally the largest meal of the day and could consist of the following courses (served separately):

amuse-bouche—a small treat to whet the appetite, literally a "mouth delight"

entrée/hors-d'oeuvre (appetizer)—cold meats or marinated vegetables, pâté, salad, soup, oysters, snails, savory pastries

plat (principal/de résistance) (main course)—meat or fish, usually with vegetables and possibly followed by a green salad

fromage (cheese)—usually several kinds, choose up to three. Slice to maintain the pointed shape. Place a bite-sized piece on a bite-sized chunk of torn-off bread. Drink a swallow of wine between types of cheese. Is often "raw" (unpasteurized) in France.

dessert (sweet or fruit)—Usually ordered at the end of the meal. Classics include *crème brûlée* (custard topped with caramelized sugar), *crème caramel* (caramel custard), *Tarte Tatin* (upside-down apple tart), and *moelleux au chocolat* (hot chocolate cake with liquid chocolate filling).

café (coffee)—strong coffee

digestif (after-dinner liqueur)

The main meal is commonly shortened to *entrée-plat-dessert* or a bare-bones *entrée-plat* or *plat-dessert*.

le dîner
(the evening meal)
The evening meal is generally available from around 7:30 to around 10, with earlier times in rural areas. In most homes, dinner is around 8 or 9. It follows the same pattern as lunch and can be large or light.

Culture note—Menu specials

Many places have a daily special menu at a fixed price (*le menu prix-fixe*); it may be called a *plat du jour* (daily special), a *formule* (formula), a *menu touristique* (tourist menu) or, for food lovers, a rich and heavy *menu gourmand*. The daily special typically includes a main course, a drink, and a dessert or appetizer. The meal is usually a good deal, often featuring the same food available on the regular menu, but at a much better price, particularly at lunch. The drawback is a limited selection. For a harried tourist overwhelmed by unfamiliar choices, however, this limitation can be a godsend.

If a menu item is especially popular, the restaurant may run out of it. They may have to substitute dishes.

Culture note—Entrée, French vs American

Don't be fooled by the French word *entrée*. Actually, we Americans somehow managed to twist the term to mean the main course of the meal. In France, it means the *entry* to the meal, the first course or appetizer.

Ordering

Do you have a table ___?	Avez-vous une table ___?	*ah-vay-voo (z)ew°n tah-bluh ___?*
for two	pour deux personnes	*pooR duh pehr-suhn*
in a no smoking section	dans une zone non-fumeur	*dah^n (z)ew°n zohn noh^n few°-muhR*
near the window	près de la fenêtre	*pReh duh lah fuh-neh-tRuh*
outside	à l'extérieur	*ah lehk-stayR-yuhR*
inside	à l'intérieur	*ah lah^n-tayR-yuhR*
Waiter!	Monsieur!	*muh-syuh!*
Waitress!	Madame!/ Mademoiselle!	*mah-dahm! / mahd-mwah-zehl!*
Excuse me! (to get attention)	Pardon!	*pahR-doh^n*
to desire	désirer	*day-zee-Ray*
=What would you like?	Vous désirez?	*voo day-zee-Ray?*
to order	commander	*kuh-mah^n-day*
You desire (=are ready) to order?	Vous désirez commander?	*voo day-zee-Ray kuh-mah^n-day?*
What would you take (=like to have)?	Qu'est-ce que vous prenez?	*kehs kuh voo pRuh-nay?*
Can you ___?	Pouvez-vous ___?	*poo-vay voo ___?*
to recommend	recommander	*Ruh-kuh-mah^n-day*
something	quelque chose	*kehl-kuh shohz*
Can you recommend something?	Pouvez-vous recommander quelque chose?	*poo-vay voo Ruh-kuh-mah^n-day kehl-kuh shohz?*
I would like ___.	Je voudrais ___.	*zhuh voo-dRay ___.*
We would like ___.	Nous voudrions ___.	*noo voo-dRee-yoh^n ___.*
I'll have/take ___.	Je prends ___	*zhuh pRah^n ___*
We'll have/take ___.	Nous prenons ___	*noo pReh-noh^n ___*

some house wine	du vin ordinaire	dew° væ^n uhR-dee-nehR
a toasted ham/cheese sandwich	un croque-monsieur	æ^n kRuhk muh-syuh
tea	un thé	æ^n tay
Enjoy your meal!	Bon appétit!	buh (n)ah-pay-tee
to like	aimer (bien)	ay-may (byæ^n)
I like ___.	J'aime (bien) ___.	zhehm (byæ^n) ___
I don't like ___.	Je n'aime pas ___.	zhuh nehm pah ___
I (don't) like it.	Je (ne) l'aime (pas).	zhuh (nuh) lehm (pah)
very much	beaucoup	boh-koo

Culture note—*Bon appétit!*

Before you start eating a meal, it is polite to wish your fellow diners *bon appétit!* [buh (n)ah-pay-tee]. The closest equivalent that we have in English is "Enjoy your meal."

Similarly, before drinking with others, it is polite to hold your glass up and say *Santé!* [sah^n-tay] (to your health!), *À la vôtre!* [ah lah voh-tRuh] (to you!), or *tchin!* [cheen] (cheers!) to your companions.

The Menu

menu (printed)	la carte	lah kahRt
fixed-price menu	le menu (prix-fixe)	luh muh-new° (pRee feeks)
today's special	le plat du jour	luh plah dew° zhooR
What's today's special?	Quel est le plat du jour?	kehl ay luh plah dew° zhooR?
house specialty	la spécialité de la maison	lah spay-syah-lee-tay duh lah meh-zoh^n
appetizers	les hors-d'oeuvre (m)	lay uhR-duh-vRuh
first course, starter	l'entrée (f)	lah^n-tRay
soups	les soupes (f)	lay soop
fish and seafood	les poissons (m) et les fruits de mer (m)	lay pwah-soh^n ay lay fRwee duh mehR

meats	les viandes (f)	*lay vyah^{n}d*
vegetables	les légumes (m)	*lay lay-gew^{o}m*
salads	les salades (f)	*lay sah-lahd*
fruit	les fruits (m)	*lay fRwee*
cheese	les fromages (m)	*lay fRuh-mahzh*
dessert	les desserts (m)	*lay day-sehR*
drinks	les boissons (f)	*lay bwah-soh^n*

Note: Menu sections are often labeled with plural forms of food types. If you would like to read about plural formation now, jump ahead to p. 112.

Culture note—L'apéritif or l'apéro

Drinks are often served before meals and during the cocktail hours in France. The term *l'apéritif* [*lah-pay-Ree-teef*], often shortened to *l'apéro* [*lah-pay-Roh*], comes from the idea that a cocktail stimulates the appetite. These drinks may be served in someone's home, or friends may meet in a *café* or *bar* to share a drink and relax, typically about 6 or 7 p.m. *L'apéro* usually includes a small, crunchy snack, such as nuts or pretzels.

French diners also like to have *un apéritif* in a restaurant, on Sundays or holidays, or with guests. Popular *apéritifs* include *kir* (white burgundy wine sweetened with a red currant liqueur), *pastis* (aniseed/water mix), *pineau* (grape juice with cognac), or something non-alcoholic, such as water, juice, or a soft drink. Beer is also popular, often ordered by the *demi* (¼ liter).

Culture note—Ice cubes

Most Europeans do not drink water or juice with ice cubes, though they might have ice in a soft drink, if the drink is warm. Waiters typically do not react well when Americans ask for ice cubes with chilled beverages. They usually respond, *"C'est frais."* ("It's chilled.") Europeans are serious about saving energy, and electricity is required to produce ice cubes. Also, a harried waiter in a café does not appreciate extra work when, in his mind, the beverage is chilled.

Drinks

I would like ___.	Je voudrais ___.	zhuh voo-dRay ___
a drink	une boisson	ew°n bwah-soh^n
some water	de l'eau (f)	duh loh
some cold water	de l'eau fraîche	duh loh fRehsh
some mineral water	de l'eau minérale	duh loh mee-nay-Rahl
carbonated	gazeuse	gah-zuhz
non-carbonated	plate	plaht
some tap-water	de l'eau ordinaire	duh loh uhR-dee-nehR

Culture note—Non-potable water

When on a train or plane (or anywhere else, for that matter), do not drink or brush your teeth with water labeled *non potable*. The warning indicates that the water is not safe to consume.

I'll have/take ___	Je prends ___	zhuh pRah^n ___
some wine	du vin	dew° væ^n
some red wine	du vin rouge	dew° væ^n Roozh
some white wine	du vin blanc	dew° væ^n blah^n
some sparkling wine	du vin mousseux	dew° væ^n moo-suh
	du vin pétillant	dew° væ^n pay-tee-yæ^n
some house wine	du vin maison	dew° væ^n meh-zoh^n
	du vin de table	dew° væ^n duh tah-bluh
the wine list	la carte des vins	lah kahRt day væ^n
a beer	une bière	ew°n byehR
a draft beer	une bière pression	ew°n byehR pReh-syoh^n
a glass of ___	un verre de ___	æ^n vehR duh ___
a carafe of ___	une carafe de ___	ew°n kah-Rahf duh ___
a bottle of ___	une bouteille de _	ew°n boo-tehy duh __
a cup of ___	une tasse de ___	ew°n tahs duh ___
a tea	un thé	æ^n tay
an iced tea	un thé glacé	æ^n tay glah-say
a soft drink	un soda	æ^n suh-dah
a cola	un coca	æ^n kuh-kah

a lemonade	une citronnade	ew°n see-tRuh-nahd
	un citron pressé	æⁿ see-tRohⁿ pRay-say
a fruit juice	un jus de fruit	æⁿ zhew° duh fRwee
an alcoholic cider	un cidre	æⁿ see-dRuh
some milk	du lait	dew° lay
a coffee	un café	æⁿ kah-fay
a strong black coffee	un café noir	æⁿ kah-fay nwahR
a decaffeinated coffee	un café décaféiné	æⁿ kah-fay day-kah-fay-ee-nay
an espresso	un café-express	æⁿ kah-fay ehks-pRehs
an espresso with a little milk	un café noisette	æⁿ kah-fay nwah-zeht
a coffee with milk	un café au lait*	æⁿ kah-fay oh lay
a coffee with cream	un café-crème	æⁿ kah-fay kRehm
an iced coffee	un café glacé	æⁿ kah-fay glah-say
a (hot) chocolate	un chocolat (chaud)	æⁿ shuh-kuh-lah (shoh)
some ice cubes	des glaçons (m)	day glah-sohⁿ

*morning only

Culture note—Coffees

The main coffees you can choose from in France are as follows. They are generally available in *grand* [gRahⁿ] and *petit* [puh-tee].

Un express [æⁿ (n)ehks-pRehs] is an espresso, made in an espresso machine and usually served in a small cup.

Un café noir [æⁿ kah-fay nwahR] is strong, dark coffee without cream or milk.

Un café noisette [æⁿ kah-fay nwah-zeht] is an espresso with a little milk.

Un café américain [æⁿ kah-fay ah-may-Ree-kæⁿ] is watered-down espresso.

Un café au lait [æⁿ kah-fay oh lay] is an espresso with frothy milk and is drunk only in the morning.

Culture note—Wine

Wine is the national drink of France, with each region producing its own specialties. French people generally drink wine with every meal but breakfast (and some do then, too), but in moderation, usually no more than a couple of glasses. It is considered very bad form to drink too much wine, and you rarely see drunken French people. To avoid over-consumption, drinkers alternate water with sips of wine, as well as leave wine in their glasses to avoid refillings. Children begin to drink wine with the family from a young age (diluted with water, at the start) and may order wine in a restaurant from the time they are fourteen.

Wine is important in France—its color, its smell, its taste. To properly pair your wine with your food, you may always ask for your waiter's recommendation. In general, you want *rosé* or white with your starters, red with meat, dry white with fish, and a sweet dessert wine with dessert.

Wine is ordered by the bottle (*une bouteille*) [ew°n boo-tehy], half-bottle (*une demi-bouteille*) [ew°n duh-mee boo-tehy], or by the *carafe* [ew°n kah-Rahf]. When the waiter opens a bottle of wine for you, he will let you taste it for quality, to make sure it's not "corked" (spoiled by a cork fungus). If the wine tastes bad or smells funny, you should tell your waiter, *"C'est bouchonné"* [say boo-shuh-nay] and send the bottle back.

It's perfectly acceptable (and kind to your budget) to order the house wine (*vin maison* [væ^n meh-zoh^n] or *vin de table* [væ^n duh tah-bluh]), be it red, white or *rosé*.

If your table has multiple glasses on it, the smallest is for white wine, the middle one is for red wine, and the largest one is for water. To properly appreciate the color and quality of the wine, you should hold the glass by the stem. To allow the wine to breath properly and enhance its aroma, your glass may be only partially filled, then added to as you drink. When you switch wines, you should wipe your lips with your napkin.

Grammar—The partitive article

Masculine, singular	Feminine, singular	Before a vowel, sing.
du (*dew⁰*)	de la (*duh lah*)	de l' (*duhl*)

We have already discussed definite articles (*the*, to refer to a specific noun) and indefinite articles (*a/an*, to refer to a non-specific noun). Now we will learn about the partitive article, to express an unspecified amount of something, or a *part* of something (the *partitive*).

Sometimes you want to order *some* of something, rather than a specific amount of it, for example, *some mineral water*. To do this in French, you use a form of *de* (see table above), as in *de l'eau minérale*. This use of *de* to express an unspecified quantity is very common in French, used in cases where we would just leave the word out in English. For example, in English you could ask someone either of the following questions: "Would you like coffee?" or "Would you like some coffee?" Both are fine. In French, though, you need to use the "some" version: *Voulez-vous du café?* The article is always required in French, even if you wouldn't say "some" in English.

The forms of the partitive are *du* for singular masculine nouns (*du sucre*—some sugar), *de la* for singular feminine nous (*de la viande*—some meat), and *de l'* before singular nouns starting with a vowel or *h* (*de l'eau*—some water).

Exercise 3.3

How would you order *some* of the following?

1. some red wine (le vin rouge)

2. some beer (la bière)

3. some cola (le coca)

4. some lemonade (la citronnade/le citron pressé)

5. some milk (le lait)

6. some tea (le thé)

7. some fruit juice (le jus de fruit)

Answers: 1) du vin rouge, 2) de la bière, 3) du coca, 4) de la citronnade *or* du citron pressé, 5) du lait, 6) du thé, 7) du jus de fruit

Culture note—Beverages customs

During meals, French people drink wine, beer, mineral water, or juice. In general, adults do not drink milk. If you order a soft drink, you will quickly notice that the servings are small by American standards, and there won't be any free refills (for coffee, either, by the way). While it is fine to order a soft drink in a café, you should not order one with a meal in a restaurant, as it might be considered an insult to the chef. Other than breakfast, coffee is never drunk during meals. Meals are frequently capped off with an espresso, however.

French restaurants do not automatically place water on the table for customers to drink. To go with local custom, you could order mineral water to drink (*de l'eau minérale*), and the waiter will ask whether you want *gazeuse* (carbonated) or *plate/non-gazeuse* (non-carbonated). If you prefer, you may ask for the perfectly safe tap water for free by requesting *une carafe d'eau*. As with other cool drinks, water will not be served with ice. You may be able to receive ice upon request during the summer, but you're fighting a losing battle. Consider giving in and drinking cool rather than ice-cold beverages.

Culture note—Breakfast drinks

Express, *café au lait*, and *chocolat* are the most popular breakfast beverages. You may be able to get orange juice, and milk may be available for cereal at a buffet. It is likely to be raw or sterilized milk, however, which tastes different from American pasteurized milk. *Un café crème* [æ^n kah-fay kRehm] or *un café au lait* [æ^n kah-fay oh lay] is an espresso with cream or frothy milk.

Breakfast

I would like ___	Je voudrais ___	zhuh voo-dRay ___
some bread	du pain	dew^p pæ^n
a loaf of French bread	une baguette	ew^{p}n bah-geht
some butter	du beurre	dew^p buhR
a roll	un petit pain	æ^n puh-tee pæ^n
a croissant	un croissant	æ^n kRwah-sah^n
some toast	du pain grillé	dew^p pæ^n gRee-yay
some eggs	des oeufs	day (z)uh
some orange juice	du jus d'orange	dew^p zhew^p duh-Rah^{n}zh
some honey	du miel	dew^p myehl
some jam	de la confiture	duh lah koh^n-fee-tew^{p}R
some milk	du lait	dew^p lay
some sugar	du sucre	dew^p sew^p-kRuh
some cream	de la crème	duh lah kRehm

Culture note—Breakfast dress code

If you eat breakfast in your hotel, be aware that it is not the casual affair of many continental breakfasts in the United States. Wear clothes, including shoes, *not* pajamas. Brush your hair. Look ready for the day. From the French point of view, you insult those around you when you don't bother to look presentable.

Culture note—Bread

French bread (*du pain*) is always on the table at no extra cost with a meal. It is to be eaten with the meal, not as an appetizer. Bread should be broken with the fingers, not cut with a knife, and the chunk you have broken off should be placed on the table next to your plate. It should not be dipped in food. Bread is usually not served with butter except at breakfast; when butter *is* served, it should be put on individual pieces of bread that are broken off with the fingers, not on a whole piece of bread.

Poultry and Game

I'll have/take ___.	Je prends ___.	*zhuh pRah^{n} ___*
chicken	du poulet	*dew^{P} poo-lay*
duck	du canard	*dew^{P} kah-nahR*
goose	de l'oie (f)	*duh lwah*
pheasant	du faisan	*dew^{P} fuh-zah^{n}*
rabbit	du lapin	*dew^{P} lah-pæ^{n}*
venison	du chevreuil	*dew^{P} shuh-vRuhy*

Meat

beef	du boeuf	*dew^{P} buhf*
steak	du bifteck	*dew^{P} beef-tehk*
pork	du porc	*dew^{P} pohR*
ham	du jambon	*dew^{P} zhah^{n}-boh^{n}*
bacon	du lard	*dew^{P} lahR*
sausages	des andouilles	*day (z)ah^{n}-dooy*
veal	du veau	*dew^{P} voh*
lamb	de l'agneau (m)	*duh lah-nyoh*

Culture note—Meat

French people are not overly sensitive about their meat or where it comes from. The production of *foie gras* (force feeding geese) is not a cause of great concern there. All parts of animals are eaten, with no effort to hide what they are. As in many other European countries, horsemeat is eaten in France and sold at special butcher shops. The French word for horse is *cheval*, easily confused with a style of serving food with an egg "riding" on top, *à cheval*. Look for the *à* in the food description, or ask your waiter, if you want to avoid eating horsemeat.

Fish and Seafood

snails	des escargots	*day (z)ehs-kahR-goh*
frog's legs	des cuisses de grenouille	*day kwees duh gRuh-nooy*
oysters	des huîtres	*day (z)wee-tRuh*
shrimps	des crevettes	*day kRuh-veht*
lobster	du homard	*dew° uh-mahR*
tuna	du thon	*dew° toh^n*
trout	de la truite	*duh lah tRweet*
anchovies	des anchois	*day (z)ah^n-shwah*

Culture note—American fast food

Travelers often dive into the local cuisine with the best intentions but find themselves hankering for familiar food after a few days. If you're dying for a Big Mac or something similar, you will find American fast-food restaurants in French cities. The food may not be identical to what you are used to, but it will be close enough to stave off cravings, and it's interesting to see what the chains do differently in their franchises abroad.

Be aware that if you "special order" anything (no toppings, for example), it will take considerably longer to get your food. My daughter's "plain" hamburger required an extra ten-minute wait and two follow-up checks by the manager. Another difference is that you are unlikely to find free refills in France, and your drink cup may not be filled to the prescribed level. Nonetheless, you should expect to pay more than at an American fast-food restaurant. Don't believe the myth that only Americans eat at "McDo"—these places are usually packed with locals. Just don't limit yourself to American fast-food chains, or you will miss a vital part of French culture.

Vegetables and Salad

English	French	Pronunciation
I would like ___	Je voudrais ___	zhuh voo-dRay ___
an artichoke	un artichaut (m)	$æ^n$ (n)ahR-tee-shoh
asparagus	des asperges	day (z)ahs-pehRzh
carrots	des carottes	day kah-Ruht
mushrooms	des champignons	day shah^n-pee-nyoh^n
corn	du maïs	dew^o mah-ees
celery	du céleri	dew^o sehl-Ree
a cabbage	un chou	$æ^n$ shoo
a cauliflower	un chou-fleur	$æ^n$ shoo-fluhR
spinach	des épinards	day (z)ay-pee-nahR
green beans	des haricots verts	day ah-Ree-koh vehR
onions	des oignons	day (z)uh-nyoh^n
green pepper	du piment	dew^o pee-mah^n
peas	des petits pois	day puh-tee pwah
a leek	un poireau	$æ^n$ pwah-Roh
potatoes	des pommes de terre	day puhm duh tehR
a tomato	une tomate	ew^{o}n tuh-maht

Cheese

English	French	Pronunciation
What is that cheese?	Quel fromage est-ce?	kehl fRuh-mahzh ehs?
Is it ___?	Est-il ___?	eh-teel ___?
low-fat	maigre	meh-gRuh
mild	doux	doo
sharp	piquant/fort	pee-kah^n/fuhR
hard	à pâte dure	ah paht dew^{o}R
soft	à pâte molle	ah paht muhl

Nuts

English	French	Pronunciation
a hazelnut	une noisette	ew^{o}n nwah-zeht
an almond	une amande	ew^{o}n ah-mahnd
a chestnut	un marron	$æ^n$ mah-Roh^n
a walnut	une noix	ew^{o}n nwah

Fruit

I would like ___	Je voudrais ___	zhuh voo-dRay ___
a fruit	un fruit	æ^n fRwee
an apple	une pomme	ew°n puhm
an orange	une orange	ew°n uh-Rah^nzh
a pear	une poire	ew°n pwahR
a banana	une banane	ew°n bah-nahn
a strawberry	une fraise	ew°n fRehz
a raspberry	une framboise	ew°n fRah^n-bwahz
a cherry	une cerise	ew°n suh-Reez
a peach	une pêche	ew°n pehsh
a grape	un raisin	æ^n Reh-zæ^n
a lemon	un citron	æ^n see-tRoh^n

Culture note—Condiments

Condiments are not necessarily placed on the restaurant table automatically, but often you do see Dijon mustard, salt, and pepper. You may need to call the waiter (*Monsieur!*) and request a condiment that you want. Season only if you must, avoid salt and pepper, and use restraint—it may insult the chef if you imply that the seasoning isn't perfect.

Seasoning

I would like ___	Je voudrais ___	zhuh voo-dRay ___
salt	su sel	dew° sehl
pepper	du poivre	dew° pwah-vRuh
mustard	de la moutarde	duh lah moo-tahRd
ketchup	du ketchup	dew° keht-shuhp
mayonnaise	de la mayonnaise	duh lah mah-yuh-nehz
vinegar	du vinaigre	dew° vee-neh-gRuh
sugar	du sucre	dew° sew°-kRuh
honey	du miel	dew° myehl
butter	du beurre	dew° buhR
olive oil	de l'huile d'olive	duh lweel duh-leev

Dessert

I'll have/take ___.	Je prends ___.	*zhuh pRah^n ___*
a dessert	un dessert	*æ^n day-sehR*
sweets	des sucreries (f)	*day sew^o-kRuh-Ree*
a candy	un bonbon	*æ^n boh^n-boh^n*
chocolate	du chocolat	*dew^o shuh-kuh-lah*
a fancy layer cake	un gâteau	*æ^n gah-toh*
an ice cream	une glace	*ew^{o}n glahs*
whipped pudding	une mousse	*ew^{o}n moos*
thin, filled pancake	une crêpe	*ew^{o}n kRehp*
an open-faced pie	une tarte	*ew^{o}n tahRt*
a caramel-topped egg custard	une crème caramel	*ew^{o}n kRehm kah-Rah-mehl*
cream puff with ice cream	une profiterole	*ew^{o}n pRuh-fee-tRuhl*

Culture note—Smoking

Public smoking is undergoing a shift in France. Long a nation of smokers, in 2008 France enacted a strict public smoking ban, severely restricting smoking in hotels, nightclubs, and eating establishments, and outlawing it completely on trains. Smoking in public buildings is allowed only if there is a separate, enclosed, air-conditioned smoking room.

An official ban is one thing; widespread compliance is another. You are likely to see the smoking ban flouted in restaurants, bars, and other public places, even on public transportation. You have the right to complain if someone lights up near you, but it's easier and probably more effective just to move.

If you are a smoker and find a smoking section (*zone fumeur*) in which to indulge, please don't light up during a meal—only at the end.

Culture note—Table manners

Manners are important in France, including table manners. To be polite, you should put your napkin on your lap (or on the table off to the left) and wait until all are served before you eat. Don't slouch. And watch how you use your silverware.

The French keep their fork in the left hand, knife in the right, throughout the meal, using the knife for cutting and for pushing food onto the fork. If you are not holding the knife in your hand, you should place your right hand and forearm on the table next to the plate, not on your lap. (No switching the fork to your right hand!) Contrary to the custom in the United States, it is considered bad manners to place a hand on the lap during a meal. It is all right to rest your hands and wrists on the table, but try not to plant your elbow there.

You should not eat the bread while waiting for the first course of the meal. Bread at the table should be torn off the loaf, not cut. Place it to the left next to the plate when you are not eating it, to keep it out of any sauces. If you want to soak up sauce with bread pieces, use your fork to do so, not your fingers. This should never be done at a fine restaurant, however, and never use bread to wipe your plate. Only tear off one chunk of bread at a time, and only eat bite-sized pieces that you tear off; never take a bite off a larger chunk of bread. During the meal, do not speak loudly, don't point with your knife, and don't talk with your mouth full. Do take an interest in the food on your plate.

Cheese is picked up with the prongs of a cheese knife and placed on a piece of bread. Choose cheese from the cheese board, cut off the slices you want, but keep the wedge shape. *Do not* cut off the point of the triangle. (That would be cutting off the "nose"!)

You are expected to eat everything on your plate. Not to do so is considered wasteful, because you generally don't take leftovers home. Do not, however, tip your soup plate for the last drops. When you are finished eating, you should lay your silverware together (parallel) on your plate, with the fork pointing up.

Tableware

I need __.	Il me faut ___.	eel muh foh ___
We need ___.	Il nous faut ___.	eel noo foh ___
a plate	une assiette	ew^on ah-syeht
a glass	un verre	$æ^n$ vehR
a fork	une fourchette	ew^on fooR-sheht
a knife	un couteau	$æ^n$ koo-toh
a spoon	une cuillère	ew^on kwee-yehR
a napkin	une serviette	ew^on sehR-vyeht

Paying

I'd like ___.	Je voudrais ___.	zhuh voo-dRay ___
to pay	payer	pay-yay
I'd like to pay.	Je voudrais payer.	zhuh voo-dRay pay-yay
Check, please.	L'addition, s'il vous plaît.	lah-dee-$syoh^n$, see voo play
together	ensemble	ah^n-sah^n-bluh
separate	séparément	say-pah-Ray-mah^n
service charge/tip	le service	luh sehR-vees
Is the tip included?	Le service est compris?	luh sehR-vees ay koh^n-pRee?
for you	pour vous	pooR voo
This is for you.	Ceci est pour vous.	suh-see ay pooR voo
a mistake	une erreur	ew^on eh-RuhR
I think that ___.	Je crois que___.	zhuh kRwah kuh ___
I think that there's a mistake.	Je crois qu'il y a une erreur.	zhuh kRwah keel yah ew^on eh-RuhR
a meal	un repas	$æ^n$ Ruh-pah
a very good meal	un très bon repas	$æ^n$ tRay boh^n Ruh-pah
That was a very good meal.	C'était un très bon repas.	say-teh (t)$æ^n$ tRay boh^n Ruh-pah

Culture note—Paying, tipping, and leaving

When you are ready to leave an eating establishment, you must ask for *l'addition, s'il vous plaît*—the waiter doesn't want to rush you by bringing over the bill before you ask for it. Check the bill for errors. French people check, too. Along with the bill, the waiter might bring a saucer or small tray for you to place your cash or credit card on, or he might bring a credit card machine right to the table. If you are paying by credit card, you should select to pay in the local currency, not in U.S. dollars, because you will get a better exchange rate.

If you are eating with a group of people, the bill may be for the entire table. You can either have one person pay and settle up afterward, or each party can figure out their own portion and pay for that. A service charge (normally of 15%) is included. The words *service compris* tell you that the price includes a service charge. If you are particularly pleased with the service, you can add 5% to 10% of the total, but anything more is too much and could be considered showing off. If the bill says *service non compris*, then you should add at least 10% for service. Most diners round up to the next convenient and appropriate euro and leave that total on the payment saucer or tray.

Exercise 3.4
How would you say the following in French?

1. Is there a restaurant near here?

2. I would like a carafe of red wine, please.

4. Can you recommend something?

5. Do you have onion soup?

6. Can you recommend a wine?

7. I would like the fixed-price menu.

8. I need a fork, please.

9. Check, please!

Answers: 1) Il y a un restaurant près d'ici? 2) Je voudrais une carafe de vin rouge, s'il vous plaît. 3) Pouvez-vous recommander quelque chose? 4) Avez-vous de la soupe à l'oignon? 5) Pouvez-vous recommander un vin? 6) Je voudrais le menu (prix-fixe). 7) Il me faut une fourchette, s'il vous plaît. 8) L'addition, s'il vous plaît.

Exercise 3.5

Say several things that you like to eat or drink. When using verbs of preference, you will include the definite article (*le, la, l', les*) for whatever you like/don't like. For example, *J'aime la salade niçoise. J'aime bien les desserts.*

Now say what you *don't* like to eat or drink. For example, *Je n'aime pas les rognons. Je n'aime pas les cuisses de grenouille.*

4 Shopping

Numbers (0-100, by ten)

Time for more numbers. Review 0-10 (p. 41) and 11-20 (p. 63)
before learning these.

0	zéro	*zay-Roh*
10	dix	*dees*
20	vingt	*væ^n*
30	trente	*tRah^{n}t*
40	quarante	*kah-Rah^{n}t*
50	cinquante	*sæ^n-kah^{n}t*
60	soixante	*swah-sah^{n}t*
70	soixante-dix	*swah-sah^{n}t dees*
80	quatre-vingts	*kah-tRuh-væ^n*
90	quatre-vingt-dix	*kah-tRuh-væ^n dees*
100	cent*	*sah^n*

* Note: Use just one word—*cent*—for "one hundred," not two
words. The correct French equivalent for one-hundred is just
"hundred."

Exercise 4.1
Translate the following numbers into French. Try not to look at
the list above.

1. ten

2. sixty

3. twenty

4. seventy

5. thirty

6. eighty

7. forty

8. ninety

9. fifty

10. one hundred

Answers: 1) dix, 2) soixante, 3) vingt, 4) soixante-dix, 5) trente, 6) quatre-vingts,
7) quarante, 8) quatre-vingt-dix, 9) cinquante, 10) cent

Exercise 4.2

Give the correct number in French.

1. Number of people on five U.S. juries

2. Years in a decade

3. Decade of bell bottoms and disco

4. Stars on the American flag

5. Complete, All = _____ %

6. Ounces in five pounds

7. The "roaring" decade

8. Hours in a standard U.S. work week

9. Six quintets

10. Minimum age for a nonagenarian

Answers: 1) soixante, 2) dix, 3) soixante-dix, 4) cinquante, 5) cent, 6) quatre-vingts, 7) vingt, 8) quarante, 9) trente, 10) quatre-vingt-dix

Useful Vocabulary

big	grand*	$gRah^n$
small	petit*	*puh-tee*
hot	chaud*	*shoh*
cold	froid*	*fRwah*
good	bon*	boh^n
bad	mauvais*	*moh-veh*
a lot (of)	beaucoup (de)	*boh-koo (duh)*
a little (of)	un peu (de)	$æ^n$ *puh (duh)*
well	bien	$byæ^n$
badly	mal	*mahl*
too	trop	*tRoh*
enough (of)	assez (de)	*ah-say (duh)*
not enough (of)	pas assez (de)	*pah (z)ah-say (duh)*
only	seulement	$suhl-mah^n$
also	aussi	*oh-see*

* Grammar note—Adjective agreement

The first six words in the list above are adjectives, so they should agree in gender and number with the noun they modify. Below is the full list of their forms. The first French options show masculine singular and plural forms, and the second part shows feminine singular and plural forms.

big	grand(s)/grande(s)	$gRah^n/gRah^nd$
small	petit(s)/petite(s)	puh-tee/puh-teet
hot	chaud(s)/chaude(s)	shoh/shohd
cold	froid(s)/froide(s)	fRwah/fRwahd
good	bon(s)/bonne(s)	boh^n/buhn
bad	mauvais/mauvaise(s)	moh-veh/moh-vehz

Here are a couple examples of how to use these adjectives, using the verb forms *est* (is) and *sont* (are):

Fem. sing.: The soup is hot. *La soupe est chaude.* [la soop ay shohd]

Fem. plural.: The bedrooms are too small. *Les chambres sont trop petites.* [lay $shah^n$-bRuh soh^n tRoh puh-teet]

Culture note—Commas and decimal points

In French numbers, commas and periods are used differently than in the American system. A comma is used to indicate decimals (where we would use a period), and a period is used to indicate thousands (where we would use a comma).

American   3,576.90

French   3.576,90

You will see the comma most frequently in prices. For example, € 7,40 means seven euros and 40 cents.

Culture note—The baguette

A *baguette* is the long, skinny loaf of French bread you will see tucked under arms and sticking out of bags all over France. The humble baguette should be of the same high quality as other

French food. The best baguettes are baked in the traditional way and can be identified by the satisfying crackle of their crusts. Most tourists will be perfectly happy with any fresh baguette, particularly if topped with luscious, fat-filled French butter.

Shopping

Virtually all travelers do some shopping, even if just for postcards or bottled water. Make your shopping easier by learning some useful question and answer forms.

As with food vocabulary, you will probably have time to look up the word for anything specific that you want to buy, so you don't need to spend a lot of time memorizing lists of shopping items, unless you have the time or you know you are going to shop a lot.

Reality check: Shopping is one of those areas where you can get by pretty well with body language (pointing, nodding, shaking your head). If you are short on language-learning time, just skim this section on shopping. You are probably best off knowing how to ask *How much?* and then being familiar with numbers so you can recognize the answer.

how much	combien	koh^n-byæ^n
How much is it?	C'est combien?	say koh^n-byæ^n?
Can you please write it down?	Pouvez-vous l'écrire, s'il vous plaît?	poo-vay voo lay-kReeR, see voo play?
Do you have ___?	Avez-vous ___?	ah-vay voo ___?
postcards	des cartes postales	day kahRt puhs-tahl
corkscrews	des tire-bouchons	day teeR-boo-shoh^n
maps	des cartes	day kahRt
umbrellas	des parapluies	day pah-Rah-plwee
I would like ___.	Je voudrais ___.	zhuh voo-dRay ___
this	ceci	suh-see
that	cela	suh-lah

Culture note—Shopping

French shopping is not the quick grab-and-go experience of the United States. Speciality shops offer a wide range of their specific items, which may be carefully examined and discussed before a choice is made. Bread is bought at a *boulangerie*, fish at a *poissonnerie*, pastries at a *pâtisserie*, meat at a *boucherie*.

Much shopping is done at fresh markets, which rotate in time and location. (The tourist office can inform you of the local schedule.) Bring your own shopping bags or basket, if you shop at the market.

Because of the emphasis on high-quality, fresh food, French people prefer to shop often—even daily—for small amounts of fresh foods to supplement their supermarket frozen foods.

Culture note—Customer service

Customer service is less a priority in France than in the U.S. (The exception might be small, family-run shops.) When approaching service personnel for help, treat them as impor-tant professionals who are doing you a favor. Respect their expertise. Value their assistance. Be grateful. And be patient. Convince yourself that time is not of the essence.

It helps to try to connect with the worker from the start, be it waiter, clerk, or shopkeeper. Greet him or her with a *Bonjour, Madame/Monsieur!* and try to make eye contact. Once you've made eye contact, remember, you've already overcome some of the distance between you. It's harder to ignore you.

If you encounter what you consider poor, even churlish, service, realize that it's not personal. Most service workers don't earn a high salary, don't enjoy high prestige, and don't necessarily like their jobs. Try to take any rudeness in stride and don't get worked up about it. That's just life in France.

When it's time to pay, it's the *customer's* responsibility to be alert for shortchanging and overcharging. To be polite, always say *Merci! Au revoir!* when leaving, with a title, of course.

I would like to see ___.	Je voudrais voir ___.	*zhuh voo-dRay vwahR ___*
to look for	chercher	*shehR-shay*
I'm looking for ___.	Je cherche ___.	*zhuh sheRsh ___*
to buy	acheter	*ahsh-tay*
I would like to buy ___.	Je voudrais acheter ___.	*zhuh voo-dRay (z)ahsh-tay ___*
some toothpaste	du dentifrice	*dew^o dah^n-tee-frees*
some deodorant	du déodorant	*dew^o day-uh-duh-Rah^n*
Where is ___?	Où est ___?	*oo ay ___?*
the cash register	la caisse	*la kehs*
a bookstore	une librairie	*ew^{o}n lee-bReh-Ree*
Where are ___?	Où sont ___?	*oo soh^n ___?*
the shoes	les chaussures (f)	*lay shoh-sew^{o}R*
to touch	toucher	*too-shay*
Don't touch!	ne pas toucher	*nuh pah too-shay*
to help	aider	*ay-day*
May I help you?	Je peux vous aider?	*zhuh puh voo (z)ay-day?*
Could you help me?	Pouvez-vous m'aider?	*poo-vay voo may-day?*
What would you like?	Vous désirez?	*voo day-see-Ray?*
I'm just looking.	Je ne fais que regarder.	*zhuh nuh feh kuh Ruh-gahR-day*
sales	les soldes	*lay suhld*
It's my turn.	C'est à moi.	*say (t)ah mwah*
to take	prendre	*pRah^n-dRuh*
I'll take it.	Je le/la prends.	*zhuh luh/lah pRah^n*
I'll take them.	Je les prends.	*zhuh lay pRah^n*
That's all, thanks.	C'est tout, merci.	*say too, mehR-see*
How are you paying?	Comment payez-vous?	*kuh-mah^n pay-yay voo?*
Do you accept ___?	Acceptez-vous ___?	*ahk-sehp-tay voo ___?*

credit cards	des cartes de crédit	*day kahRt duh kRay-dee*
I'll pay ___.	Je paie ___.	*zhuh pay __*
with credit card	avec une carte de crédit	*ah-vehk ew^{o}n kahRt duh kRay-dee*
in cash	en liquide	*ah^n lee-keed*

Culture note—Outdoor markets

France is famous for its outdoor markets, which range from vibrant vegetable markets to ones specializing in birds or stamps. Market day varies according to neighborhood or city, but most of them start around 8 or 9 and finish before lunch.

You might be able to negotiate on price right before closing time, but otherwise don't expect to haggle at an outdoor market. You should expect to wait before you are served, because the discussion and selection of items can take a while. Mireille Guilano's *French Women Don't Get Fat* provides an excellent description of buying a melon at a market, explaining the importance of discussing every aspect of the desired melon with the vendor. The grocer needs to know the customer's needs before he can choose the perfect fruit *for that customer*, primed to be at its peak at the time she wants to serve it.

If you want to buy something at a market, you should try to talk with the vendor a little, even if you can't manage anything beyond an appreciative comment about his wares. Don't pick up the produce yourself; the vendor will do that. *You* just point. Order produce in metric weights, and bring your own shopping bags.

Another type of outdoor market is the flea market. There are two kinds flea markets in France, the *marchés aux puces* which are fixed to a certain location, and the *brocantes*, which are travelling flea markets. You are expected to bargain at either kind of flea market. Payment is in cash.

Grammar—Question forms

1. Intonation (*Vous acceptez des cartes de crédit?* = You accept credit cards?)

2. Add *Est-ce que* (ehs-kuh) at the front of a phrase. (*Est-ce que vous parlez anglais?* = Do you speak English?)

3. Inversion (*Parlez-vous anglais?* = Do you speak English?)

The easiest way to form questions in French is simply to use the same word order as a declarative sentence (a statement) and raise your intonation at the end so it sounds like a question (version 1, above). If you want to remove any doubt that it's a question, you can add *Est-ce que* at the front of it, as a question marker (version 2).

You can also invert the subject and the verb in French to form a question (version 3), as we usually do in English ("Are you sleeping?"), but there are several rules for doing so, including adding a hyphen between the verb and the subject (*Dormez-vous?*). Don't bother learning the inverted question form except with questions that you will use a lot and will learn in the vocabulary sections (*Avez-vous?, Parlez-vous?, Pouvez-vous?*). For most other questions, just use a simple statement form, possibly with an *Est-ce que* at the start.

Exercise 4.3
Translate these questions into French.

1. Do you have rooms available?

2. Can you recommend a wine?

3. Do you want the house specialty?

4. Do you accept credit cards?

Answers: 1.1) (Est-ce que) vous avez des chambres libres?, 1.2) Avez-vous des chambres libres?, 2.1) (Est-ce que) vous pouvez recommander un vin?, 2.2) Pouvez-vous recommander un vin?, 3.1) (Est-ce que) vous désirez la spécialité de la maison?, 3.2) Désirez-vous la spécialité de la maison?, 4.1) (Est-ce que) vous acceptez des cartes de crédit?, 4.2) Acceptez-vous des cartes de crédit?

Stores

English	French	Pronunciation
I'm looking for ___.	Je cherche ___.	zhuh sheRsh ___
Is there ___ close to here?	Il y a ___ près d'ici?	eel yah ___ pReh dee-see?
a bank	une banque	ew°n bah^n k
a store/shop	un magasin	æ^n mah-gah-zæ^n
a grocery store	une épicerie	ew°n ay-pees-Ree
a market	un marché	æ^n mahR-shay
a supermarket	un supermarché	æ^n sew°-pehR-mahR-shay
a pharmacy	une pharmacie	ew°n fahR-mah-see
a perfumery	une parfumerie	ew°n pahR-few°m-Ree
a gift shop	un magasin de cadeaux	æ^n mah-gah-zæ^n duh kah-doh
a bakery	une boulangerie	ew°n boo-lah^n-zhRee
a pastry shop	une pâtisserie	ew°n pah-tees-Ree
a bookstore	une librairie	ew°n lee-bReh-Ree
a department store	un grand magasin	æ^n grah^n mah-gah-zæ^n
a newstand	un kiosque à journaux	æ^n kyuhsk ah zhooR-noh
a tobacconist's shop	un tabac	æ^n tah-bah
a liquor store	un marchand de vin	æ^n mahR-shah^n duh væ^n
a camera store	un magasin de photos	æ^n mah-gah-zæ^n duh fuh-toh

Culture note—Specialized food stores

France enjoys an abundance of specialized food shops, including the following: *la boulangerie* (bakery), *la boucherie* (butcher shop), *la boucherie chevaline* (horse butcher shop), *le chocolatier* (chocolate shop), *la charcuterie* (pork butcher shop/delicatessen), *la confiserie* (candy store), *la fromagerie* (cheese and dairy shop), *la laiterie* or *la crèmerie* (dairy shop), *la pâtisserie* (pastry and cake shop), *la poissonnerie* (fish shop), and *la rôtisserie* (roast-chicken shop).

Culture note—Bargains

France is an expensive country. Don't expect to find a lot of bargains. If your budget extends to shopping, consider buying wine and housewares. Scarves and ties are also affordable.

Culture note—Mom-and-Pop shops

While chain stores certainly exist in France (Monoprix, for example), most French shops are of the mom-and-pop variety. They are smaller, more individual, and more intimate than chains, but may have more restricted hours of business than Americans would expect. French shops specialize as much as possible, resulting in such diverse specialties as perfume shops (not general toiletries) and pork butcher shops (not a general butcher shop).

It's been said that shopping in France is not a convenience but an art form. You must find the right shop at the right time of day on a day the store is not closed. As with so many things French, shopping in small stores is also a social experience for locals, an opportunity to preserve and strengthen established relationships.

Common Signs

entrance	l'entrée (f)	*lah^n-tRay*
exit	la sortie	*lah suhR-tee*
stairs	les escaliers (m)	*lay (z)ehs-kahl-yay*
escalator	les escaliers roulant (m)	*lay (z)ehs-kahl-yay Roo-lah^n*
elevator	l'ascenseur (m)	*lah-sah^n-suh^{o}R*
toilets	toilettes (f)	*twah-leht*
push	poussez	*poo-say*
pull	tirez	*tee-Ray*
open	ouvert	*oo-vehR*
closed	fermé	*fehR-may*
business hours	heures d'ouverture	*uhR doo-vehR-tew^{o}R*

Culture note—Business hours

French stores are open more than those in many European countries, but they're still a long way from 24/7. Stores are frequently closed on Sundays or Mondays. Stores and businesses usually open around 9, close a couple of hours for lunch, and open again until 7 or even later. Bakeries open earlier, usually by 7:30 a.m. Most outdoor food markets are usually open only in the morning and shut down before lunch.

Post offices are generally open all day in France, typically from 8 or 9 a.m. to anywhere from 5 to 7 p.m., as well as Saturday morning. (In smaller towns, they may be closed from 12 to 2 for lunch.) These hours would also be typical for large stores and department stores.

Common banking hours are 9 to 4:30, but banks also close for a long lunch, as well as Saturday or Monday. If a bank is open for business but you are unable to open the door, that is because of the security system that allows only one person in at a time. There should be a red button to push by the outside door, which will turn green when it unlocks. Do the same to enter through the inside door.

Exercise 4.4

Translate the following into French.

1. Is there a gift shop near here?

2. I'm looking for the cash register.

3. How much does that cost?

4. Excuse me. I'm looking for a pharmacy, please.

5. I'm looking for a supermarket.

6. I'm just looking.

Answers: 1) Il y a un magasin du cadeaux près d'ici? 2) Je cherche la caisse. 3) C'est combien? 4) Excusez-moi/Pardon. Je cherche une pharmacie, s'il vous plaît. 5) Je cherche un supermarché. 6) Je regarde seulement./Je ne fais que regarder.

Culture note—Common stores

Tabacs (tobacco shops) offer basic items such as tobacco, transportation tickets, stamps, postcards, phone cards, cell phone credits, gum, mints, parking disks, and trinkets. Many sell food, as well, to the point where they look like full-fledged *cafés* or bars. The sign indicating a *tabac* is in the shape of a red cigar.

La presse (*la maison de la presse*) sells the expected newspapers and magazines, as well as transportation tickets and maps.

La pharmacie (pharmacy) offers anything related to health or hygiene—medicine, foot pads, razors, shampoo, facial tissues, sanitary napkins, thermometers, disinfectants, cough drops—but not general merchandise, as American drug stores do.

Pharmacists also diagnose minor ailments and provide stronger medicines than U.S. pharmacies provide over the counter. The stores are identified by a flashing green cross.

L'epicerie (grocery store) is a traditional small grocery store that will probably be a bit higher priced and require cash.

Hypermarchés or **grandes surfaces** (supermarkets) offer a wide range of food and other products, although the store may be small by American standards. (Those in suburbs or on the edge of town tend to be larger.) Look for personal products here for lower prices than in a pharmacy. Have your money at the ready to pay and be prepared to bag your own purchases. You may have to pay for plastic bags, if you need them.

Grands magasins (department stores) provide kitchenwares, clothing (including bra-fitting consultations), electronics, food stuffs, household items, and much more.

Clothing

clothing	des vêtements	day veht-mah^n
blouse	un chemisier	æ^n shuh-meez-yay
shirt	une chemise	ew^{o}n shuh-meez
pants	un pantalon	æ^n pah^n-tah-loh^n
skirt	une jupe	ew^{o}n zhew^{o}p
dress	une robe	ew^{o}n ʀuhb
pullover sweater	un pull	æ^n pew^{o}l
cardigan sweater	un cardigan	æ^n kahʀ-dee-gah^n
hat	un chapeau	æ^n shah-poh
tie	une cravate	ew^{o}n kʀah-vaht
jacket	une veste	ew^{o}n vehst
coat	un manteau	æ^n mah^n-toh
shoes	des chaussures (f)	day shoh-sew^{o}ʀ
gloves	des gants (m)	day gah^n
swimsuit	un maillot de bain	æ^n mah-yoh duh bæ^n
swim trunks (small briefs)	un slip de bain	æ^n sleep duh bæ^n
shorts	un short	æ^n shuhʀt

Colors

____ color	de couleur ____	duh koo-luhʀ ____
black	noire	nwahʀ
white	blanche	blah^{n}sh
red	rouge	roozh
yellow	jaune	zhohn
green	verte	vehʀt
blue	bleue	bluh
brown	marron	mah-ʀoh^n
purple	violette	vyuh-leht
gray	grise	gʀeez
pink	rose	ʀohz
orange	orange	uh-ʀah^{n}zh
beige	beige	behzh

light	___ clair	___ *klehʀ*
dark	___ foncé	___ *fohⁿ-say*

To indicate that a color is light or dark, you use the color name followed by the word *foncé* (for dark) or *clair* (for light).

light green	vert clair	*vehʀ klehʀ*
dark gray	gris foncé	*gʀee fohⁿ-say*

Culture note—French style

French people have a reputation for looking extremely good, for always being elegant. Surprisingly, their distinction does not rest entirely on dressing well. In fact, many people don't dress "fashionably" at all. What really makes people stand out favorably in France is the way they carry and present themselves. With confidence and pride. No slouching allowed. Always being conscious of looking good.

Is that too tall an order for a visitor? Try blending in on the clothing front, then. They do dress differently in France; there's no denying that. Good dress is a way to show your good taste, your classiness. To fit in, wear primarily dark or neutral colors, possibly with a bright piece or two on the upper half. (French women love scarves for changing the looks of their basic outfits.) Shoes should be dark, ideally fashionable, but definitely comfortable for walking. Women should favor dresses, skirts, and well-fitting slacks. French people also wear jeans now, but paired smartly to make a nice-looking outfit. No one wears shorts in the city, but the "rules" are more relaxed in the country (and *all* the clothing rules are more relaxed during August vacation time). A good haircut goes a long way in creating the right image, as well. The goal is to look well-cared-for and pulled together. Incidentally, the emphasis on elegance and fashion starts very young. It's common to see children who are not dressed as children, but as miniature, *stylish* adults.

Exercise 4.5

What colors are the following items?

1. pearl
2. lettuce
3. cardinals
4. harvest moon
5. mud

6. Barbie toys
7. sunflower
8. a cloudless sky
9. pigeons
10. lilacs

Answers: De couleur... 1) blanche 2) verte, 3) rouge, 4) orange, 5) marron/noire, 6) rose, 7) jaune (marron/noire), 8) bleue, 9) grise, 10) violette

Culture note—Shoes and socks

The ubiquitous white tennis shoe is also seen in France—mostly on American tourists. French people wear few sport shoes, and most of those aren't white. They do not regularly wear white sport socks. Shoes and socks are usually dark.

Miscellaneous Purchases

English	French	Pronunciation
I need ___.	Il me faut ___.	*eel muh foh ___*
I would like ___.	Je voudrais ___.	*zhuh voo-dRay ___*
I'm looking for ___.	Je cherche ___.	*zhuh sheRsh ___*
a newspaper	un journal	*æ^n zhooR-nahl*
an American newspaper	un journal américain	*æ^n zhooR-nahl ah-may-Ree-kæ^n*
an English newspaper	un journal anglais	*æ^n zhooR-nahl ah^n-gleh*
a magazine	un magazine	*æ^n mah-gah-zeen*
a battery	une pile	*ew^{o}n peel*
some paper	du papier	*dew^o pah-pyay*
a pen	un stylo	*æ^n stee-loh*
some facial tissues	des mouchoirs en papier	*day moosh-wahR ah^n pah-pyay*
some toilet paper	du papier toilette	*dew^o pah-pyay twah-leht*
sunglasses	des lunettes (f) de soleil	*day lew^o-neht duh suh-lay*
aspirin	de l'aspirine (f)	*duh lahs-pee-Reen*
shampoo	du shampooing	*dew^o shah^n-pwuh^n*

Exercise 4.6

Match the following items with where you could buy them.

1. livre   A. pharmacie
2. journal   B. boulangerie
3. vin   C. marchand de vin
4. tarte   D. librairie
5. aspirine   E. pâtisserie
6. pain   F. kiosque à journaux

Answers: 1) D, 2) F, 3) C, 4) E, 5) A, 6) B

(Note: You could find some of these items in more than one type of store.)

Exercise 4.7

Translate the following into French.

1. I need a battery, please.

2. Where are the shoes?

3. I'm looking for a blouse.

4. I would like facial tissues, please.

5. I need a pen.

6. Do you have sunglasses?

7. Where is the shampoo?

8. I'm looking for a jacket.

9. I would like an American newspaper.

10. Where are the pants?

Answers: 1) Il me faut une pile, s'il vous plaît. 2) Où sont les chaussures? 3) Je cherche un chemisier. 4) Je voudrais des mouchoirs en papier, s'il vous plaît. 5) Il me faut un stylo. 6) Avez-vous des lunettes de soleil? 7) Où est le shampooing? 8) Je cherche une veste. 9) Je voudrais un journal américain. 10) Où sont les pantalons?

Culture note—Bags

It's very common to carry a bag in France, even for men, but not a fanny pack. A fanny pack screams "tourist" and could even become a security risk.

Culture note—Toiletries

If you are choosy about the toiletries you use, bring plenty along with you. France has a wide selection of personal hygiene products, but finding a specific American brand of shampoo or deodorant can be difficult. You may note that the French are more accepting of natural body odors than Americans are. In contrast, looking through the French cultural lens, many Americans seem obsessed with hygiene.

Culture note—Quality

Americans love a bargain and often choose quantity over quality. Most French people are the reverse—they prefer quality over quantity and are willing to pay for it. Don't be surprised if prices are higher for goods in France, especially if the dollar is weak.

Useful Vocabulary

early	tôt	*toh*
late	tard	*tahʀ*
more	plus	*plew^p*
less	moins	*mwæ^n*
expensive	cher	*shehʀ*
inexpensive	bon marché	*boh^n mahʀ-shay*
near (to)	près (de)	*pʀeh (duh)*
very near to	tout près	*too pʀeh*
far (from)	loin (de)	*lwæ^n (duh)*
up(stairs)	en haut	*ah^n oh*
down(stairs)	en bas	*ah^n bah*

Culture note—Showing skin

Social norms for showing skin are definitely different in France than in the U.S. Women and men may go nude at the pool or beach. Nudity is common in magazines, newspapers, and on TV. Women wearing shirts that show a bit (or a lot) of cleavage is quite common. Yet people don't wear shorts in the city. If you are exposed to nudity "in the flesh," don't consider it a come-on. It's just an earthy acceptance of the body.

5   Sightseeing

Numbers (21-99)

Once you learn how to count in the twenties, thirties, etc., up to 100, you will have the hardest part of the number system behind you. Review the numbers you already know before you attack the new ones: count from 0 to 20, then from 0 to 100 by tens. Then look at the new numbers below.

20	vingt	$væ^n$
21	vingt et un	$væ^n$ (t)ay $æ^n$
22	vingt-deux	$væ^n$t-duh
23	vingt-trois	$væ^n$t-tRwah
24	vingt-quatre	$væ^n$t-kah-tRuh
25	vingt-cinq	$væ^n$t-sæ^{n}k
26	vingt-six	$væ^n$t-sees
27	vingt-sept	$væ^n$t-seht
28	vingt-huit	$væ^n$t-weet
29	vingt-neuf	$væ^n$t-nuhf
30	trente	tRah^{n}t
31	trente et un	tRah^{n}t ay $æ^n$
32	trente-deux	tRah^{n}t-duh
40	quarante	kah-Rah^{n}t
41	quarante et un	kah-Rah^{n}t ay $æ^n$
43	quarante-trois	kah-Rah^{n}t tRwah
50	cinquante	sæ^n-kah^{n}t
54	cinquante-quatre	sæ^n-kah^{n}t-kah-tRuh
60	soixante	swah-sah^{n}t
65	soixante-cinq	swah-sah^{n}t-sæ^{n}k

Note: "*number*" *and one* is always three separate words (e.g., *trente et un*). For the 2-9 numbers, use hyphens.

Using the table below as a guide, count from 21-69. Combine the numbers of the right column with the number 20 to get 21-29, then go through all combinations with the number 30, and so on, until you reach 69. Run through all the numbers a couple of times, until they start to feel a little more natural.

Forming numbers 21-69

20	1
30	2
40	3
50	4
60	5
	6
	7
	8
	9

Numbers 70-99 deserve their own section, because they break with the pattern of 21-69.

70s—You may remember that the number 70 in French is the equivalent of our English *sixty-ten* (*soixante-dix*). Keep going up from ten to get other numbers in the 70s—71 is *soixante et onze* (*sixty and eleven*), 72 is *sixty-twelve*, all the way up to *sixty-nineteen* for 79.

80s—French for the number 80 is *quatre-vingts*, like *four-twenties* in English. You add numbers 1 through 9 to get numbers in the eighties—81 is *quatre-vingt-un* (note that there is no *et* and all numbers are hyphenated), 86 is *quatre-vingt-six*. Once you get past an even 80, you drop the -*s* on *vingts*.

90s—Ninety in French is literally *four-twenty-ten* in English, *quatre-vingt-dix*. You go up from ten through eleven, twelve, and the teens to get numbers 91-99, as you did to get the 70s. (Again, in 91, *quatre-vingt-onze*, there is no conjunction *et* and all numbers are hyphenated.) Numbers like *four-twenty-fifteen* sound very awkward to our English-speaking ears and take a moment to mentally convert to, say, *ninety-five*, but with a little practice it gets easier.

70	soixante-dix	*swah-sah^{n}t-dees*
71	soixante et onze	*swah-sah^n (t)ay oh^{n}z*
72	soixante-douze	*swah-sah^{n}t-dooz*
73	soixante-treize	*swah-sah^{n}t-tRehz*
74	soixante-quatorze	*swah-sah^{n}t-kah-tuhRz*
75	soixante-quinze	*swah-sah^{n}t-kæ^{n}z*
76	soixante-seize	*swah-sah^{n}t-sehz*
77	soixante-dix-sept	*swah-sah^{n}t-dee-seht*
78	soixante-dix-huit	*swah-sah^{n}t-dee-(z)weet*
79	soixante-dix-neuf	*swah-sah^{n}t-dees-nuhf*
80	quatre-vingts	*kah-tRuh-væ^n*
81	quatre-vingt-un	*kah-tRuh-væ^n-æ^n*
82	quatre-vingt-deux	*kah-tRuh-væ^n-duh*
83	quatre-vingt-trois	*kah-tRuh-væ^n-tRwah*
84	quatre-vingt-quatre	*kah-tRuh-væ^n-kah-tRuh*
85	quatre-vingt-cinq	*kah-tRuh-væ^n-sæ^{n}k*
86	quatre-vingt-six	*kah-tRuh-væ^n-sees*
87	quatre-vingt-sept	*kah-tRuh-væ^n-seht*
88	quatre-vingt-huit	*kah-tRuh-væ^n-weet*
89	quatre-vingt-neuf	*kah-tRuh-væ^n-nuhf*
90	quatre-vingt-dix	*kah-tRuh-væ^n-dees*
91	quatre-vingt-onze	*kah-tRuh-væ^n-oh^{n}z*
92	quatre-vingt-douze	*kah-tRuh-væ^n-dooz*
93	quatre-vingt-treize	*kah-tRuh-væ^n-tRehz*
94	quatre-vingt-quatorze	*kah-tRuh-væ^n-kah-tuhRz*
95	quatre-vingt-quinze	*kah-tRuh-væ^n-kæ^{n}z*
96	quatre-vingt-seize	*kah-tRuh-væ^n-sehz*
97	quatre-vingt-dix-sept	*kah-tRuh-væ^n-dees-seht*
98	quatre-vingt-dix-huit	*kah-tRuh-væ^n-dee-(z)weet*
99	quatre-vingt-dix-neuf	*kah-tRuh-væ^n-dees-nuhf*

Now practice the upper numbers. Using the table below as a guide, count from 70-99 a few times.

Forming numbers 70-99

70	1
80	2
90	3
	4
	5
	6
	7
	8
	9

Exercise 5.1

Can you read the following numbers out loud?

1. 27	6. 72
2. 34	7. 88
3. 49	8. 93
4. 56	9. 61
5. 65	10. 41

Answers: 1) vingt-sept [*væ^n-sehf*], 2) trente-quatre [*tRah^{n}t-kah-tRuh*], 3) quarante-neuf [*kah-Rah^{n}t-nuhf*], 4) cinquante-six [*sæ^n-kah^{n}t-sees*], 5) soixante-cinq [*swah-sah^{n}t-sæ^{n}k*], 6) soixante-douze [*swah-sah^{n}t-dooz*], 7) quatre-vingt-huit [*kah-tRah-væ^n-weet*], 8) quatre-vingt-treize [*kah-tRuh-væ^n-tRehz*], 9) soixante et un [*swah-sah^{n}t ay æ^n*], 10) quarante et un [*kah-Rah^{n}t ay æ^n*]

Culture note—City structure

As you read your city map to locate the sights, you may notice that the city streets intersect not to form a grid, but often a star pattern. The star pattern is very common in France—stand at the top of the Arc de Triomphe, where twelve streets meet, and you can't miss it.

Units of Time

how long?	combien de temps?	koh^n-$by\alpha^n$ duh tah^n
a year	un an	α^n (n)ah^n
a month	un mois	α^n mwah
a week	une semaine	ew^on suh-mehn
a day	un jour	α^n zhooR
an hour	une heure	ew^on uhR
a minute	une minute	ew^on mee-new^{o}t
a second	une seconde	ew^on suh-goh^{n}d

Excercise 5.2

Complete the following statements about units of time.

1. Soixante secondes font (make) _____.
2. Soixante minutes font _____.
3. Vingt-quatre heures font _____.
4. Sept jours font _____.
5. Quatre semaines font _____.
6. Douze mois font _____.

Answers: 1) une minute, 2) une heure, 3) un jour, 4) une semaine, 5) un mois, 6) un an

Culture note—Counting in Switzerland and Belgium

In French-speaking parts of Switzerland and Belgium, they follow the "regular" number pattern for 70-99. The number for 80 is *huitante* [wee-tah^{n}t], and 90 is expressed as *nonante* [nuh-nah^{n}t].

Culture note—The *OT*

The local tourist office—*l'Office du Tourisme*—is sometimes referred to as the *OT* and can offer excellent information and services when you arrive in a town. You can usually find an OT at the train station and in city centers, but certainly your hotel can direct you to one. Follow the signs marked with an *i*, for *information*.

Culture note—Cobblestone streets and street signs

Many French streets are paved with cobblestones, which are picturesque but can be rough on the feet. The stones can get very slick when wet. If you will walk a lot (and most tourists do), wear thick-soled, sturdy shoes that are well broken in. Any blisters you develop will hurt twice as badly on the uneven walking surface. (Be aware that feet often swell for a couple of days after long flights, and bring shoes that allow your feet enough room.)

Street signs may be on the corners of buildings at an intersection rather than at the street on a pole. Be prepared to search a bit to identify your location.

Grammar—Plurals, nouns and articles

Masculine

Singular	Plural
le/un livre (*the/a book*)	les/des livres (*the/some books*)
le/un lit (*the/a bed*)	les/des lits (*the/some beds*)
l'/un hôtel (*the/a hotel*)	les/des hôtels (*the/some hotels*)

Feminine

Singular	Plural
la/une chambre (*the/a room*)	les/des chambres (*the/some rooms*)
la/une carte (*the/a map*)	les/des cartes (*the/some maps*)
l'/une amie (*the/a friend*)	les/des amies (*the/some friends*)

We don't get very far in a new language before we want to start talking about more than one thing at a time, using plural forms, in other words. This is a good time to discuss plural forms, because we frequently want to talk about more than one minute, hour, day, or other unit of time.

I'm happy to tell you that the French rules for making plural forms are easy: add an -s to most nouns, but don't pronounce it. That's it! Thus, *un hôtel* goes to *deux hôtels, une carte* to *trois cartes.* Most nouns ending in *au*, such as *château*, add an -*x* instead of an -*s* (*châteaux*), but again, you don't pronounce the plural marker.

When we change from singular to plural, not only is the form of the noun affected, but the form of the definite article (*the*) and indefinite article (*a/an*) is, too. This may sound like it's complicated, but it's really not, because the masculine and feminine forms look the same in the plural. (In other words, you don't have to learn a separate version for each.)

Let's look first at definite articles and see how they change to show plural. When we are discussing one particular book (masculine), it is *le livre*. If we start discussing a couple of specific books, we add an *-s* to *livre* and also to *le*, to get *les livres*. Turning to the feminine version, we can change *la chambre* (the room) to *les chambres* (the rooms).

When we are talking about non-specific nouns, remember, rather than specific ones, we use indefinite articles (*a/an*). In French, the masculine indefinite article is *un* (*un lit*—a bed) and the feminine is *une* (*une carte*—a map). They both have the same plural form: *des* (some)—*des lits* (some beds), *des cartes* (some maps). While we can often leave the word "some" out in English—"There are tables outside."—in French you *must* include the article: *Il y a des tables à l'extérieur* [*eel yah day tah-bluh ah lehk-stayR-yuhR*].

While *le* or *la* is usually contracted to *l'* in front of singular nouns starting with a vowel or an *h* (*l'hôtel, l'amie*), there is no contraction when you use the other definite or indefinite articles (*un, une, les, des*); thus, we see *des hôtel* and *une amie*.

Culture note—Queues and breaking the rules

French people understand rules, such as waiting their turn for something, or parking in approved spaces, but they also believe that people who break the rules probably have a good reason to do so and, consequently, they don't get too worked up about the infraction. The same logic applies to shrugging their shoulders if someone violates a no-smoking sign, or no-parking sign, or any other sign of authority. As a visitor, it's best if you don't make a big deal about these things.

Exercise 5.3
Make the plural forms for units of time.

1. l'an

2. le mois

3. la semaine

4. le jour

5. la heure

6. la minute

7. la seconde

Answers: 1) les ans, 2) les mois, 3) les semaines, 4) les jours, 5) les heures, 6) les minutes, 7) les secondes

Exercise 5.4
Can you answer the following questions? Remember that *combien de/d'* means *how many*.

1. Combien de mois a (= has) un an?

2. Combien de semaines a un mois?

3. Combien de jours a une semaine?

4. Combien d'heures a un jour?

5. Combien de minutes a une heure?

6. Combien de secondes a une minute?

Answers: 1) Un an a 12 (douze) mois. 2) Un mois a 4 (quatre) semaines. 3) Une semaine a 7 (sept) jours. 4) Un jour a 24 (vingt-quatre) heures. 5) Une heure a 60 (soixante) minutes. 6) Une minute a 60 (soixante) secondes.

Travel tip: Check museum times carefully as you plan your sightseeing schedule. Many are closed on Mondays, some on Tuesdays, and some on Wednesdays. Many are closed over a long lunch hour. Many have free entry on certain days, which you may try to avoid because crowds will be heavier.

Culture note—Petty crime

Violent crime is relatively rare in France, but petty crime occurs, especially in cities, around tourist sights, around train and bus stations, on crowded public transportation, and in restaurants and cafés, especially with outdoor seating. Smart tourists are always on guard against pickpockets. Any distraction (watch out for manufactured ones, such as a bump or an interruption) can be an invitation for theft.

Don't get so involved in admiring the sights that you won't notice someone lifting your wallet. Better yet, keep most of your money in a money belt under your clothes. Don't carry a purse or bag slung loosely over your shoulder, where it could easily be snatched away.

Don't use a purse that hangs to the back. Don't keep valuables in a backpack or fanny pack that could be slit open and emptied while you are distracted. Don't wear expensive jewelry. When in a crowd, be alert, be cautious, be super-sensible, even a little suspicious. Traveling or sightseeing is not the time to rely on the honesty of strangers.

Culture note—Religion

France is an overwhelmingly Roman Catholic country, but only officially. When it comes to actual church attendance, the number of practicing Christians drops dramatically.

The church nonetheless plays an important role in society through church baptisms, first communions, and weddings. In addition to Roman Catholicism, France is home to a large and growing Muslim community, primarily from North Africa.

When visiting a church, do not wear shorts, as that would be considered disrespectful.

Sightseeing

Where is ___?	Où est ___?	*oo ay ___?*
I need ___.	Il me faut ___.	*eel muh foh ___*
Can you recommend __?	Pouvez-vous recommander _?	*poo-vay-voo Ruh-kuh-mah^n-day ___?*
a sightseeing tour	une visite touristique	*ew°n vee-zeet too-Rees-teek*
a boat trip	une promenade en bateau	*ew°n pRuhm-nahd ah^n bah-toh*
an excursion	une excursion	*ew°n ehks-kew°R-syoh^n*
tourist information office	l'office (*m*) du tourisme	*loh-fees dew° too-Reesm*
a map	une carte	*ew°n kahRt*
city	la ville	*lah veel*
a city map	un plan de ville	*æ^n plah^n duh veel*
downtown area	le centre ville	*luh sah^n-tRuh veel*
old part of town	la vieille ville	*lah vyehy veel*
cathedral	la cathédrale	*lah kah-tay-dRahl*
church	l'église (f)	*lay-gleez*
museum	le musée	*luh mew°-zay*
palace	le palais	*luh pah-lay*
castle	le château	*luh shah-toh*
bridge	le pont	*luh poh^n*
fountain	la fontaine	*lah foh^n-tehn*
market	le marché	*luh mahR-shay*
park	le parc	*luh pahRk*
garden	le jardin	*luh zhahR-dæ^n*
square	la place	*lah plahs*
main square	la place principale	*lah plahs pRæ^n-see-pahl*
street	la rue	*lah Rew°*
Is it open/closed?	C'est ouvert/fermé?	*say oo-vehR/fehR-may?*
entrance	l'entrée (f)	*lah^n-tRay*
exit	la sortie	*lah suhR-tee*

Culture note—Pedestrian hazards

Most tourists in France walk a lot. You should be alert to the following potential hazards for pedestrians.

—Quiet cars can sneak up on you. Look carefully before you step into a street, even if you don't hear any traffic.

—City streets can teem with traffic. Cross carefully at intersections. Don't attempt to cross any extremely busy streets, such as the multi-laned ring around the Arc de Triomphe, where there is a safe underground walkway. Look for a protected crosswalk or underground passage, then use it. It's there for a reason.

—Do *not* expect French drivers to stop for pedestrians in crosswalks. They may not, even if the pedestrians have a green walk light. Do not attempt to challenge a driver with your right to cross unless you are sticking closely to locals who lead the way.

—Keep an eye on the ground for dog messes. Paris is famous for them. The French supposedly think it is good luck to step in dog poop. You probably won't.

—Watch out for bicyclists. Tourists on bikes may not know where they are going, and locals may rush and cut corners.

admission	l'entrée (f)	*lah^n-tRay*
admission charge	le prix d'entrée	*luh pRee dah^n-tRay*
How much is the entrance fee?	Combien coûte l'entrée?	*koh^n-byæ^n koot lah^n-tRay?*
ticket	le billet	*luh bee-yay*
admission ticket	le billet d'entrée	*luh bee-yay dah^n-tRay*
adult	l'adulte (m/f)	*lah-dew^{o}lt*
child	l'enfant (m/f)	*lah^n-fah^n*
free admission	l'entrée gratuite/libre	*lah^n-tRay gRah-tweet/lee-bRuh*
prohibited/no ___	défense de ___ / ___ interdit(e)	*day-fah^{n}s duh ___ /___ æ^n-tehR-dee(t)*
no entry	défense d'entrer	*dah-fah^{n}s dah^n-tRay*
no flash photos	photos avec/aux flash interdites	*fuh-toh (z)ah-vehk/ (z)oh flahsh æ^n-tehR-deet*

Travel tip: If you will be visiting more than one sight in a city, see whether combination tickets are available. Not only will you be able to save money, but you can often skip the long ticket lines. This is something you can probably take care of before your outing by visiting the local tourist office, sparing you a wait even at your first sightseeing stop.

Exercise 5.5
Translate into French.

1. Where is the entrance?

2. I need a city map, please.

3. I need an entrance ticket.

4. How much does an entrance ticket cost?

5. Where is the cathedral?

6. I'm looking for the city center.

7. Straight ahead and then left.

8. I see the park.

9. I would like to buy two entrance tickets.

10. Two adults.

Answers: 1) Où est l'entrée? 2) Il me faut un plan de ville, s'il vous plaît. 3) Il me faut un billet d'entrée. 4) Combien coûte l'entrée/un billet d'entrée? 5) Où est la cathédrale? 6) Je cherche le centre ville? 7) Tout droit et ensuite/puis à gauche. 8) Je vois le parc. 9) Je voudrais acheter deux billets d'entrée. 10) Deux adultes.

Bathrooms
Let's not overlook the obvious. Some vital vocabulary. . . .

bathrooms	les toilettes	*lay twah-leht*
ladies	les dames	*lay dahm*
women	les femmes	*lay fahm*
gentlemen	les messieurs	*lay may-syuh*
men	les hommes	*lay (z)uhm*
some toilet paper	du papier toilette	*dew° pah-pyay twah-leht*

Culture note—Bathroom terms and customs

The bathroom, that is, *where the bath is*, is called the *salle de bains*. The toilet may also be in there, but more often it is in a separate room. If you want to make sure you get to a room with a toilet, ask for *les toilettes*.

Toilets are marked in public places as "WC" or *toilettes*. The men's room is identified by a figure of a man or by H (for *Hommes*) or M (for *messieurs*). The women's room could have a female figure on the door, an F (for *Femmes*) or a D (for *Dames*).

If you see something that looks like a strange, low sink, it is a *bidet* and is used for intimate washing. Face the control knobs and straddle the basin, if you wish to use the bidet. Be aware that some toilets include a bidet function, so be cautious about activating any unknown controls while you are using the facilities.

In rural France and in some very old buildings, you may run across old-fashioned "Turkish" toilets (*les toilettes turques*), porcelain holes in the floor that you squat over to use. (There are foot markings to get you properly situated.)

Be prepared to pay for public toilets. If an attendant is working, he or she probably expects to be paid or given a tip. Keep coins on hand for that purpose.

Don't use toilets in an eating establishment unless you at least buy a small drink. You may see a unisex *cabine* on the street, which you can use for a small fee. *Libre* (or a green light) means "available"; *occupé* (or a red light) means "occupied."

To flush in France, look for a button or lever on the tank or on the wall. You may need to pull a chain or pull up on a knob. If there are two choices for flushing, the smaller side (usually the left) is for a smaller amount of water, to conserve resources. Finally, it's a good idea to have a stash of toilet paper along when you're out for the day, just in case.

Mail Service and Email

the post office	la poste	*lah puhst*
	le bureau de post	*luh bew^o-Roh duh puhst*
a mailbox	une boîte aux lettres	*ew^{o}n bwaht oh leht-Ruh*
a letter	une lettre	*ew^{o}n leht-Ruh*
a stamp	un timbre	*æ^n tæ^n-bRuh*
a postcard	une carte postale	*ew^{o}n kahRt puhs-tahl*
by airmail	par avion	*pahR ah-vyoh^n*
to the U.S.	aux Ètats-Uni	*oh (z)ay-tah-zew^o-nee*
email	l'e-mail	*lee-mayl*
	le mail	*luh mayl*
the Web	le web	*luh wehb*
	la toile	*la twahl*
a Web page	une page Internet	*ew^{o}n pahzh æ^n-tehR-neht*
Internet	Internet (m)	*æ^n-tehR-neht*
an Internet point	un point Internet	*æ^n pwah^n æ^n-tehR-neht*
Internet café	un cybercafé	*æ^n see-buhR-kah-fay*
a computer	un ordinateur	*æ^n (n)ohR-dee-nah-tuhR*
a printer	une imprimante	*ew^{o}n æ^n-pRee-mah^{n}t*
to print	imprimer	*æ^n-pRee-may*
to download	télécharger	*tay-lay-shahR-zhay*
Wi-Fi	le Wi-Fi	*luh wee-fee*
an electrical outlet	une prise	*ew^{o}n pReez*

Culture note—Mail service

As with government services in many countries, you may some-times encounter long lines and less-than-friendly workers at a French post office, or you may be waited on quickly by a perfectly pleasant employee. Avoid going first thing in the morning and during lunchtime, and remember to say, *"Bonjour, Monsieur/ Madame"* and *"Merci, Monsieur/Madame."*

You can buy stamps not just at the post office but at a tobacconist shop, and you can mail postcards at yellow postal boxes around town. Make sure you get airmail stamps or stickers (*Prioritaire*) if sending to the U.S.

Post offices are generally open at least from 9 to 5, with a possible lunch break. If you don't see *la Poste* on your map, ask for directions at your hotel or the tourism office.

Culture note—Internet access

If you prefer to contact friends at home via the Internet, you will have options for doing so in France, but if you don't have Wi-Fi in your hotel, Internet access is not always easy to find (especially in August, when shops often close for vacation) and can get expensive when you factor in slow connections and an unfamiliar keyboard. You can access the Internet in cybercafés, some laundromats, and some hotels. You usually pay for an amount of time up front and receive a username and password so you can log on to an open terminal. Keep an eye on the clock, or you could be cut off mid-message.

Fortunately, more and more cafés and *brasseries* offer free Wi-Fi now, and you can ask a server for the code (assuming, of course, that you ordered something to eat or drink). Try *Quel est le code wifi, s'il vous plaît?* [*kehl ay luh kuhd wee-fee, see voo play?*] If you have a smartphone, you can send emails via Wi-Fi even if your phone has no international service.

To get the @ symbol on a French keyboard, press the Alt-Gr key (right of the space bar) along with the key where you see the @ symbol (check on the zero key). Use the shift key (marked with an up arrow or "Maj") to type numbers. Notice that Q and A are switched, along with W and Z. Some other letters and punctuation are also not where you expect them, so you probably don't want to touch type, or your message will be littered with peculiarities. Use the Alt-Gr key to type any third character on a key.

Exchanging Money

money	l'argent (m)	*lahR-zhah^n*
a euro	un euro	*æ^n (n)uhR-oh*
a euro cent	un centime (d'euro)	*æ^n sah^n-teem (duhR-oh)*
to exchange	échanger	*ay-shah^n-zhay*
an exchange office	un bureau de change	*æ^n bew^o-Roh duh shah^{n}zh*
an automatic teller machine (ATM)	un distributeur (automatique de billets) (=DAB)	*æ^n dee-stRee-bew^o-tuhR (oh-tuh-mah-teek duh bee-yay) (=day ah bay)*
a cash card	une carte de retrait	*ew^{o}n kahRt duh Ruh-tRay*
a debit card	une carte bancaire	*ew^{o}n kahRt bah^n-kehR*

Culture note—Money

Money is not a socially acceptable topic of conversation. It is rude to ask people what they do to make money. Culture, intellect, and the ability to engage others are much more important than money in France. It is far better to downplay any wealth than to flaunt it.

Exercise 5.6

What would you say in the following situations?

1. You're looking for a bathroom.

2. You're looking for an ATM.

3. You need euros.

4. You're looking for a post office.

5. You need stamps to America.

6. You would like to exchange dollars.

Answers: 1) Où sont les toilettes? *or* Je cherche les toilettes. 2) Où est un distributeur (automatique)? *or* Je cherche un distributeur (automatique). 3) Il me faut des euros. 4) Où est la poste? *or* Je cherche une poste. 5) Il me faut des timbres aux États-Unis. 6) Je voudrais échanger des dollars.

Culture note—ATMs

With the rapid spread of ATMs, exchanging money has become obsolete. It's easier and cheaper to get money from an ATM than to exchange it. If your cash or debit card has a Plus or Cirrus logo on it, just look for an ATM (*un distributeur*) that shows Plus or Cirrus affiliation. Make sure you have a four-digit PIN, and know your number rather than an alphabetic equivalent. French keypads don't include letters the way American ones do.

Only very large bank branches offer currency exchange or traveler's check cashing services. That leaves exchange booths (*un bureau de change*) at the train station, airport, or tourist center, where you pay exorbitant fees for terrible exchange rates.

Plan to use credit cards and ATMs to pay for your stay, and notify your bank and credit card company of your plans so they do not shut down unexpected (to them) cash withdrawals and card use in France.

Do make sure you keep cash (in euros) on hand, for visiting rural areas or other places where it may be hard to find an ATM and where credit card use may not be as common.

For my own peace of mind, I always take along some cash when I travel, *just in case* I have trouble getting cash abroad. Between credit cards and ATMs, though, I haven't had to exchange money in more than a decade. I always bring the unused American dollars home and redeposit them in the bank.

ATMs are easy to find in public—every bank has one. You may need to swipe your card in order to gain access to a locked vestibule where the ATM is located. At the airport, it's best to go straight to information and look around there or ask where a *distributeur* is. Do be careful withdrawing money—withdraw during daylight, not in a bus or train station if you can help it, and be secretive when entering your PIN.

Culture note—Credit cards

Credit cards are widely used across France. MasterCard and VISA are the most widely accepted American credit cards. Make sure a restaurant displays in its window the logo of the card you want to use, or they may not accept yours.

Different banks charge wildly different fees for using their credit cards abroad, so investigate to find which of your cards has the lowest fee for international use (possibly 0%) before you go.

When you pay with a credit card, the merchant is supposed to ask you whether you want the charge in euros or dollars. Despite the comforting familiarity of dollars, choose the local currency, or you will get gouged by a bad exchange rate. Confirm that the charge is in euros before signing.

Realize that you probably cannot use your American credit cards in self-service situations, such as a ticket machine in a train station, because they do not have the "smart chip" technology ("chip and PIN") that European credit cards do.

Finally, do not use your credit card to get cash from an ATM, or you'll pay a boatload of interest. Debit cards, however, work fine in ATMs as long as currency is being withdrawn from a checking account and you have previously notified your bank of your travel plans.

6   Arrival and Transportation

Numbers (100-1000, by 100)

Let's take on the last of French numbers—hundreds and thousands. Again, review the previous number sections to imprint them a little more deeply in your memory before starting this new section.

100*	cent	*sah^n*
200	deux cents	*duh sah^n*
300	trois cents	*tRwah sah^n*
400	quatre cents	*kah-tRuh sah^n*
500	cinq cents	*sæ^n sah^n*
600	six cents	*see sah^n*
700	sept cents	*seht sah^n*
800	huit cents	*wee sah^n*
900	neuf cents	*nuhf sah^n*
1.000*	mille	*meel*

* Remember that although we say <u>one</u> hundred or <u>one</u> thousand in English, in French it's just *cent* or *mille*.

Reality check: It will not affect communication if you ignore how numbers are sometimes pronounced a little differently in different contexts (e.g., *cinq*—with a k-sound at the end—versus *cinq cents*—with no k-sound). Only the most motivated learners will care about these small distinctions.

You now have the building blocks to build numbers up to (and past) one thousand. Notice that when the numbers are not straight multiples of 100, they lose the plural *-s*.

101	cent un [*sah^n æ^n*]
102	cent deux [*sah^n duh*]
213	deux cent treize [*duh sah^n tRehz*]
16.400	seize mille quatre cents [*sehz meel kah-tRuh sah^n*]
48.930	quarante-huit mille neuf cent trente [*kah-Rah^{n}t-wee meel nuhf sah^n tRah^{n}t*]

Exercise 6.1

Can you say these numbers in French without looking at the list above?

1. 165

2. 647

3. 812

4. 231

5. 597

6. 956

7. 328

8. 783

9. 479

10. 1 014

11. 3 285

12. 8 937

Answers: 1) cent soixante-cinq [*sah^n swah-sah^{n}t sæ^{n}k*], 2) six cent quarante-sept [*see sah^n kah-ʀah^{n}t-seht*], 3) huit cent douze [*wee sah^n dooz*], 4) deux cent trente et un [*duh sah^n tʀah (t)ay æ^n*], 5) cinq cent quatre-vingt-dix-sept [*sæ^n sah^n kah-tʀuh-væ^n-dees-seht*], 6) neuf cent cinquante-six [*nuhf sah^n sæ^n-kah^{n}t-sees*], 7) trois cent vingt-huit [*tʀwah sah^n væ^{n}t-weet*], 8) sept cent quatre-vingt-trois [*seht sah^n kah-tʀuh-væ^n- tʀwah*], 9) quatre cent soixante-dix-neuf [*kah-tʀuh sah^n swah-sah^{n}t-deez-nuhf*], 10) mille quatorze [*meel kah-tuhʀz*], 11) trois mille deux cent quatre-vingt-cinq [*tʀwah meel duh sah^n kah-tʀuh-væ^n-sæ^{n}k*], 12) huit mille neuf cent trente-sept [*wee meel nuhf sah^n tʀah^{n}t-seht*]

Reality check: If you really hate learning numbers, you can probably get by just fine without the high numbers. Concentrate on being able to count comfortably from one to twenty and then make do if you need to communicate larger numbers.

Culture note—24-hour clock

Europeans use the 24-hour clock (also known as military time) for official designations of time (for example, on train, bus, or TV schedules) and often in casual usage. If you see a time listed as 20.00, for example, just remember to subtract twelve to get the "normal" time, eight p.m. In conversation, French speakers usually do not use the 24-hour clock. They differentiate between a.m and p.m. by saying *du matin* for morning times and *de l'après-midi* for afternoon times. Evening times use *du soir*. Time is generally listed with an *h* separating the hour and minutes: 1h30 (for 1:30), 21h15 (for 9:15 p.m.).

Arrival

Your arrival in France will be less confusing if you know what some of the words around you mean. You should be able to recognize most of these terms when you see them, as well as be able to say a few basics.

Here is ___.	Voici ___.	*vwah-see ___*
my passport	mon passeport	*moh^n pahs-puhR*
passport control	le contrôle des passeports	*luh koh^n-tRuhl day pahs-puhR*
customs	la douane	*lah dwahn*
nothing to declare	rien à déclarer	*Ryæ^n ah day-klah-Ray*
goods to declare	marchandises/ articles à déclarer	*mahR-shah^n-deez/ ahR-teek-luh ah day-klah-Ray*
luggage	les bagages	*lay bah-gahzh*
suitcase	la valise	*lah vah-leez*
information	les renseignements	*lay Rah^n-seh-nyuh-mah^n*
"Do you speak English?"	Parlez-vous anglais?	*pahR-lay-voo ah^n-gleh?*

Culture note—Typical daily schedule

A typical French person rises around 7, breakfasts on coffee, bread, or toast, and starts work at 9. The long lunch stretches for up to two hours somewhere between noon and 2:30. Then it's back to work until 6, 7, or later (depending on how long lunch was), followed by errands, with an evening meal generally around 8 o'clock.

Culture note—Punctuality

French people have a flexible concept of punctuality; anytime within fifteen minutes is considered to be on time. When visiting others, French people may arrive up to thirty minutes late without cause for censure.

The Alphabet

You sometimes need to spell words as a traveler, such as your name. Also, announcements in airports and train stations may include letters identifying boarding gates or platform locations. In addition, you need to know how to pronounce letters if you want to properly be able to say abbreviations such as the following: RATP (Paris public transportation system), A6 (express highway number), N13 (national highway number), USA (the country), UE (European Union), TVA (sales tax), and TGV (superfast train). Consequently, while it's not necessary to be able to say the alphabet forward and backward in French, it's not a bad idea to familiarize yourself with it a little bit.

a ah	**j** zhee	**s** ehs
b bay	**k** kah	**t** tay
c say	**l** ehl	**u** ew°
d day	**m** ehm	**v** vay
e uh	**n** ehn	**w** doo-
f ehf	**o** oh	bluh-vay
g zhay	**p** pay	**x** eeks
h ahsh	**q** kew°	**y** ee-gRehk
i ee	**r** ehR	**z** zehd

Exercise 6.2

What French words do the following series of letters spell?

1. say / ehR / oh / ee / ehs / ehs / ah / ehn / tay

2. ehs / uh / ehr / vay / ee / uh / tay / tay / uh

3. bay / oh / ew° / tay / ee / kew° / ew° / uh

4. ehm / ah / day / uh / ehm / oh / ee / ehs / uh / ehl / ehl / uh

5. ehs / oh / ee / eeks / ah / ehn / tay / uh

6. day / oh / ew° / zehd / uh

7. ehf / oh / ew° / ehR / say / ahsh / uh / tay / tay / uh

8. ahsh / oh / ehr / ehl / oh / zhay / uh

9. pay / ee-gRehk / zhee / ah / ehm / ah

10. vay / oh / ee-gRehk / ah / zhay / uh / ehR

Answers: 1) croissant, 2) serviette, 3) boutique, 4) mademoiselle, 5) soixante, 6) douze, 7) fourchette, 8) horloge , 9) pyjama, 10) voyager

Culture note—Transportation passes

In Paris, you can buy single-use public transportation tickets (*un ticket à l'unité*) or a discounted set of ten tickets (*un carnet*). Other cities may use a long card that allows for numerous rides, which can be purchased at a central location. Different cities have different rules about how long you can ride on one ticket, how many transfers you can have, and whether you can combine below-ground and above-ground transportation. You may choose to simplify your ticket purchases and use by buying a multi-zone, multi-day pass, which typically allows unlimited travel during the specified time period. Tickets in Paris are available at ticket offices, *cafés*, *tabacs*, and newspaper kiosks. Be aware that any ticket with a magnetic strip on it could be invalidated if you store it next to a magnet. (Watch out for sunglass clips and bag closures.)

Culture note—Taxis

Taxis are expensive in France and difficult to find. In Paris and many other cities, it's not common to flag one down as it passes by. Rather, you must usually telephone for one or find one at a taxi stand (*une borne/ station de taxi*) where they wait for customers. Check the main square, the train station, and major tourist sights. Available taxis have a white light on top; the yellow lights show taxis in use. As when interacting with other service personnel, greet your driver with a *Bonjour, monsieur*. Be aware that many factors affect the rate charged for a taxi: mileage, travel and waiting times, bags in the trunk, time of day, day of the week. Pay what's on the meter, plus a small tip, usually 5-7% of the fare. Rounding up to a good figure and telling the driver to keep that amount works well. You may ask for a receipt (*un reçu*).

Culture note—Strikes

Strikes are an occasional nuisance in France, particularly in public transportation. Fortunately, they are usually announced in advance. If you have important travel plans, it would be wise to check the news (or ask your hotel clerk) to make sure no strikes are planned then. The French word for strike is *grève (f)*. Don't be surprised if you want to take a train, bus, or subway someday and everything is shut down.

Culture note—Public transportation

France has an extensive public transportation system. It is reasonably priced, highly used, and well run. You will easily find trains, subways, buses, and streetcars to transport you around the country and its cities.

Validate your ticket either when entering the station (the subway and train) or on the vehicle (the bus). Signs saying *Compostez votre billet!* are there to remind you of that. Look around for an orange *composteur* machine (possibly yellow, at the train station) that will stamp your ticket with the date and time. If you feed your ticket through an automatic turnstile to reach a train platform, that will take care of validating your ticket.

You are on your honor to validate your ticket, but you can be asked to show it to a *contrôleur [koh^n-tRoh-lew°R]* (inspector) at any time on the trip or even as you exit. You may need to run your ticket through a turnstile again as you exit, so hold on to it. You must validate your ticket each time you transfer. (A transfer is referred to as a *correspondance*.) If you are caught riding without a valid ticket—even unintentionally—you could face a hefty fine.

Beware of pickpockets on public transportation, especially on the Paris *Métro*. Realize that it is not French custom to wait patiently in line for the bus; crowd in as necessary. For a detailed explanation of French public transportation modes and practices, see the book *France: Instructions for Use*, by Alison Culliford and Nan McElroy.

Transportation

Unless you are with a tour group with all transportation provided, you should be familiar with the most important means of getting around.

English	French	Pronunciation
Where is ___?	Où est ___?	oo ay ___?
I would like ___.	Je voudrais ___.	zhuh voo-dRay ___
I'm looking for ___.	Je cherche ___.	zhuh shehRsh ___
a taxi stand	une station de taxi	ew^{o}n stah-syoh^n duh tahk-see
a bicycle	un vélo	æ^n vay-loh
a bus	un bus	æ^n bew^{o}s
the bus stop	l'arrêt de bus	lah-reh duh bew^{o}s
entrance	l'entrée (f)	lah^n-tRay
exit	la sortie	lah suhR-tee
subway	le métro	luh may-tRoh
train	le train	luh tRæ^n
connections	la correspondance	lah kuh-Reh-spoh^n-dah^{n}s
train station	la gare	lah gahR
arrivals	les arrivées	lay (z)ah-Ree-vay
departures	les départs	lay day-pahR
platform	le quai	luh kay
airport	l'aéroport (m)	lah-ay-Ruh-puhR
airplane	l'avion (m)	lah-vyoh^n
flight	le vol	luh vuhl
ferry	le ferry-boat	luh feh-Ree-boht
a ticket	un billet	æ^n bee-yay
from. . . to	de . . . à	duh . . . ah
for ___ people	pour ___ personne(s)	pooR ___ pehR-suhn

Culture note—Subways and the RER

You may ride *le Métro* in Paris, Lyon, Rennes, Marseille, Lille, and Toulouse. Subway stops are marked with an M sign for *Métro*. Each line is identified by its end stations. (Make sure you choose the end station that lies in the direction you want to go.) If you need to transfer, look for the correct *correspondance* sign (don't forget to check the direction of the second line, too) and follow it. You may use the same *Métro* ticket when you transfer.

Feed your ticket through the machine at the turnstile or gate in the subway tunnel. It will shoot out farther along for you to pick up. And don't forget it—you could be required to show your ticket on the subway train or when you leave the subway, or you may need to feed it through the exit gate to leave.

RER is the abbreviation for the Paris suburban train system, which runs partially above ground (outside of Paris) and partially below (in the city). Within Paris, the RER connects with the *Métro* system. Outside Paris, the RER system extends to both Paris airports, Disneyland, and Versailles, although the outer reaches require a separate, more expensive RER ticket.

While the *Métro* is a convenient way to cover distances in the city, be prepared to walk substantial distances and climb endless sets of stairs between train platforms and the street. If you have physical challenges or heavy bags, you may want to consider alternate transportation.

Culture note—Regional Buses

Beyond the familiar network of city buses, comfortable regional buses (called *autocars* or just *cars*) connect towns and villages. You buy a bus ticket at the bus station (*la gare routière*), at the local tourist office, or often on the bus itself. Make sure you validate the ticket by stamping it in the machine on the bus. Town-to-town buses leave either around the train station or in the city center. Regional buses are run by private companies, and isolated areas may have infrequent bus service.

Exercise 6.3

How can you best get from place to place?

1.	across Paris (quickly)	A. un bus
2.	in most towns and cities	B. un ferry-boat
3.	Marseille to Corsica	C. un avion
4.	Paris to New York	D. le métro
5.	Paris to Lille	E. un train

Anwers: 1) D, 2) A, 3) B, 4) C, 5) E

Renting a Car

Virtually anyone you would rent a car from is used to dealing with tourists and should be proficient in English. If you'd feel better knowing how to rent a car in French (just in case), here are some words and phrases to use.

a car	une voiture	$ew^{o}n$ vwah-tew^{o}R
to rent	louer	loo-ay
I would like to rent a car.	Je voudrais louer une voiture.	zhuh voo-dRay loo-ay $ew^{o}n$ vwah-tew^{o}R
I have a reservation.	J'ai une réservation	zhay $ew^{o}n$ Ray-zehR-vah-syoh^{n}
from. . . to	de . . . à	duh . . . ah
for ___ people	pour ___ personne(s)	pooR ___ pehR-suhn
with automatic transmission	à transmission/ boîte automatique	ah tRah^{n}s-mees-yoh^{n}/ bwaht uh-tuh-mah-teek
with air conditioning	avec climatisation	ah-vehk klee-mah-tee-zah-syoh^{n}
I need ___.	Il me faut ___.	eel muh foh ___
some insurance	de l'assurance (f)	duh lah-sew^{o}-Rah^{n}s
a road map	une carte routière	$ew^{o}n$ kahRt Roo-tyehR
a driver's license	un permis de conduire	$æ^{n}$ pehR-mee duh koh^{n}-dweeR

Travel tip: Should you rent a car or not? If you will be traveling from city to city, you are better off taking the train. It's safe, convenient, and fast (up to 180 mph). If you are going to visit small towns, you can probably get around on buses. If, however, you intend to visit hard-to-access sights or spend all your time off the beaten path, it might make sense to rent a car.

Driving a Car

a gas station	une station-service	ew^on stah-syoh^n-sehR-vees
Fill it up, please.	Le plein, s'il vous plaît.	luh plæ^n, see voo play
some gasoline	du l'essence (f)	duh lay-sah^{n}s
leaded, high octane	supercarburant	sew^o-pehr-kahR-bew^o-Rah^n
unleaded	sans plomb *or* SP95	sah^n ploh^n
some diesel	du gasoil *or* gazole	dew^o gah-zwahl *or* gah-zuhl
__(30)__ Liters gas	__(30)__ litres d'essence	___ lee-tRuh day-sah^{n}s
self-service	le libre-service	luh lee-bRuh-sehR-vees
some oil	de l'huile (f)	duh lweel
a battery	une batterie	ew^on bah-tRee
a tire	un pneu	æ^n pnuh
a breakdown	une panne	ew^on pahn
broken(down)	en panne	ah^n pahn
an express highway	une autoroute	ew^on uh-tuh-Root
a road(way)	une route	ew^on Root
a street	une rue	ew^on Rew^o
a toll	un péage	æ^n pay-ahzh
an exit	une sortie	ew^on suhR-tee
a parking lot	un parking	æ^n pahRk-ing
a parking meter	un parcmètre	æ^n pahRk-meh-tRuh

Travel tips: Make sure you have a decent road map (*une carte routière*). You may not get a map with your rental car, so you definitely want to bring a good one along with you, if you plan to drive a lot. It's hard enough to find the right roads even with a good map; you don't want to be stuck with a lousy one. Consider renting a GPS system with your car, especially if you won't have a co-pilot to help out. Navigation really is different in France. First, it's not uncommon for the same stretch of road to have multiple names or numbers, and they will not all be identified on road signs. And second, road directions are not indicated by compass directions (e.g., A10 *West*) but rather by *what cities* lie in that direction, which are likely to be unfamiliar to you.

Your U.S. driver's license is all you need to drive in France, but an international driver's license (which includes your license information in multiple languages) is recommended. They are available through AAA. Check your auto insurance policy and your credit cards to see whether they include international auto insurance in their coverage.

Be prepared to drive a manual transmission in France. If you can't, make sure you order a car with automatic transmission (*une voiture automatique*) and expect to pay more.

Driving in France

Fueling up

Make sure you know what kind of fuel your car takes and be vigilant when filling up to avoid a mix-up. If you put diesel in your lead-free car or vice versa, you're in trouble. Don't plan to coast into a station on empty to fill up; they're harder to find in France than in the U.S. (bathrooms, too, by the way) and may be closed midday and Sundays. Stations at rest stops on the expressways (look for signs indicating *une aire de repos*) are always open, and you will find bathrooms, food, and fuel there. Because U.S. credit cards don't have the required "chip and PIN" technology needed for pay-at-the-pump, use a self-service pump that allows you to pay inside: fill with the right fuel, then go in and pay the attendant. (A receipt for fuel is called a *ticket.*) You can probably use your credit or debit card for this, but make sure you have cash on hand in case of a problem.

Car requirements

When driving in France, you must have a driver's license, be at least 20, have auto insurance that covers you while driving the vehicle, and have a red warning triangle and a first-aid kit. Everyone must wear a seatbelt. Children must sit in the back seat and use a child seat or booster. (Ask your rental company about current age requirements.) Drunken driving is strictly prohibited.

Road rules

Slower traffic keeps to the right. That probably means you, too, or you will quickly have a string of angry French drivers flashing their headlights at you in your rearview mirror. (An oncoming car flashing its lights, however, is probably trying to warn of a police speed trap ahead. There are also plenty of radars and cameras set up to catch speeders, by the way.) If you see arrows down the center of the pavement pointing to your lane, that means you are approaching a no-passing zone. Get over quickly, if you are in the wrong lane.

At intersections in cities, the vehicle at the right has the right of way, except in a traffic circle, where entering traffic yields to the traffic already in the circle, or if there is a sign indicating otherwise. When at a traffic light, look carefully before entering the intersection on green; red lights are routinely ignored and another car could come speeding through on the cross street. Always use your turn signals to indicate your intentions, but don't be surprised if other drivers don't. Also, don't cut in front of other vehicles or stop suddenly in traffic, even if you are about to miss your turn. It's not worth getting rear-ended and starting a small international incident. French drivers are assertive and risk-taking and have no patience with indecision on the street.

When approaching a blind intersection or curve, a light horn honk alerts others to your presence. And speaking of honking, don't be surprised if you get honked at in a less friendly way by locals; just remember that driving rules are different in France and don't take the honk personally. The French, after all, believe in expressing their displeasure.

Types of roads

There are three main types of roads in France. *Autoroutes* (marked with a large blue sign showing an A followed by a number, such as A4) are like our interstate highways. *Routes nationales* are main national roads (indicated on signs with an N followed by a number) and are more like our old two-lane state highways. *Routes départementales* are minor local roads (indicated by a D followed by a number), rather like our county roads.

Autoroutes are well-maintained and direct, allow the fastest driving, and are by far the best-marked type of road (worth taking for that, alone!). They are often toll roads, where you either pay a few coins when you enter, or you take a ticket and then pay when you exit the road or that section of the road. (Don't count on your credit cards being accepted; plan to pay in cash. Look for a lighted green down-arrow above the lanes to find ones that accept cash— probably at the right). Remember, *péage* means a toll.

The toll-free *routes nationales* (also called N roads, because of their abbreviations) often run next to the *autoroutes* but are less direct, even going through town centers, and require slower speeds. Look for green signs that show destinations on N roads.

Routes départementales are narrower, picturesque, and toll-free. D roads noted on white signs are particularly small or indirect. Expect to have trouble locating your desired route if you plan to take minor roads.

Toutes directions (All directions)

The listing of All Directions on a road sign looks a little strange to visitors, but it's a great fail-safe for when you aren't able to find the sign for the particular destination you want. The *Toutes directions* option is particularly helpful at a roundabout when you have already gone around a few times and still can't find the best exit for your destination.

Road stops

French expressways offer periodic rest areas (*les aires*) and service centers that vary greatly in the amenities they offer, from basic toilets and picnic tables to motels and restaurants. Signs are posted in advance of the rest area exits and indicate which services are available. If you have car trouble or otherwise need assistance, free telephones are posted every 2 km on the *autoroutes*. Don't forget to use the emergency triangle in your car to warn other drivers you have pulled over.

Holiday warning

Don't plan to drive much during holidays in France, as the roads will be clogged with French holidaymakers. The entire month of August is vacation time for locals, making drives at the beginning and end of the month torturous. Ascenscion Day weekend around Aug. 15 also causes plentiful traffic jams. Routes from Paris to the Mediterranean coast are particularly popular with vacationers.

Parking rules

"No parking" is indicated by yellow lines or when a section is marked by a sign with a red circle that has either an X or a diagonal line across it. (Add-on signs show whether no-parking is limited to certain days or hours.) Blue lines indicate "blue zones" that allow free parking up to 1 ½ hours (longer on nights and Sundays). If your rental car doesn't have one, get a parking disc (*un disque de stationnement*) from a *tabac* or a tourist office, show your arrival time, and put the disc on your dashboard so it's easily visible from the outside.

Parking is also allowed where there are broken white lines ending in solid white lines, but expect to pay for it—the key word is *payant*. Look for a blue/green machine to get your pre-paid ticket. (Insert your cash, choose the length of time you need (*choisir la durée*), confirm (*valider*), and remove your ticket from the machine to place on your dashboard.) If the sign indicates you must pay for certain hours, that means you *don't* have to pay for the complementary times (such as overnight).

If you park in a lot or a garage, you may need to pay for your parking before returning to your car. Look for a cashier (*le caissier*), then keep your paid ticket handy for exiting at the gate.

Be aware that city parking is in short supply and French drivers try to shoehorn their cars into impossibly tight spaces, lightly bumping the cars on either side to gain a little more room. If you are in a *café* and should be so fortunate as to have a very small parking space open on the street before you, plan to stay awhile and enjoy the entertainment as car after car is sure to stop and attempt to squeeze in. Of course, if you are on the driving side of this spectacle, it is not so amusing.

Grammar—Negation (ne . . . pas)

There are multiple ways to express negation in French, but we will look at the most common here.

$$ne + verb + pas$$

Let's look at some examples we've already seen. *J'ai le livre* [zhay luh leev-Ruh] (I have the book) becomes *Je n'ai pas le livre* [zhuh nay pah luh leev-Ruh] (I don't have the book). Notice that *je* is no longer contracted when it is split from the verb, but the *ne* is then shortened to *n'*. That is because of elision; when one word starts with a vowel, certain words that precede that word (*je, te, le, ne, la, se*) contract and the dropped vowel is replaced by an apostrophe.

Je comprends [zhuh koh^n-pRah^n] (I understand) is negated to *Je ne comprends pas* [zhuh nuh koh^n-pRah^n pah] (I don't understand).

The trickiest part (other than knowing when to contract words, which is unlikely to interfere with comprehension) is remembering that the negation has two parts—*ne* and *pas*—and they bookend the verb.

Note: Be aware that indefinite articles change to *de* or *d'* after a negative. You don't need to learn this, but don't be surprised if you hear it. For example,

I'll have a salad.	Je prends une salade.	*zhuh pRah^n ew^{o}n sah-lahd*
I'll not have salad.	Je ne prends pas de salade.	*zhuh nuh pRah^n pah duh sah-lahd*

At the Train Station

The French national railway is known as the SNCF. Trains are reliable, punctual, fast, clean, and convenient. There are many different types, from superfast trains that require a surcharge to pokey local ones. You can figure out the kind of train you want by looking at the large poster that shows departures (*départs*) and reading how long it takes to reach your destination or by going online to www.sncf.fr. You can buy a train ticket from a travel agent or at the train station, but don't wait until the last minute or you could face a long line or an already-full train.

You need to choose first or second class. If you are taking a popular route or traveling on a weekend or holiday, you want to buy a seat reservation, even if it's not required with your ticket. If you are taking an overnight train and want a (non-private) sleeping bunk, ask for a *couchette*. You should be able to get discounted tickets for children and for adults over 65. Wherever you buy your ticket, you should double check the date on both your ticket and your seat reservation. (Warning: As of this writing, the yellow self-service ticket machines in train stations do not accept U.S. bank cards or credit cards. You may use the machines to get information, but you can only purchase tickets there with a European bank card.) If you buy a railpass in the U.S., you still need to pay for reservations and certain upgrades, such as high-speed service or *couchettes*.

Different types of train tickets (national, international, suburban) may be sold in different places. Ask at the help desk (*accueil*) to make sure you get in the right line. Before you go to the platform (*le quai*) next to the track (*la voie*) to wait for or board your train, check the large, elevated departure (*départs*) boards that are constantly updated. The trains are listed according to their *final destination*, not by the stops along the way (which may include *your* destination), so make sure you know the final stop of your train or you might miss a change in departure time or platform and then miss the train itself. (Check the large departure schedule posters if you need to find the final destination of your train.)

If you have trouble locating your train information or platform, visit the help desk (*accueil*) in the station. Before boarding your train, you *must* stamp your ticket in one of the yellow or orange validating machines. Look for them on the platform or around the station. Then find the board that displays diagrams of major trains and look for your train. If your train is listed, find the car you want to board, then stand in the area where that car is supposed to stop. Use the letters hanging from the roof above you or sticking out somewhere along the platform as guides. Those letters correspond to the letters you will see on the diagram.

Before you board your car, check the destination that is posted on the side of the car next to the door. Not all parts of the train go to the same place, so you want to make sure you board a car that travels to your destination. Also make sure that the car is the same class as your ticket. When you arrive at your destination, leave the train quickly and look for the *Sortie* signs.

If you are joining a train as it progresses from a different starting point, make sure you locate your platform and are ready to board well before its scheduled arrival time. French trains are very punctual and will not linger past their allotted stopping time. Be prepared to board and exit quickly, especially on the high-speed (TGV) trains, where passengers are routinely left on the platform (or on the car) as the automatic doors shut and the train continues on schedule.

Culture note—Luggage lockers

Luggage storage (*la consigne*) and luggage lockers (*les consignes automatiques*) are sometimes available at the train station, if you don't want to haul your baggage around with you. Fees are very reasonable. If you deposit your luggage with workers at a counter, make sure you get their hours of operation, so you know when you can get your bags back. Self-service lockers may also be off-limits at certain times. Because of security concerns, luggage lockers are not as prevalent as they used to be.

Culture note—Types of trains

International trains include the Eurostar (or "chunnel" train, as Americans sometimes refer to it) to London and the Thalys train to Belgium, Germany, and The Netherlands. These trains are fast, comfortable, and require reservations.

National trains include the super-fast TGV (*train à grande vitesse*) and the express Corail trains. The TGV runs only between certain major cities and requires a reservation. Corail trains, though not quite as fast as the TGV, offer more routes, and require reservations on some routes (advised on all). Both types of trains have air conditioning.

Regional Ter trains make more stops, do not have a first-class section, do not require reservations, but do have air conditioning.

Commuter trains are concentrated around Paris (Transilien and RER).

Culture note—Night trains

Overnight trains can be an efficient way to maximize your time in France. You must be vigilant on night trains, however, because they are not always safe. Watch your belongings at all times on a train, but especially on overnight trips.

Culture note—Trains and toilets

Each train car has bathrooms at the ends. A small sign next to the handle will show whether the room is occupied or vacant, probably by displaying either a red or green shape. Train toilets can be rather dirty. Don't use them when the train is in the station, as some older models may flush directly onto the tracks.

7   Emergencies and Additional Vocabulary

Emergencies

Odds are that you will not encounter any emergencies abroad, but if you do, you might not have time to look up how to say something. Learning some basic emergency vocabulary can be a life-saving investment. If nothing else, at least learn how to say "Help!"

Help!	Au secours!	*oh suh-koo$R$!*
Watch out!	Attention!	*ah-tah^n-syoh^n!*
Look!	Regardez!	*Ruh-gah$R$-day!*
Go away!	Allez-vous-en!	*ah-lay-voo-zah^n!*
	(*informal*) va-t-en!	*vah-tah^n!*
Fire!	Au feu!	*oh fuh!*
Call ___!	Appelez ___!	*ah-play ___!*
the police	la police	*lah puh-lees*
an ambulance	une ambulance	*ew^{o}n ah^n-bew^o-lah^{n}s*
the fire department	les pompiers	*lay poh^n-pyay*
a doctor	un médecin	*æ^n mehd-sæ^n*
I need ___.	Il me faut ___.	*eel muh foh ___*
a telephone	un téléphone	*æ^n tay-lay-fuhn*

Exercise 7.1
How would you say the following in French?

1. Call the police!
2. Help!
3. Call an ambulance!
4. Call a doctor!

5. I need a telephone.
6. Watch out!
7. Fire!
8. I need a doctor!

Answers: 1) Appelez la police! 2) Au secours! 3) Appelez une ambulance! 4) Appelez un médecin! 5) Il me faut un téléphone. 6) Attention! 7) Au feu! 8) Il me faut un médecin!

Culture note—Making phone calls

French telephone numbers have ten digits, and when calling in France, you should always use all ten of them. The first two digits are the area code. Any number starting with 01 is for Paris; any number starting with 06 is for a cell phone.

To call France from outside the country, you need to dial the correct international calling code from the country you are in (011 from the U.S.), followed by the destination country code for France (33), then the area code (omitting the 0 at the start of the number), then the rest of the phone number. For example, a call from the U.S. to Paris (using a fake French number 01.23.54.87.xx for illustration) could be placed using this number: 011 33 1 23 54 87 xx.

If you want to call the United States from France, start with the code for international calls originating in France (00), followed by the destination country code for the U.S. (1), followed by the area code and local number. For example, I could call Iowa from France by dialing 00 1 319 885 744x.

Calling directly from your hotel or with a credit card is ridiculously expensive. An economical option is to purchase a phone card (*télécarte*) from a *tabac* or the post office. To call internationally, get a *carte internationale*. (Make sure the sales-person realizes you want to call the U.S.) This card will allow you to call within France *or* to other countries and can be used on public or private phones. It works as a U.S. phone card does—scratch the strip on the back to uncover the PIN, dial the toll-free access number on the back of the card, enter the PIN and the complete destination phone number (starting with 00 1 for calls to the U.S.). The on-phone instructions will be in French, but if you follow the English instructions on the back of the card, you'll be fine.

You can also use your U.S. phone card to call from France, provided you have a French access number, but the units will fly by more quickly than if you buy a local card. In either case, if you are able to call from your hotel phone, most likely you will first need to dial a "0" to get an outside line. Not all phones in hotel rooms allow this, but, in that case, the hotel probably provides a public phone you can use.

If you want to make calls at reasonable rates without messing with a phone card, try to find a phone bank—individual phone booths in a shop that may also offer fax, Internet, and photocopying services. Phone rates should be posted. Pay the cashier when you have completed your call.

Another option is to rent a French cell phone for your stay. Incoming calls are usually free. Outgoing calls have different rates for calls within France ($.78 per minute, in a phone rental agreement recent to this writing) and for international calls ($1.78 per minute, in the same rental agreement).

cell phone	le portable	*luh puhR-tah-bluh*
SIM card	la carte SIM	*lah kahRt seem*
battery	la batterie	*lah bah-tRee*
to recharge (elec.)	charger	*shahR-zhay*

Culture note—Pharmacies

Pharmacies in France function as mini-clinics. People go there for advice and treatment in place of visiting a doctor. (Heads up: The treatment, in France, often includes a suppository.) In addition to medicine and herbal remedies, pharmacies offer pretty much anything that has to do with health or personal hygiene. They are identified by a large green neon cross outside the door.

At the doctor / At the pharmacy

No one wants to get sick or hurt while away from home (and if you do, your healthcare worker may know English), but there's peace of mind in knowing some rudimentary health vocabulary.

It hurts here.	J'ai mal ici.	*zhay mahl ee-see*
I'm sick.	Je suis malade.	*zhuh swee mah-lahd*
I have ___.	J'ai ___.	*zhay ___*

a fever	de la fièvre	*duh lah fyeh-vRuh*
constipation	la constipation	*lah koh^n-stee-pah-syoh^n*
diarrhea	la diarrhée	*lah dyah-Ray*
a headache	un mal de tête	*æ^n mahl duh teht*
	un mal à la tête	*æ^n mahl ah lah teht*
a stomach ache	mal à l'estomac	*mahl ah leh-stoh-mah*
a cold	un rhume	*æ^n Rew^{o}m*
Can you please write it down for me?	Pouvez-vous me l'écrire, s'il vous plaît?	*poo-vay voo muh lay-kReeR, see voo play?*

Note: If you have a chronic health condition, know how to say it in French, just as a precaution.

I'm diabetic.	Je suis diabétique.	*zhuh swee dyah-bay-teek*
I have a heart condition.	Je souffre du coeur.	*zhuh soo-fRuh dew^o kuhR*
I have high blood pressure.	J'ai de l'hypertension.	*zhay duh lee-pehR-tah^n-syoh^n*
I'm allergic ___.	Je suis allergique ___.	*zhuh swee (z)ah-lehR-zheek ___*
to penicillin	à la pénicilline	*ah lah pay-nee-see-leen*
to peanuts	aux cacahuètes	*oh kah-kah-weht*

Culture note—At the doctor

Many French doctors understand English or can at least read it. If you need to visit a doctor (remember to try a pharmacy first, if your condition is not serious), you may want to write down your symptoms.

Before traveling to France, make sure you are covered by your medical policy. Payment is expected at the time of treatment, but get copies of all paperwork so you can be reimbursed by your insurance company. Most likely, you will need to visit an emergency room (*le service des urgences*) [*luh sehR-vees day (z)ew^{o}R-zhah^{n}s*] if you want treatment to be covered by a U.S. policy.

Medication

I need ___.	Il me faut ___.	*eel muh foh ___*
a prescription	une ordonnance	*ew^{o}n ohR-duh-nah^{n}s*
some aspirin	de l'aspirine (f)	*duh lah-spee-Reen*
a decongestant	un décongestion-nant	*æ^n day-koh^n-zhehs-tyoh-nah^n*
an antihistamine	un antihistami-nique	*æ^n (n)ah^n-tee-ees-tah-mee-neek*
some cough syrup	du syrop pour la toux	*dew^o see-Roh pooR lah too*
a cough drop	une pastille pour la toux	*ew^{o}n pah-steey pooR lah too*

Culture note—Medical emergencies

If you have a medical emergency, the quickest response will be from the fire department (*Sapeurs-Pompiers*). Dial number 18 on the telephone, and a paramedic will soon be on the way.

Travel tips: When traveling abroad, take any medicine in its original container, so customs officers can identify it. Take extra medicine along as a precaution. Take a copy of your prescription with you. Know the generic names for your medicines, because specific brand names may not be available or recognized.

Additional Vocabulary

Travelers frequently want to know how to say things beyond the bare necessities. This section includes three common topics: family, occupations, and the weather. Remember, though—stay away from personal topics with French people unless *they* bring them up. More extensive vocabulary is included in the dictionaries at the back of this book.

Family

English	French	Pronunciation
I'm with ___.	Je suis avec ___.	*zhuh swee (z)ah-vehk___.*
my children	mes enfants	*may (z)ah^n-fah^n*
my son	mon fils	*moh^n fees*
my daughter	ma fille	*mah feey*
my husband	mon mari	*moh^n mah-Ree*
my wife	ma femme	*mah fahm*
my friend (male)	mon ami	*moh^n (n)ah-mee*
my friend (female)	mon amie	*moh^n (n)ah-mee*
man	l'homme (m)	*luhm*
woman	la femme	*lah fahm*
boy	le garçon	*luh gahR-soh^n*
girl	la fille	*lah feey*
baby	le bébé	*luh bay-bay*
I'm ___.	Je suis ___.	*zhuh swee ___*
married	marié(e)	*mahR-yay*
single	célibataire	*say-lee-bah-tehR*
separated	séparé(e)	*say-pah-Ray*
divorced	divorcé(e)	*dee-vuhR-say*
widowed (woman)	veuve	*vuhv*
widowed (man)	veuf	*vuhf*

Culture note—Family life

Historically, family life is sacrosanct in France—private, tightly woven, separate from public life, and incurring deep obligations. Children may live with their parents until marriage and sometimes beyond. Those who don't live together try to be together on Sundays and holidays, reinforcing their strong familial ties.

The separation of French family life from public life is reinforced by their houses—guarded by walls, hedges, and curtains closed at dusk. Generally, it is rare for non-family members to be included in family events, and a great honor because of that.

Culture note—Children

Traditionally, French children have not been given the run of the house or, indeed, much freedom at all. They are expected to learn proper behavior and dress and to act as little adults, conforming to society's rules or else face sometimes harsh rebukes. Historically (although this has loosened considerably in France, as it has elsewhere, depending on social class, family situation, and cultural background), French parents are considered to have a social obligation to produce good citizens and family members (polite and well-mannered), and to fail at this—that is, to have poorly behaved or poorly groomed children—can make the entire family look bad.

This often strict child rearing in no way means the French don't like children, however. On the contrary, most like children very much, but they expect them to be civilized and not act like little savages. I have traveled in France with a well-behaved child (she was on a good streak, at the time) and can report that it opened doors of French friendliness to me that I had not seen before. Strangers would address my then-eight-year-old daughter with playfulness and warmth, and she became a gateway through which we adults could connect. If you want to have actual interactions with the notoriously private French, I highly recommend taking a (polite) child along!

Grammar—Third-person singular

If you want to talk about another person or a thing (my wife, my son, the man, the room, the wine), you need to use the grammar forms for third-person singular (he, she, it). Most of us, however—beginners that we are—don't really want to be overwhelmed by more grammar rules right now. Fortunately, we don't need to be, if all we care about for the moment is getting by.

Here is an easy "cheat" to use third-person singular: the pronunciation of he/she/it verb forms is usually the same as the *I*-forms (*je* __) you are already familiar with, even if the verb-ending is sometimes different. Therefore, you can use spoken *I*-forms as a shortcut if you want to talk about other individual things or persons. For example, the verb in *Je bois* (I drink) sounds the same as in *Mon mari boit* (My husband drinks). Very often, the present-tense verb forms also *look* identical.

The vital verbs *to be* and *to have* are, as always, irregular, and we must learn the forms for he/she/it. You have seen the forms throughout this book, however, and may already be familiar with them: "is" = *est* [ay] and "has" = *a* [ah].

Grammar—Third-person singular pronouns

he	il [*eel*]
she	elle [*ehl*]
one	on [*oh^n*]

If you don't want to repeat a name (Marc) or noun phrase (my wife) over and over in a conversation, you need to use pronouns. The French word for *he* is il [*eel*]. The word for *she* is elle [*ehl*]. And the very handy *one* (used more widely in French than in English) is *on* [*oh^n*].

Culture note—French work life

Rules in French work life are wildly different than work conventions in the United States. For starters, French workers have a shorter work week—officially 35 hours, for most of them—and are required to take at least five weeks of vacation a year. Work has its place, but is not the be-all and end-all in France. Workaholics are not admired.

On the job itself, relationships again take priority. Before getting down to the business at hand, it is important to develop trust and a connection between those doing business together. Business relationships are long-term and need to be nurtured, but in the proper business sphere. Unlike in the U.S., business associates do not generally socialize outside of work.

Occupations

Remember, it is considered ill-mannered to ask strangers or new acquaintances about their occupations. At some point, however, the topic may come up. If someone asks about your job, then you can talk about it and ask about theirs without fear of offense. You do not use an *a* or *an* when telling about occupations in French. Literally, you would say, "I'm accountant" or "I'm engineer," for example. When the feminine form of an occupation differs from the masculine, it is shown below with a slash. Check the dictionaries in the back of this book for more job titles.

a job	un métier	$æ^n$ may-tyay
What is your job?	Quel est votre métier?	kehl ay vuh-tRuh may-tyay?
I'm a(n) ___.	Je suis ___.	zhuh swee ___
My wife is ___.	Ma femme est ___.	mah fahm ay ___
My husband is ___.	Mon mari est ___.	moh^n mah-Ree ay ___
doctor	médecin	$mehd\text{-}sæ^n$
lawyer	avocat/e	ah-voh-kah/-kaht
manager	directeur/-trice	dee-Rehk-tuhR/-tRees
minister	pasteur	pahs-tuhR
musician	musicien/ne	mew^p-zee-syæ^n/-syehn
professor	professeur	pRuh-feh-suhR
student	étudiant/e	ay-tew^p-dyah^n/-dah^{n}t
teacher	professeur	pRuh-feh-suhR
retired	retraité/e	Ruh-tRay-tay

Culture note—Education

Education, especially the "right" education, at the most elite schools, is of paramount importance in France. Many parents push their children to excel at academics in the hope they can attain the highest education possible and join the leaders of French government and business. Education is valued far more than experience, and the right education can open doors for the rest of a person's life. Consequently, the pressure to succeed in school can be immense.

Weather

weather	le temps	*luh tah^n*
How is the weather?	Quel temps fait-il?	*kehl tah^n feh-teel?*
It's ___.	Il fait ___.	*eel feh ___*
nice	beau	*boh*
bad	mauvais	*moh-vay*
cold	froid	*fRwah*
cool	frais	*fReh*
hot	chaud	*shoh*
It's ___.	Il y a ___.	*eel yah ___*
cloudy	des nuages	*day new^{p}ahzh*
windy	du vent	*dew^p vah^n*
foggy	du brouillard	*dew^p bRoo-yahR*
sunny	du soleil	*dew^p suh-lay*
It's raining	Il pleut.	*eel pluh*
It's snowing.	Il neige.	*eel nehzh*

Culture note—The mistral

The mistral is a strong wind that blows from the north or north-west toward the Mediterranean. It occurs most frequently in winter or spring, but can appear anytime weather conditions are right. The mistral can last for days or even more than a week, and it particularly affects Provence and the Rhone Valley. While the mistral appears only with bright, clear skies, it can produce winds exceeding 50 mph and can cause storms on the Mediterranean.

If you are exposed to the mistral, take great care to hold on to your belongings. Hats can quickly fly aloft. The mistral can instantly snatch any paper—including tickets and euro bills—and permanently remove them from your possession.

Exercise 7.2

What do you need to prepare yourself for the following weather conditions? Match the listings in columns A and B.

A	B
1. Il fait frais.	A. un maillot/slip de bain ou un short
2. Il pleut.	
3. Il y a du soleil.	B. un chapeau ou des lunettes de soleil
4. Il fait froid et il neige.	C. une veste ou un pull
5. Il fait chaud.	D. un parapluie
	E. un manteau et des gants

Answers: 1) C, 2) D, 3) B, 4) E, 5) A

Culture note—Celsius

Remember that France uses the Celsius temperature scale. Water freezes at zero degrees Celsius and boils at 100 degrees. Twenty degrees Celsius is the quite pleasant temperature of 68 degrees Fahrenheit, while 32 degrees Celsius is a steamy 90 degrees Fahrenheit.

For a rough conversion of Celsius temperatures to Fahrenheit, double the Celsius number and add 30. For example, start with 20 degrees Celsius, double it to 40, add 30 for 70, which gets you close to the correct Fahrenheit reading of 68. While it's not perfect, this shortcut will at least get you in the ballpark.

$$\text{Celsius reading} \times 2 + 30 = \text{approximate Fahrenheit reading}$$

If you have time or need a very accurate conversion, you can always check the temperature on a conversion chart. Here is an abbreviated version of one.

Temperature Conversion Chart

C	F
40	104
35	95
30	86
25	77
20	68
15	59
10	50
5	41
0	32
-10	14
-20	-4

A final word

That's it! You have covered the basics of French that will serve you well as a visitor in that glorious country and many others. You have learned a little grammar, quite a bit of vocabulary, and a lot about French social customs. Congratulations! Whatever effort you were able to put into your preparation will pay off handsomely in France, I promise. You *will* be able to communicate with French speakers, understand some of what is going on around you, and experience daily life without the paralyzing fear of complete uncertainty. So dive in and enjoy your French visit!

And then tell me about it. Please. The good, the bad, what you learned, what surprised you. I'd love to hear about your experiences with this book and abroad. Write me in care of World Prospect Press, P.O. Box 253, Waverly, IA 50677 (on the Web at worldprospect.com), or you can reach me via email at bingham@worldprospect.com.

Have a great trip, and I look forward to hearing from you!

Self-Test

Can you remember what to expect and how to communicate in the following situations? Test yourself, then review what you need to work on.

❑   Bare-bones French
　　yes
　　no
　　please
　　thank you
　　excuse me
❑   Greetings
　　day
　　evening and night
　　informal
❑   Introductions
　　introduce yourself
　　ask others their names
❑   Origins
　　say where you are from
　　ask others where they are from
❑   Leave-taking
　　most of the time
　　informal
❑   Manners
　　please
　　thank you
　　you're welcome
　　excuse me
❑   Useful expressions
　　yes/no/and/or
　　"I don't understand."
　　"Please repeat."
　　"Please speak more slowly/loudly."
❑   Numbers 0-10
❑   Concrete vocabulary
　　identify items in the room around you
❑   Days of the week

- ❏ Times of day
  morning
  afternoon
  evening
  night
- ❏ Months
- ❏ Directions
  there
  right
  left
  straight ahead
- ❏ Lodging
  "Where is a hotel, please?"
  "Do you have rooms available?"
  "I would like a double room."
  with a shower
  for three nights
  "How much does that cost?"
  "Do you have something less expensive?"
  "I'll take it."
- ❏ There is ___ / There are ___
- ❏ Numbers 11-20
- ❏ Eating out
  meals
  how to order
  some foods and drinks
  how to pay, tip
  "Check, please!"
  "For you."
- ❏ Numbers 10-100, by ten
- ❏ Shopping
  "Do you have _____?"
  "I would like. . ."
  types of stores
  clothing
  colors
  miscellaneous items
- ❏ Numbers 21-99
- ❏ Units of time

❑　Sightseeing
places to visit
❑　Rest rooms
"bathroom"
men's
ladies'
❑　Mailing letters
post office
stamps
by airmail
to America
❑　Email
Wi-Fi
❑　Exchanging money
"Where's an ATM?"
❑　Numbers 100-1000, by 100
❑　Alphabet
❑　Transportation
public transportation
renting and driving a car
at the train station
❑　Negation
❑　Emergencies
"Help!"
"Watch out!"
"Call a doctor!"
"Fire!"
"I need a telephone."
❑　At the doctor/pharmacy
"It hurts here."
❑　Medication you need
❑　Family and occupations
tell what you have for family and occupations
❑　Weather
"Quel temps fait-il?"
Celsius temperature conversion

Resource Guide

Culture Shock! France, 3rd ed., by Sally Adamson Taylor, Cavendish Square Publishing, 2008, ISBN 978-0761454809, $15.95

Culture Smart! France: The Essential Guide to Customs and Culture, 2nd rev. ed., by Barry Tomalin, Kuperard, 2013, ISBN 978-1857336733, $9.95

France for Dummies, 4th ed., by Darwin Porter, Danforth Prince, and Cheryl A. Pientka, For Dummies, 2007, ISBN 978-0470085813, $21.99

France: Instructions for Use: The Practical, On-Site Assistant for the Enthusiastic (Even Experienced) Traveler, by Alison Culliford and Nan McElroy, Illustrata Press, 2007, ISBN 978-1885436405, $14.95

French or Foe? Getting the Most Out of Visiting, Living and Working in France, 2nd ed., by Polly Platt, Culture Crossings, 1998, ISBN 978-0964668409, $16.95

French Women Don't Get Fat, by Mireille Guiliano, Vintage, 2007, ISBN 978-0375710513, $14.95

Just Enough French: How to Get By and Be Easily Understood, 2nd ed., by D. L. Ellis, McGraw-Hill, 2005, ISBN 978-0071451390, $8.00

Kiss, Bow, or Shake Hands, 2nd ed., by Terri Morrison and Wayne A. Conaway, Adams Media, 2006, ISBN 978-1593373689, $24.95

Living, Studying, and Working in France: Everything You Need to Know to Fulfill Your Dreams of Living Abroad, by Saska Reilly and Lorin David Kalisky, Henry Holt, 1999, ISBN 978-0805059472, $16.00

Paris, Paris: Journey Into the City of Light, by David Downie, Broadway Paperbacks, 2011, ISBN 978-0-307-88608-8, $15.00

Stuff Parisians Like: Discovering the Quoi in the Je Ne Said Quoi, by Olivier Magny, Berkley Publishing Group, 2011, ISBN 978-0425241189, $15.00

Xenophobe's Guide to the French, 2nd rev. ed., by Nick Yapp and Michel Syrett, Oval Books, 2009, ISBN 978-1906042325, $7.95

French-English Dictionary

How to use this dictionary

The purpose of this dictionary is to help you decipher written and spoken French. Because you will be exposed to more French than you will need to produce, this dictionary contains more entries than the English-French dictionary that follows it. It is by no means comprehensive however.

French words are listed in bold. Verbs are listed in the infinitive form, as well as separate listings for some common inflected forms. Nouns are listed in singular form, followed by the definite article and, if necessary, *m* or *f* to show whether the noun is masculine or feminine. Adjectives are listed in their masculine forms with alternate feminine endings. Pronunciations are not located here but are included in the English-French dictionary.

a has
à to, until, at (a time)
  à bientôt so long, see you soon!
  à bord aboard, on board
  à côté de beside, next to
  à demain until tomorrow
  à droite to the right
  à gauche to the left
  à la in the style of
  à la prochaine until next time
  à point medium rare (meat)
à bientôt so long, see you soon!
abîmé(e) damaged
à bord aboard
abribus, l' *m* bus shelter
abricot, l' *m* apricot
absolument absolutely
accepter to accept
accès aux trains to the trains
accident, l' *m* accident
accompagnement, l' *m* side dish
accord, l' *m* agreement
  d'accord OK
accueil, l' *m* help desk, welcome, check-in
acheter to buy
à côté de beside, next to

actualités, les *f* news
actuellement currently
addition, l' *f* bill, check
à demain until tomorrow
admirer to admire
adresse, l' *f* address
  adresse domicile home address
à droite to the right
ADSL DSL
adulte, l' *m/f* adult
aérogare, l' *f* airport, terminal
aéroport, l' *m* airport
affaire, l' *f* matter
affaires, les *f* business
affirmer to affirm
affranchir to frank, to put postage on
affranchissement, l' *m* postage
à gauche to the left
âge, l' *m* age
agence, l' *f* agency
  de spectacles ticket agency
  de voyages travel agency
agent de police, l' *m* police officer
agneau, l' *m* lamb
agréable pleasant
aide, l' *f* help, aid
aider to help

aiglefin, l' *m* haddock
aïgo bouïdo garlic soup
aigre sour
aigreurs d'estomac, des *f* heartburn
aiguille, l' *f* needle
aiguillettes de canard au vinaigre
fillet of duck in vinegar
ail, l' *f* garlic
aimable kind, friendly, likeable
aimer to like, to love
aïoli, l' *m* garlic mayonnaise
aire (de repos/de service/de
stationnement), l' *f* rest area
à la in the style of
à la prochaine until next time
alcool, l' *m* alcohol
alcoolique alcoholic
alcoolisé(e) alcoholic (content)
alimentation générale, l' *f* grocery
store
aliments, les *m* food
allée, l' *f* path, aisle
allemand(e) German
aller to go
aller-retour round trip
aller-simple one-way
allergie, l' *f* allergy
allergique à allergic to
allez go (you, formal)
allumer to light
allumette, l' *f* match
alors then, so
alose, l' *f* shad
alouette, l' *f* lark (bird)
alouettes sans têtes small veal
cutlets, stuffed and rolled
alpinisme, l' *m* mountaineering
alsacien(ne) (food) with sauerkraut
amande, l' *f* almond
ambassade, l' *f* embassy
ambulance, l' *f* ambulance
amende, l' *f* fine, penalty
amer/amère bitter
américain(e) American
Americano, l' *m* watered-down
espresso
ameublement, l' *m* furniture
ami(e), l' *m/f* friend
amour, l' *m* love
ampoule, l' *f* light bulb

amuse-bouche/-gueule, des
appetizers, munchies
amygdales, les *f* tonsils
an, l' *m* year
ananas, l' *m* pineapple
anchois, l' *m* anchovy
ancien(ne) old, former
andouille(tte), l' *f* pork sausage,
strongly-flavored tripe sausage
(andoillette is coarser and can
contain colon)
aneth, l' *m* dill
angine, l' *f* sour throat
anglais(e) English
Anglais(e), l' *m/f* Englishman/-
woman
anglaise breaded and fried, cooked
vegetables
Angleterre, l' *f* England
anguille, l' *f* eel
animal, l' *m* animal
anis, l' *m* aniseed
année, l' *f* year
anniversaire, l' *m* birthday
annuaire, l' *m* phone book
annuler to cancel
antibiotique, l' *m* antibiotic
antiquités, les *f* antiques
antivol, l' *m* lock
août August
apéritif, l' *m* aperitif/before-dinner
drink
apéro, l' *m* aperitif
à point medium rare (meat)
appareil photo digital, l' *m* digital
camera
appartement, l' *m* apartment
appartenir to belong
appel téléphonique, l' *m* phone call
appeler to call
appendicite, l' *f* appendicitis
appétit, l' *m* appetite
apporter to bring
apprendre to learn
appuyer (sur) to press (on), to push
appuyer pour ouvrir press to open
après after
après-demain the day after
tomorrow
après-midi, l' *m* or *f* afternoon

arbre, l' *m* tree
architecte, l' *m/f* architect
argent, l' *m* silver, money
argenté(e) silver (color)
Argenteuil, la crème d' cream of
  asparagus soup
Armagnac a wine brandy
Armistice, l' *m* Armistice Day
armoire, l' *f* wardrobe, closet
arobase, l' *f* @ symbol
arranger to adjust, to arrange
arrêt, l' *m* stop
  arrêt interdit no stopping
arrêter to stop
arrêtez votre moteur turn off your
  engine
arrivée, l' *f* arrival
arriver to arrive
arrondissement, l' *m* administrative
  district within Paris/Marseille
art, l' *m* art
artichaut, l' *m* artichoke
  à la vinaigrette in vinaigrette
  dressing
artiste, l' *m/f* artist
ascenseur, l' *m* elevator
Ascension, l' *f* Ascension Day
asperge, l' *f* asparagus
  asperges à la crème, les asparagus
  in cream
aspic, l' *m* meat or fish in aspic jelly
aspirine, l' *f* aspirin
assaisonnement, l' *m* seasoning
assez (de) enough (of)
assiette, l' *f* plate
  __ anglaise plate of cold cuts
  __ de charcuterie plate of cold
cuts
Assomption, l' *f* Assumption
assurance, l' *f* insurance
asthme, l' *m* asthma
atelier, l' *m* workshop
  atelier d'artiste studio
attachez vos ceintures fasten your
  seat belt
attendez votre billet wait for your
  ticket
attendre to wait (for)
attention! caution!
au to the, at the

au revoir goodbye
auberge, l' *f* inn
  __ de jeunesse youth hostel
aubergine, l' *f* eggplant
au choix choice of
aucun(e) none; no __
au-dessous (de) under, below
au-dessus (de) above
audiophone, l' *m* hearing aid
aujourd'hui today
aussi also
auteur, l' *m* author
autobus, l' *m* local bus
autocar, l' *m* tour bus
automatique automatic
automne, l' *m* fall, autumn
autoroute, l' *f* expressway, highway
autour de around
autre other
  autre jour, l' the other day
  un(e) autre another
Auvergnate, la salade ham/cheese
  salad
aux to the, at the, in the
  aux États-Unis to/at/in the
  U.S.
avant (de) before
  en avant in front, forward
  avant-hier the day before yesterday
avec with
  avec plomb leaded
averse, l' *f* rainshower
avertir to warn
Avez-vous ___? Do you have ___?
avion, l' *m* airplane
  par avion airmail
avocat, l' *m* avocado
  avocat aux crevettes avocado with
  shrimp
avocat(e), l' *m/f* lawyer
avoir to have
  avoir besoin de to need, have need
  of
avril April
baba au rhum, le rum baba, rum-
  soaked sponge cake
babeurre, le buttermilk
baby-sitter, le babysitter
baby-sitting, faire du to babysit
bac, le river ferry, ferry boat

bagages, les *m* luggage
bagnole, la car (slang)
bague, la ring
baguette, la long loaf of French bread
baignoire, la bathtub
bain, le bath
baiser, le a kiss
balcon, le balcony
banane, la banana, fanny pack
banc, le bench
bande dessinée, la comic book
banlieue, la suburbs
banon soft, mild cheese from sheep or goat milk
banque, la bank
bar, le bar, restaurant car, sea bass
barbe, la beard
barbue, la monkfish
barquette, la boat-shaped pastry shell with fruit
barré(e) closed
barre de chocolat, la chocolate bar
bas low
  en bas downstairs
bas, les *m* stockings
basilic, le basil
baskets, les *m* basketball shoes, sneakers
bâtard, le narrower loaf of French bread
bateau, le boat, ship
  bateau-mouche river cruise boat
batterie, la battery (car)
baume pour lèvres, le lip balm
bavarois Bavarian cream cakes
bazar, le general store
bd boulevard
béarnaise white egg/butter sauce with white wine, shallots, tarragon
beau *m* beautiful
  beau-frère, le brother-in-law
beaucoup a lot, too, many, much
  beaucoup de ___ a lot of, much
Beaujolais, le a fresh, fruity red wine
bébé, le baby
béchamel white sauce
beige beige
beignet, le usually-filled fritter, doughnut

beignets aux pommes apple doughnuts
belle *f* beautiful
  belle-soeur, la sister-in-law, stepsister
besoin, le need
betterave, la beet
beurre, le butter
  beurre blanc sauce: butter with white wine, vinegar and shallots
  beurre noir browned butter sauce
biberon, le baby bottle
bibliothèque, la library
bidet, le bidet
bien well
  bien cuit well done (meat)
  bien sûr of course
bientôt soon
  à bientôt see you soon
bienvenue! welcome!
bière, la beer
  bière blonde light beer
  bière brune dark beer
  bière sans alcool non-alcoholic beer
bifteck, le (beef) steak
bigarade (sauce) with oranges
bigoudis, les hair curlers
bijou, le (les bijoux) jewel
bijouterie, la jewelry store
bikini, le bikini
billet, le ticket, bill (paper money)
billeterie, la ticket distributor
bio organic
biscuit, le cookie
  biscuit salé cracker
bise, la kiss
bisque, la chowder or stew with seafood
  bisque d'écrevisses crawfish soup
bistro, le bar, simple restaurant
blanc(he) white
blanchaille herring
blanchisserie, la laundry
blanquette de veau, la veal with cream sauce
blazer, le blazer
bleu, le blue cheese

bleu d'auvergne very sharp soft, veined cheese made from cow's milk
bleu(e) blue, very rare (meat)
bloc-notes, le notepad
blouse, la smock
blouson, le jacket
blues, le blues music
boeuf, le beef
  boeuf bourguignon beef/red wine stew
  boeuf mode beef chunks/carrots/ onions in red wine
  boeuf salé corned beef
boire to drink
bois, le wood(s)
boisson, la drink
boîte, la box, dance club
  boîte aux lettres mail box
bolet, le a kind of mushroom
bombe glacée, la formed ice cream or sherbet
bon(ne) good, right
  bon marché inexpensive
bonbon, le candy
bonjour hello, good day
bon(ne) good, right
  bonne journeé have a good day
  bonne soirée have a nice evening
bonnet, le hat
bonsoir hello (good evening)
bordelaise beef marrow, mushroom, red wine sauce
bordereau de transport, le shipping form
borne de taxi, la taxi stand
botte, la boot
bouche, la mouth
bouchée à la reine vol-au-vent—puff pastry filled with savory or sweet filling
boucherie, la butcher shop
bouchon, le cork (bottle)
  bouchons, les *m* traffic jams
boucles d'oreilles, les *f* earrings
boudin, le blood pudding/sausage
bouillabaisse, la stew of fish and seafood
bouilli(e) boiled (often beef)
boulangerie, la bakery

boulette, la meatball
bouquet, le bouquet
bourguignon(ne) dish prepared with Burgundy wine
bourride, la soup made from fish or seafood
boursin mild soft cheese from cow's milk
bout, le tip, point, end
bouteille, la bottle
boutique, la small store, shop
bracelet, le bracelet
braisé(e) braised, stewed
bras, le arm
break, le station wagon ("brek")
brebis, la sheep's cheese
bretonne includes beans
brie, le mild to strongly flavored cow's milk cheese
brioche, la rich, eggy roll
briquet, le lighter
brocante, la traveling flea market
broche, la brooch
broche, à la on a spit or skewer
brochet, le pike
brosse à dents, la toothbrush
brouillard, le fog
brouillé(e) scrambled
brugnon, le nectarine
bruit, le noise
brûler to burn
brun(e) brown, brunette
brut very dry (wine)
bruyant(e) loud, noisy
buffet, le buffet
  de salades salad bar
bureau, le desk, office
  d'accueil reception office
  de change money exchange office
  de poste post office
  de tabac tobacco shop
  de vente ticket office
bus, le bus
ça that (thing)
  ça va How're things going?/Fine
cabillaud, le cod
cabine, la booth, cabin
  d'essayage fitting room
  téléphonique phone booth
cabri, le baby goat

cacahuètes, les *f* peanuts
cachet, le   tablet (medicine)
   cachet contre la douleur   pain killers
   cachet contre les maux de tête headache pills
cadeau, le   (les cadeaux) gift
cadenas, le   padlock
Caen   dish made with apple brandy
café, le   coffee, café
   café au lait   coffee with milk
   café complet   coffee with bread/rolls, butter, jam
   café crème   coffee with cream
   café décaféiné   decaffeinated coffee
   café express   espresso
   café frappé   cold coffee, shaken
   café liégeois   iced coffee with whipped cream
   café noir   black coffee
caféine, la   caffeine
cahier, le   notebook
caille, la   quail
caisse, la   cash register, check-out
calculatrice, la   calculator
caleçon, le   underwear (men), leggings
calmar, le   squid
calme   quiet, calm
calvados   apple brandy
camembert, le   firm cow's milk cheese
caméscope, le   camcorder
camion, le   truck
camionnette, la   van
camomille, la   chamomile
campagne, la   countryside
camping, le   camping
   faire du camping   to camp
   camping-car, le   motorhome
Canada, le   Canada
canadien(ne)   Canadian
canal, le   canal
canapé, le   decorative, bite-sized appetizer
canard, le   duck
   canard à l'orange   duck à l'orange
   canard laqué   Peking duck
caneton, le   duckling
canicule, la   heat wave
cannelle, la   cinnamon

câpres, les *f*   capers
car, le   tour bus
carafe, la   carafe, pitcher
caravane, la   camper, camping trailer
carbonnade   meat grilled over charcoal
caricole, la   sea snail
carnaval, le   Carnival
carnet, le   book of Métro tickets
carotte, la   carrot
carpe, la   carp
carré d'agneau, le   rack of lamb
carrefour, le   intersection
carrelet, le   flounder
carte, la   menu
   carte à puce   smart card
   carte banqcaire   bank card
   carte de crédit   credit card
   carte de téléphonique   telephone card
   carte d'identité   ID card
   carte géographique   map
   carte internationale   international phone card
   carte parking   pre-paid parking card
   carte postale   postcard
   carte routière   roadmap
   carte SIM   SIM card
carton, le   box
casquette, la   cap
cassé(e)   broken
casse-croûte, le   snack (e.g., sandwich)
cassis, le   black current, black current liqueur
cassoulet, le   bean/sausage stew
cathédrale, la   cathedral
caution, la   deposit
ça va?   How are you?
   ça va   OK, it's OK
   ça va bien   I'm well, it's going well
   ça vous plaît?   Do you like it?
cave, la   cellar
CD, le   CD, compact disk
ce   this (adj.)
ceci   this, it
céder le passage   to yield
cédez   yield
ceinture, la   belt

ceinture de sécurité (pour enfants) seat belt (for children)
cela that
céleri, le celery
célibataire single (unmarried)
celle-ci *f* this one
celle-là *f* that one
celui-ci *m* this one
celui-là *m* that one
cendrier, le ashtray
cent one-hundred
cent, le cent
centre, le center
  centre-ville town center
cèpe, le type of mushroom
céréales, les *f* cereal
cerf, le venison
cerfeuil, le chervil (like mild parsley)
cerise, la cherry
certes certainly
cerveau, le brain
cervelas, le garlic pork sausage
cervelle, la brains
ce soir this evening
c'est ___ it's ___
  ce n'est pas ___ it's not ___
chabichou, le goat/cow milk cheese
chaise, la chair
  chaise d'enfants, la high chair, child's seat
chaleur, la heat (natural)
chambre, la room
  chambre à deux lits room with two beds
  chambre d'hôte bed and breakfast
  chambre à deux personnes double room
chambré(e) room temperature (e.g., wine)
champ, le field
champagne, le champagne
champignon, le mushroom
chance, la luck
changer to change, to exchange
chantilly, le sweetened whipped cream; hollandaise sauce with whipped cream
chapeau, le hat, cap
  chapeau de soleil sun hat

chapelle, la chapel
chapon, le capon
chaque each
charcuterie, la cooked pork, cold cuts, pork butcher shop
charger, recharger to charge (battery)
charlotte, la pudding in a lining of sponge cake or ladyfingers
charmant(e) charming
chasseur mushroom/white wine sauce with shallots and parsley
chat, le cat
château, le castle
châteaubriand, le beef tenderloin, porterhouse steak
chaud(e) hot, warm
chaudrée fish/seafood stew
chauffage, le heat
  chauffage-central central heat
chauffer to heat
chaussette, la sock
chausson aux pommes, le apple turnover
chaussure, la shoe
chemin, le small road/path/route
chemise, la shirt
chemisier, le blouse
chèque, le check
  chèque de voyage, le traveler's check
cher/chère expensive
  le moins cher the least expensive
chercher to look for
chéri(e), le/la dear one
chérir to cherish
cheval, le (les chevaux) horse
  à cheval with an egg on top
cheveux, les *m* hair
cheville, la ankle
chèvre, la goat
chèvre, le goat's cheese
chevreuil, le venison
chez at the house/place of
chicorée, la chicory
chien, le dog
chips, les *f* potato chips
chocolat, le chocolate
  chocolat chaud hot chocolate

chocolatine, la chocolate-filled puff
pastry
choisir to choose
chômage, au unemployed
choron, le tomato béarnaise sauce
chose, la thing
chou, le cabbage
    chou fassum stuffed cabbage
    chou de Bruxelles Brussels
    sprout
choucroute, la sauerkraut
    choucroute garnie sauerkraut
    with sausage and pork
chou-fleur, le cauliflower
choux, aux with cabbage
chute de pierres falling rocks
ciboulette, la chives
cidre, le cider, apple wine
ciel, le sky
cigare, le cigar
cigarette, la cigarette
cimetière, le cemetery
cinéma, le movie
cinq five
cinquante fifty
    cinquante-cinq fifty-five
    cinquante-deux fifty-two
    cinquante et un fifty-one
    cinquante-huit fifty-eight
    cinquante-neuf fifty-nine
    cinquante-quatre fifty-four
    cinquante-sept fifty-seven
    cinquante-six fifty-six
    cinquante-trois fifty-three
cintre, le clothes hanger
circulation, la traffic
circuler to move (traffic)
ciseaux, les *m* scissors
    ciseaux à ongles manicure
    scissors
citoyen, le citizen
    du Canada of Canada
    des États-Unis of the US
citron, le lemon
    citron pressé lemon juice
    citron vert lime
citronnade, la lemonade
civet, le game stew
clafoutis, le fruit baked in pancake-
like batter

clair(e) light, clear
clavier, le keyboard
clef/clé, la key
climatisation, la air conditioning
climatisé(e) air-conditioned
cliquer sur click on
clous de girofle, les *m* cloves
cochon de lait, le suckling pig
coco, le coconut
cocotte, (en) stewed
code postal, le postal code
coeur, le heart
    coeurs d'artichauts artichoke
    hearts
coffre, le trunk (car)
Cognac a wine brandy
coiffeur, le barber, hair stylist
coiffure, la hairstyle
coin, le corner
    coin de la rue street corner
colin, le pollack
colis, le package
collant, le pantyhose, tights
colle, la glue
collier, le necklace
colombière soft, mild cow's milk
    cheese
combien? how much? how many?
commande, la order
comme like, as
commencer to begin
comment? how? What did you say?
commissariat, le police station
commission, la fee, commission
communication, la telephone call
    communication en ville, la local
    call
    communication interurbaine, la
    long-distance call
compagnie aérienne, la airline
compagnon, le partner, companion
compartiment, le compartment
complet/complète complete, full,
    no vacancy
composter to validate/cancel a ticket
comprendre to understand
comprimé, le tablet (medicine)
compris(e) included
comptable, le accountant
compte, le account

compte bancaire bank account
concierge, le/la doorman, building caretaker
concombre, le cucumber
conduire to drive
confirmation, la confirmation
confiserie, la confectioner's shop
confit, le salt-cured meat
  confit de canard salt-cured duck
confiture, la jelly, jam
congolais, le coconut cake
congre, le conger eel
congrès, le convention
connaître to know (people, places)
connecter to connect
consigne, la check-in luggage storage, bottle deposit
  consigne automatique luggage lockers
consommation, la drink, beverage
consommé, le clear broth, usually with chicken or beef stock
  consommé à l'oeuf consummé with raw egg
  consommé de poulet chicken soup
constipé(e) constipated
contenir to contain
contenu, le contents
contraceptif, le contraceptive
contraire, le contrary, opposite
contravention, la parking ticket
contre against, for (medicine)
contre-filet, le strip steak
contrôle des passeports, le passport control
contrôle-radar, le radar control
contrôleur, le conductor, ticket collector
copain, le friend, boyfriend
copine, la friend, girlfriend
coq au vin, le chicken/red wine stew
coque, (œuf) à la soft-boiled (egg)
coquelet à l'estragon, le tarragon spring chicken
coquillage, le shellfish
coquilles Saint-Jacques, les *f* scallops
corde à linge, la clothesline
cordonnerie, la shoe repair
coriace tough

coriandre, le coriander
cornichon, le pickle
corps, le body
correspondance, la connection, transfer (transportation)
corsé(e) full-bodied (wine)
costume, le suit (man's)
côte, la coast, rib, chop
  côte de boeuf beef rib steak, T-bone
côté (de), à beside, next to
côtelette, la cutlet, chop
coton, le cotton
  coton-tige, le cotton swab
cotriade, la fish and potato soup
cou, le neck
couche (pour bébés), la diaper
  couche jetable disposable diaper
couchette, la sleeping bunk (train)
coude, le elbow
couette, la duvet, quilt
couleur, la color
coulibiac, le served in a pastry shell
coulis, le creamy sauce, soup
couloir, le aisle, center aisle, corridor, hallway
coup de soleil, le sunburn
coupe, la cut (of clothing), ice-cream sundae
  coupe de cheveux haircut
  coupe maison ice cream of the house
  coupe-ongle, le nail clippers
courgette, la zucchini
courrier, le letter, mail
cours du change, le exchange rate
court(e) short
cousin(e), le/la cousin
couteau, le knife
coûter to cost
couvert, le cover charge, silverware
couverture, la blanket
crabe, le crab
crampe, la cramp
cravate, la necktie
crayon, le pencil
crécy, à la featuring carrots
crédit, n'a plus de out of credit
crème, la cream, cream of, creamy soup

crème anglaise custard
crème brûlée custard with caramelized sugar topping
crème caramel caramel custard
crème chantilly whipped cream
crème fouettée whipped cream
crème hydratante moisturizer
crème pâtissière composed of egg, flour, sugar and milk
crème Sabayon zabaglione cream
crème solaire sunscreen
crème, le (café) frothy coffee with milk
crémeux/euse creamy (as in cheese)
crêpe, la thin pancake
crêpe à la confiture jam-filled crêpe
crêpe au sucre crêpe with sugar
crêpe suzette large crêpe with orange juice and orange liqueur set on fire
crépinette, la small, flat sausage
cresson, le watercress
crevette, la shrimp
crevette rose prawn
cristal, le crystal
croire to believe
croissant, le flaky, buttery crescent roll
croque au sel, à la raw, with salt and French dressing
croque-madame, le ham and cheese on toast with an egg on top
croquembouche, le puff pastry balls coated with caramel piled in a cone
croque-monsieur, le ham and cheese on toast
croustade, la savory filled pie or pastry shell
croûte, la crust
croûte au fromage toast topped with melted cheese, ham and a fried egg
cru(e) uncooked, raw
cruche, la pitcher
crudités (variées), les f (assorted) raw vegetables
crustacés, les m shellfish
cuillère, la spoon
cuir, le leather

cuisine, la cooking, kitchen
cuisinier/cuisinière, le/la cook
cuisinière, la stove
cuisse, la thigh
cuisse de poulet chicken drumstick
cuisse de grenouilles frog's leg
cuissot de chevreuil, le venison haunch
cuit(e) cooked
cuit(e) à la vapeur steamed
cuit(e) au four baked
bien cuit(e) well-done, medium well (meat)
très cuit(e) well-done (meat)
culotte, la (petite) pair of panties
culture, la culture
cumin, le cumin
cure-dent, le toothpick
d'accord of course, OK, agreed
dame blanche, la vanilla ice cream with chocolate sauce
dames, les f ladies
dans in, into
danser to dance
dartois, le jam or fruit pastry, tart, or strudel
date, la date
date de naissance date of birth
datte, la date (fruit)
daube, (en) casserole, (beef) stew
daurade, la bream (fish)
de from, of
de. . . à from. . . until/to
décaféiné(e) decafeinated
décembre December
déclaration, la declaration
déclaration de valeur declaration of value
déclaration d'origine declaration of origin
déclaration en douanes customs declaration
déclarer to declare
décompte, la discount
décrochez pick up receiver
défendre to forbid
défense de stationner no parking
dehors outside
déjà already

déjeuner, le lunch
  petit déjeuner, le breakfast
de l' some (bef. vowel, sing.)
de la some (fem. sing.)
délice, la delight, chef's specialty
  dessert
délicieux delicious
demain tomorrow
  à demain until tomorrow
  demain matin tomorrow
  morning
  demain soir tomorrow evening
demander to request
demi, (un) one-half, ¼-liter glass of
  beer
  demi-bouteille de half-bottle of
  demi-deuil chicken with truffle
  slices under the skin
  demi-heure half-hour
  demi-journée half-day
  demi-portion, la half-portion
  demi-poulet grillé half a roasted
  chicken
dent, la tooth
  mal de dent, le toothache
dentelle, la lace
dentifrice, le toothpaste
dentiste, le/la dentist
déodorant, le deodorant
départ, le departure
départs departures
déposer to drop off, to deposit
depuis since
déranger to bother, to disturb
dernier/dernière last, previous
derrière behind
des some (pl.)
descendez go down
descendre to descend, get off (train,
  bus)
désirer to desire, to want
Désirez-vous quelque chose?
  Would you like something?
désolé(e) sorry
dessert, le dessert
dessiner to draw
dessous under
destinataire, le recipient, addressee
destination, la destination
détour, le detour

deux two
  deux cents two hundred
  deux mille two thousand
deuxième second
devant ahead, in front of
déviation, la detour
devis, le estimate
devoir have to, ought to
diabétique diabetic
diable hot sauce
diarrhée, la diarrhea
Dieu, le God
difficile difficult
digestif, le after-dinner drink
dimanche Sunday
dinde, la turkey
  dinde aux marrons turkey with
  chestnuts
  dinde truffée turkey with truffles
dîner, le dinner, supper
dire to say
direct(e) direct
direction, la direction
disponible available
dispute, la argument
disque de stationnement, le parking
  disk
dissolvant, le nail polish remover
distributeur (de billets), le ATM,
  cash machine, ticket machine
divorcé(e) divorced
dix ten
  dix-huit eighteen
  dix-neuf nineteen
  dix-sept seventeen
docteur, le doctor
doigt, le finger
domicile, le residence
donner to give
doré(e) gold (color)
dormir to sleep
dos, le back
  douleurs au dos back pain
d'où from where
douane, la customs
  formalités de douanes, les
  customs regulations
doubler to double, overtake, pass
  (driving)
douce *f* sweet, soft, mild

douche, la shower
douleur, la pain
doux *m* sweet, soft, mild
douze twelve
drap, le sheet (bed)
droguerie, la hardware store
droit(e), (à) (to the) right
droit, tout straight ahead
du some (masc. sing.)
dur(e) hard, tough, hard-boiled
durée, la duration
duxelles with mushrooms
DVD, le DVD
eau, l' *f* water
   eau dentifrice mouthwash
   eau minérale mineral water
   eau non potable non-drinkable
   water
   eau potable drinkable water
échalote, l' *f* shallot
échanger to exchange
écharpe, l' *f* scarf
éclair, l' *m* lightening, long filled
   pastry
écluse, l' *f* river/canal lock
école, l' *f* school
écouter to listen (to)
écouteurs, les *m* headphones
écran, l' *m* screen
écrevisse, l' *f* crawfish
écrire to write, to write down
église, l' *f* church
électricité, l' *f* electricity
électroménager, l' *m* electrical goods
elle she
e-mail, l' *m* email
emballage, l' *m* packing
embarquement, l' *m* boarding
embarquer to board, to load
embouteillage, l' *m* traffic jam
embrachement, l' *m* junction,
   secondary road
embrasser to kiss
émincé de boeuf aux morilles, l' *m*
   beef stew with morel mushrooms
emporter, à to take out
en in
   en avant forward, ahead
   en bas below, downstairs
   en espèces in cash

en face de across from
en haut up, upstairs
en voiture all aboard
enceinte pregnant
enchanté(e) pleased to meet you
encore still, yet
en-dessous below
endive, l' *f* endive, chicory
endormir to go to sleep
enfant, l' *m/f* child
enfin finally
ennuyer to annoy
ennuyeux(euse) boring
enregister to check bags
enrhumé(e) (have a) cold
enseigne, l' *f* sign
enseigner to show, to teach
ensemble together
ensoleillé(e) sunny
entendre to hear
entre between, among
entrecôte, l' *f* ribeye
   entrecôte grillée grilled ribeye
entrée, l' *f* entry, entrance, appetizer
   entrée interdite no entry
entremets, l' *m* dessert
entrer to enter
enveloppe, l' *f* envelope
   enveloppe à papier bulle, l' *f*
   padded envelope
envoi, l' *m* sending, something sent
envoyer to send
   envoyer un mail to send an e-mail
épaule, l' *f* shoulder
éperlan, l' *m* smelt (fish)
épice, l' *f* spice
épicerie, l' *f* grocery store
épinards, les *m* spinach
épingle de sûreté, l' *f* safety pin
Epiphanie, l' *f* Epiphany
époux/épouse, l' *m/f* spouse
erreur, l' *f* error
escalier, l' *m* stairs
   escalier roulant escalator
escalope, l' *f* cutlet
   escalope à la crème veal scallops
   with cream
   escalope de veau veal cutlet
   escalope panée breaded veal
   cutlet

escalope viennoise breaded veal cutlet
escargot, le snail
  escargots à la bourguignonne snails in garlic butter
espace, l' *f* space
espadon, l' *m* swordfish
Espagne, l' *f* Spain
espagnol(e) Spanish
Espagnol(e), l' *m/f* Spaniard
espèces, les *f* cash
  en espèces in cash
essayer to try (on)
essence l' *f* gasoline
est is
est, l' *m* east
estomac, l' *m* stomach
estouffade de boeuf, l' *f* beef stew
estragon, l' *m* tarragon
et and
étage, l' *m* floor, story
États-Unis, les *m* United States
  aux États-Unis to the U.S.
été, l' *m* summer
étiquette, l' *f* label
étoile, l' *f* star
étouffée, à l' steamed
étranger/étrangère foreign
être to be
étudiant(e), l' *m/f* student
étuvée, à l' braised
euro, l' *m* euro
Europe, l' *f* Europe
éviter to avoid
exactement exactly
excellent(e) excellent
exceptionel(le) exceptional
excursion, l' *f* excursion, trip
excusez-moi excuse me, sorry
expédier to ship
expéditeur, l' *m* sender
express, l' *m* espresso
exquis(e) exquisite
extraordinaire extraordinary
façade, la façade
face de, en across from
facile easy
facture, la bill, invoice
facultatif/facultative on request, optional

faible weak
faim, la hunger
faire to do, to make
  faire de la musique to play/make music
  faire du baby-sitting to babysit
  faire la cuisine to cook
  faire le plein to fill up (gas tank)
  fais (I) do/make
  faites (you) do/make
fais (I) do/make
faisan, le pheasant
faites (you) do/make
famille, la family
far, le prune flan
farci(e) stuffed
fard à paupières, le eye shadow
farine, la flour
fatigué(e) tired
faubourg, le working-class suburb
faut, il it is necessary
faute, la mistake
fauteuil, le armchair
  fauteuil roulant wheelchair
faux/fausse false, fake
faux filet, le filet steak
fax, le fax
félicitations, les *f* congratulations
femme, la woman, wife
  femme de chambre cleaning lady, housekeeper
fenêtre, la window
fenouil, le fennel
fer, le iron
ferme, la farm
fermé(e) closed
fermer to close
fermeture à glissière/éclair, la zipper
ferry-boat, le ferry, ferryboat
fête, la celebration, festival
  Fête des Rois, la Epiphany
  Fête-Dieu, la Feast of Corpus Christi
  Fête du Travail, la Labor Day (May 1)
feu, le fire, traffic light, light (cigarette)
feuilleté de chèvre chaud, le warm goat cheese in dough
fèves, les *f* broad beans

février February
fiancé(e) engaged
fiancé(e), le/la fiancé(e)
ficelle, la string, thin loaf of bread
fiche, la electrical plug, form
fidèle faithful
fièvre, la fever
figue, la fig
figure, la face
fil de fer, le wire
fil dentaire, le dental floss
filet, le fillet steak
 filet de boeuf beef fillet
 filet mignon beef tenderloin fillet
fille, la daughter, girl
film, le film
fils, le son
fin, la end
finalement finally
finir to finish, to end
flageolets, les *m* kidney beans
flamiche, la cheese and onion pie,
 leek flan
flan, le custard tart
flash, le (camera) flash
fleur, la flower
fleuriste, le/la florist
fleuve, le (large) river
flocons d'avoine, les *m* oatmeal
florentine, (à la) with spinach
foie, le liver
 foie gras fresh goose or duck
 liver, possibly uncooked
foncé(e) dark (color)
fond, au in back, at far end/bottom
fondue, la melted cheese dip with
 wine
fontaine, la fountain
football, le soccer
 football américain, le (American)
 football
forestière (sauce) with mushrooms,
 shallots, white wine
forêt, la forest
formalités de douane, les *f* customs
 regulations
formidable great, terrific
formulaire, le form
formule, la form, formula
fort(e) strong, spicy

forteresse, la fortress
foulard, le headscarf, shawl
four, le oven
 (au) four baked
fourchette, la fork
frais/fraîche fresh, chilled (beverage)
frais de commission, les *m*
 commission charge
frais du transaction, les *m*
 transaction charge
fraise, la strawberry
framboise, la raspberry
Framboise raspberry brandy
français French
Français/Française, le/la
 Frenchman/Frenchwoman
France, la France
frange, la bangs
frappé chilled (coffee)
frappé, le milkshake
frère, le brother
frêt aérien, le air freight
frêt maritime, le surface freight
 (shipping)
friandises, les *f* sweets
fricassée braised or stewed meat,
 usually chicken, in a thick sauce
frisé(e) curly
frisée, la lettuce, curly endive
frit(e) fried
frites, les *f* French fries
froid(e) cold
fromage, le cheese
 fromage à pâte molle soft cheese
 fromage blanc creamy dessert
 cheese
 fromage crémeux creamy cheese
 fromage de brebis sheep's milk
 cheese
 fromage de chèvre goat cheese
front, le forehead
frontière, la border
fruit, le fruit
 fruit de la passion passion fruit
 fruit frais fresh fruit
 fruit sec dried fruit
fruité(e) fruity
fruits de mer, les *m* seafood
fumé(e) smoked
fumer to smoke

fumeur, le smoking car, smoker
  non fumeur no-smoking car
gage, le security deposit
galerie, la gallery
galette, la round, flat cake
  galette complète egg-, fish- or
  meat-filled crêpes
gamba, la large prawn
gant, le glove
  gant de toilette, le washcloth
garage, le garage, (repair)
  garage/service station
garantie, la guarantee
garbure, la cabbage soup with pork
  or goose
garçon, le boy, waiter
garderie, la daycare, child-care facility
gare, la train station
  gare routière, la bus station
garer to park (car)
garniture au choix, la choice of side
  dish
gasoil, le diesel
gâteau, le usually fancy layer cake
  gâteau au chocolat chocolate
  cake
  gâteau breton Brittany butter cake
  gâteau de riz rice pudding
  gâteau lyonnais chocolate and
  chestnut cake
gauche, (à) (to the) left
gaufre, la waffle
gazéifié(e) carbonated
gazeux(euse) carbonated, sparkling
gazole, le fuel oil
gel, le frost
  gel pour les cheveux, le hair gel
gelée, (à la) in aspic
gemme, la gem
gendarme, le state policeman
génial(e) great, brilliant
génoise, la a light sponge cake
genou, le knee
gens, les *m/f* people
gentil(le) nice
gibelotte de lapin, la rabbit/wine
  stew
gibier, le wild game
gigot, le leg of lamb/mutton

gigot à la bretonne roast leg of
  lamb with white beans
  gigot d'agneau leg of lamb
gilet, la vest
gingembre, le ginger
gîte, la B&B
glace, la ice cream, ice
  glace à la fraise strawberry ice
  cream
  glace à la vanille vanilla ice cream
  glace au chocolat chocolate ice
  cream
glacé(e) iced
glaçon, le ice cube
gluten, le gluten
gorge, la throat
  mal de gorge, le sore throat
goulasch, le goulash
goût, le taste
gouttes, les *f* drops
goyave, la guava
gramme, le gram
grand(e) big
  grand magasin, le department
  store
  grand-mère, la grandmother
  grand-père, le grandfather
granité, le fruit ice
gras(se) fat, fatty
gratin(e) breaded, baked until crusty
gratiné(e) breaded, au gratin,
  browned
gratuit(e) free of charge
gril, sur le from the grill
grillade, la grilled meat
grillé(e) grilled, broiled
grippe, la the flu (influenza)
gris(e) gray
gros(se) fat, large
groseilles, les *f* red currants
  groseilles à maquereau
  gooseberries
gruyère, le Gruyere cheese
guerre, la war
guichet, le counter, ticket counter,
  cashier's booth
  guichets automatiques, les ticket
  machines
guide, le guide
  guide touristique, le visitors' guide

habiter to live in
habits, les *m* clothes
hâché(e) chopped, minced
hachis parmentier, le shepherd's pie
hamburger, le hamburger
　hamburger à cheval hamburger
　topped with an egg
hanche, la hip
handicapé(e), le/la handicapped
　person
harcèlement sexuel, le sexual
　harassment
hareng, le herring
haricots, les *m* beans
　haricots blancs white beans
　haricots verts green beans
haut(e) high
havre, le harbor
herbes, aux with herbs
heure, l' *f* hour
　heure du déjeuner lunch hour
heure(s) o'clock
heureusement fortunately
hier yesterday
hiver, l' *m* winter
hollandaise sauce of egg yolks,
　butter, lemon or vinegar
homard, l' *m* lobster
　homard thermidor lobster with
　cheese baked over it
homme, l' *m* man
hôpital, l' *m* hospital
horaire, l' *m* schedule, timetable
horloge, l' *f* clock
hors d'oeuvre, les *m* appetizers
　_ variés assorted appetizers
hors service out of service
hotdog, le hotdog
hôtel, l' *m* hotel
　hôtel de ville town hall
hôtesse de l'air, l' *f* flight attendant,
　airline stewardess
huile, l' *f* oil
　huile d'olive olive oil
　huile solaire suntan oil
huit eight
huître, l' *f* oyster
humide damp
hypertension, l' *f* high blood pressure
hypotension, l' *f* low blood pressure

ici here
idée, l' *f* idea
identité, l' *f* identity
il he, it
île, l' *f* island
ils they
il y a there is, there are
immédiatement right away
imperméable, l' *m* rain coat
important(e) important
impossible impossible
impressionnant(e) impressive
imprimante, l' *f* printer
imprimer to print
incroyable unbelievable
Indépendance, la fête de l'
　Independence Day
indice de protection, l' *m* SPF
indienne, sauce curry sauce
infirmier/infirmière, l' *m/f* nurse
informaticien(ne), l' *m/f* computer
　scientist
information, l' *f* information
informatique, l' *f* computer science
informer to inform
infusion, l' *f* herbal tea
instant, l' *m* moment
insuline, l' *f* insulin
intelligent(e) intelligent
interdiction de doubler no passing
interdiction de stationner no
　parking
interdit(e) forbidden
intéressant(e) interesting
Internet l' *m* Internet
　point Internet, le Internet point
interrompu(e) suspended,
　interrupted
interrupteur, l' *m* switch, light switch
introduisez votre carte insert your
　card
inviter to invite
itinéraire, l' *m* itinerary
jamais never
jambe, la leg
jambon, le ham
　jambon-beurre ham and butter
　sandwich
　jambon de Bayonne raw ham
　from Bayonne

jambon fumé smoked ham
janvier January
jardin, le garden
jardiner to garden
jardinière (de légumes) cooked mixed vegetables
jaune yellow
je I
 je le crois I believe so
 je m'appelle ___ My name is ___
 je ne sais pas I don't know
 je ne comprends pas I don't understand
 je ne pense pas I don't think so
 je vous écoute I'm listening (= What would you like?)
 je vous en prie You're welcome, Don't mention it
jean, le jeans
jeton, le token
jeudi Thursday
jeune young
 jeune fille, la girl
joaillerie, la jewelry store
jogging, le jogging suit
joie, la joy
joli(e) pretty
joue, la cheek
jouet, le toy
jour, le day
 jours fériés national holidays
journal, le newspaper, news (TV)
journée, Bonne Have a good day!
juillet July
juin June
julienne cut into thin strips, shredded vegetables
jupe, la skirt
jupon, le slip
jus, le juice
 au jus in its natural juices
 jus d'orange orange juice
 jus de fruits fruit juice
 jus de pommes apple juice
 jus de tomate tomato juice
jusqu'à until (distance)
jusqu'au until (a date)
juteux(euse) juicy
ketchup, le ketchup
kilo, le kilogram

kilomètre, le kilometer
kiosque, le stand
 kiosque à journaux newspaper stand
kir, le white wine and black currant liqueur
 kir royal made with champagne instead of wine
kirsch, le cherry liqueur
la the (fem.)
là there
lac, le lake
lacet, le lace
laine, la wool
lait, le milk
 lait écrémé, le skim milk
 lait solaire, le suntan lotion
laitue, la lettuce
lames de rasoir, les *f* razor blades
lampe, la lamp
lamproie, la lamprey
landaise, la salade ham, foie gras, gizzard salad
langouste, la spiny lobster
langoustine, la scampi, large shimp
langue, la tongue, language
lapin, le rabbit
laque, la hairspray
lard, le bacon, lard
large wide
laurier, le bay leaf
lavabo, le sink, washroom
laverie, la laundromat
 laverie automatique, la laundromat
laxatif, le laxative
le the (masc.)
lecteur de CD, le CD player
léger/légère light (wine, weight)
légume, le vegetable
le/la moins ___ the least ___
lent(e) slow
lentement slowly
lentille, la contact lens, lentil
les the (plural)
lessive, la laundry detergent
lettre, la letter
leur their
lèvre, la lip
 rouge à lèvres, le lipstick

librairie, la bookstore
libre available, empty, unoccupied
lieu, le place
   lieu de naissance, le place of birth
lieu jaune, le pollack
lièvre, le wild hare
ligne, la line, route (bus)
lilas purple, lilac
limonade, la lemonade, soft drink
lin, le linen
lire to read
liste des prix, la price list
lit, le bed
   à deux lits twin beds
   lit d'enfant child's bed
   lits jumeaux twin beds
litre, le liter
livre, la pound (weight)
livre, le book
   livre de cuisine cookbook
livrer to deliver
logement, le lodging
loger to lodge, to stay at
loin (de) far (from)
   loin d'ici far from here
long(ue) long
lotion, la lotion
   lotion après-rasage, la after-shave lotion
lotte, la monkfish
louer to rent, to hire
loup de mer, le sea bass
lourd(e) humid
lui him
lumière, la light
lundi Monday
   lundi de Pâques, le Easter Monday
   lundi de Pentecôte, le Pentecost Monday
lune, la moon
lunettes, les f eyeglasses
   lunettes de soleil sunglasses
lycée, le high school
Lyonnaise (food) with onions
ma f my
macaroni, les m macaroni
macédoine de fruits, la fruit salad
machine à laver, la washing machine
madame Mrs., Madam, ma'am

mademoiselle miss, Miss
madère (sauce) with Madeira wine
madrilène consommé with tomatoes
magasin, le store
   grand magasin department store
   magasin de chaussures shoe store
   magasin de photos camera store
   magasin de souvenirs gift store
   magasin de spiritueux liquor store
   magasin de vêtements clothing store
   magasin de vins wine store
magazine, le magazine
magnifique magnificent, fantastic
magret de canard, le duck breast
mai May
maigre lean, thin, mild, light
maillot de bain, le swimsuit, swim trunks
main, la hand
maintenant now
mairie, la town hall
mais but
maïs, le corn
maison homemade
maison, la house
maître d'hôtel, le head waiter, butter/parsley/lemon sauce
mal badly
mal, le ache
   mal de dents toothache
   mal de mer seasickness
   mal de tête headache
   mal des transports motion sickness
malade sick
maladie, la illness
malheureusement unfortunately
manche, la sleeve
mandarine, la tangerine, mandarin orange
manger to eat
manque, le lack
manteau, le coat, overcoat
maquereau, le mackerel
maquillage, le make-up
marais, le swamp
marchand, le merchant

marchand de journaux
newspaper seller
marchand de vin wineseller, meat
stock and red wine sauce
marché, le market
marché alimentaire food market
marché aux puces flea market
mardi Tuesday
mardi gras, le Mardi gras
margarine, la margarine
mari, le husband
mariage, le marriage
marié(e) married
mariné(e) marinated
marjolaine, la marjoram
maroquinerie, la leather store
marron brown
marron, le chestnut
marque, la brand
mars March
mascara, le mascara
masculin(e) masculine
massage, le massage
matin, le morning
mauvais(e) bad
mauve purple
maux d'estomac, les *m*
stomachaches
maux de tête, les *m* headaches
mayonnaise, la mayonnaise
me (to) me
mécanicien, le mechanic
médaillon, le veal, pork or lamb
tenderloin
médecin, le doctor
médicament, le medicine
mél, le email
mélangé(e) mixed
melon, le melon
melon au porto melon and port
wine
même same, even
menthe, la mint
menton, le chin
menu, le menu
menu à prix fixe fixed-price
menu with set choices
menu enfant children's menu
menu gastronomique rich, heavy
menu for food lovers

menu touristique fixed-price
menu with options
mer, la sea, ocean
merci thank you
mercredi Wednesday
mercredi des cendres, le Ash
Wednesday
mère, la mother
fête des mères, la Mothers' Day
merlan, le merlin, whiting
merveilleux/merveilleuse
marvelous
messagerie, la voice mail
messe, la mass
mètre, le meter
métro, le subway
meubles, les *m* furniture
meunière floured and sautéed,
served with brown butter/lemon
sauce
midi, le midday, noon
miel, le honey
mignon(ne) cute, sweet, kind
migraine, la migraine
milieu, le middle
mille thousand
millefeuille, le napoleon (cream-filled
pastry)
million, le million
mince thin, slender
minibar, le mini-bar
minuit midnight
minute, la minute
mirabelle, la plum brandy
miroir, le mirror
mi-saignant(e) medium rare (meat)
mode, la fashion, style
moelle, la bone marrow
moi me
moins less, minus
le/la moins ___ the least ___
mois, le month
mojhettes à la crème, les *f* creamed
dried beans
molle/mollet soft, medium-boiled
mon my
monde, le world
tout le monde everybody
monnaie, la coins, change (money)

monsieur (pl: messieurs) mister, sir, Waiter!
montagne, la mountain
montant, le amount, sum
monter (dans) to board/get on (e.g., train), to go up
montez go up!
montre, la wristwatch
morille, la morel mushroom
mornay, sauce cheese sauce
mortadelle, la bologna
morue, la cod
mot, le word
motel, le motel
moto, la motorbike, motorcycle
mouchoir, le handkerchief
  mouchoir en papier facial tissue
mouillé(e) wet
moule, la mussel
mousse, la whipped pudding
  mousse au chocolat chocolate mousse
  mousse à raser shaving cream
  mousse de foie liver pâté
  mousse gel shower gel
mousseline, la mousse, hollandaise sauce with whipped cream
mousseux(euse) sparkling
moutarde, la mustard
mouton, le mutton
moyen, le way, means
muesli, le musli, cereal
munster soft, tangy cow's milk cheese
mur, le wall
mûre, la blackberry, mulberry
muscade, la nutmeg
muscle, le muscle
musée, le museum
musique, la music
musli, le muesli, cereal
myrtille, la blueberry
nager to swim
naissance, la date de date of birth
naissance, le lieu de place of birth
nantua sauce made with cream and shellfish
nappe, la tablecloth
nationalité, la nationality
nature plain, black (tea)

naturellement naturally, of course
nausée, la nausea
navet, le turnip
navette, la shuttle bus
ne ... pas not
ne ... rien nothing
neige, la snow
neiger to snow
nettoyer to clean
  nettoyer à sec to dry-clean
neuf nine
neuf/neuve new
nez, le nose
niçoise, (à la) with tomatoes, anchovies, garlic, olives, onions
Noël, le Christmas
noir, le espresso
noir(e) black
noisette, la hazelnut, espresso with dash of milk; tenderloin, small fillet
noix, la nut, walnut
  noix de coco, la coconut
nom, le name
  nom de famille family name, last name
  nom de jeune fille, le maiden name
nombre, le number
non no
non-fumeur no-smoking
nord, le north
normande, (à la) with mushroom/egg/cheese sauce; oyster or shrimp sauce; sauce with apples
nos our
note, la bill (hotel), receipt
notre our
nouilles, les *f* noodles
nourriture, la food
nous we, us
nouveau/nouvel(le) new
  Nouvel An, le New Year's Day
  nouvelles, les news
novembre November
nuage, le cloud
nuageux/nuageuse cloudy
nuit, la night
numéro, le number

numéro de téléphone telephone number

numéro vert toll-free number

objet, l' *m* object

obtenir to get, to obtain

occasion, l' *f* occasion, opportunity

   d'occasion used

occupé(e) occupied, busy

océan, l' *m* ocean

octobre October

oeil, l' *m* (pl: yeux) eye

oeuf, l' *m* egg

   oeuf à la coque soft-boiled egg

   oeuf à la diable deviled egg

   oeuf à la neige soft meringue forms in a custard sauce

   oeuf à la poêle egg sunny-side up

   oeuf à la russe Russian-style egg (deviled/stuffed)

   oeuf au bacon egg and bacon

   oeuf au jambon egg and ham

   oeuf au plat fried egg

   oeuf bercy baked egg with sausage and tomato sauce

   oeufs brouillés scrambled eggs

   oeuf cocotte soft-baked egg in cup

   oeuf dur hard-boiled

   oeuf en gelée salad of cold poached egg in jellied consommé

   oeuf frit deep-fried egg

   oeuf mollet medium-boiled egg

   oeuf poché poached egg

offrir to offer

oie, l' *f* goose

   oie aux marrons goose with chestnut stuffing

oignon, l' *m* onion

oiseau, l' *m* bird

olive, l' *f* olive

omelette, l' *f* omelet

   omelette au fromage cheese omelet

   omelette au jambon ham omelet

   omelette aux champignons mushroom omelet

   omelette aux fines herbes herb omelet

   omelette nature plain omelet

   omelette norvégienne baked Alaska

on one (person)

ongle, l' *m* fingernail

onze eleven

opéra, l' *m* opera, chocolate/nut cake

opticien(ne), l' *m/f* optician

or, l' *m* gold

   en or of gold

orage, l' *m* storm

orange, l' *f* orange

ordinateur, l' *m* computer

ordonnance, l' *f* prescription

ordures, les *f* trash, garbage

oreille, l' *f* ear

oreiller, l' *m* pillow

origan, l' *m* oregano

origine, l' *f* beginning

orteil, l' *m* toe

os, l' *m* bone

oseille, l' *f* sorrel

otite, l' *f* inner ear infection

ou or

où where

   Où se trouve ___? Where is ___?

oublier to forget

ouest, l' *m* west

oui yes

ouvert(e) open

ouvre-boîtes, l' *m* can opener

ouvre-bouteilles, l' *m* bottle opener

ouvrir to open

page, la page

   page Internet Web page

   pages jaunes, les yellow pages

paiement, le payment

paille, la straw

pain, le bread

   pain au chocolat croissant with chocolate

   pain bis pumpernickel

   pain blanc white bread

   pain complet whole-wheat bread

   pain de froment whole-wheat bread

   pain de seigle rye bread

   pain grillé toast

   pain noir black bread

   petit pain roll

paire, la pair

palais, le palace

palourde, la clam

pamplemousse, le grapefruit
panier, le basket
panne, la break down
panneau, le sign
pansement adhésif, le adhesive
  bandage
pantalon, le pair of pants
pantoufle, la slipper
papeterie, la stationery store
papier, le paper
  papier à lettres writing paper
  papier d'emballage wrapping
  paper
  papier hygiénique toilet paper
Pâques, le Easter
paquet, le package
par by, per
  par avion by airmail
  par exemple for example
  par ici this way
parapluie, le umbrella
parc, le park
parce que because
parcmètre, le parking meter
pardessus, le overcoat
pardon excuse me, pardon me
parents, les m parents, relatives
parfait(e) perfect
parfum, le perfume, flavor
parfumerie, la perfume shop
parisienne, sauce (à la) sauce with
  white wine/mushroom
parking, le parking lot
parler to talk, to speak
Parlez-vous anglais? Do you speak
  English?
parmi among
part, la piece
partager to share
partie, la part
partir to depart, to leave
  partir de to depart from
  partir pour to depart for
partout everywhere
pas not
  pas de souci no problem
  pas loin not far
passager/passagère, le/la passenger
passeport, le passport
pastèque, la watermelon

pâte, la paste
  à pâte molle soft (cheese)
  pâte dentifrice toothpaste
pâté, le meat purée (liver and other
  meats)
  pâté de campagne country pâté
  (course-textured pâté with small
  amount of liver)
  pâté de foie, le goose liver pâté
pâtes, les f pasta
pâtisserie, la pastry, pastry shop
patron, le owner, boss
paupiette, la thin slice of meat or fish
  wrapped around a meat, vegetable,
  or fruit filling
pauvre poor
payer to pay
pays, le country, nation
paysage, le countryside
péage, le toll booth, toll, road fee
peau, la skin
pêche, la peach, fishing
pêcher to fish
peigne, le comb
peignoir, le bathrobe
peindre to paint
peintre, le/la painter
pellicule, la roll of film
pendant during
pendule, la clock
péniche, la houseboat
penser (à) to think (about)
pension (de famille), la guest house,
  boardinghouse
pente, la slope
Pentecôte, la Pentecost
perche, la perch
perdre to lose
perdreau, le partridge
perdrix, la partridge
perdu(e) lost
père, le father
  fête des pères, la Fathers' Day
périgourdine, sauce sauce with
  truffles
périphérique, le beltway
perle, la pearl
permis, le permit, license
  permis de conduire, le driver's
  license

permis(e) permitted
perruque, la wig
persil, le parsley
personne, la person
  ne personne no one
peser to weight
petit(e) small
  petit ami, le boyfriend
  petite amie, la girlfriend
  petit déjeuner, le breakfast
  petite culotte, la pair of panties
  petite friture, la small fry (fish)
  petite marmite, la meat/vegetable
  consommé
  petit four, le small cake
  petit pain, le roll
  petits-enfants, les grandchildren
  petits pois, les *m* peas
  petit Suisse dessert of creamy
  fresh cow's milk cheese topped with
  sugar
peu (de), un a little (of)
peut-être maybe, perhaps
pharmacie, la pharmacy
photo, la photo
photocopie, la photocopy
pichet, le pitcher
pièce, la coin
  pièce d'identité, la I.D.
  pièce de monnaie, la coin
pied, le foot
  pied de cochon pig's feet
  pied de porc pig's feet
piéton, le pedestrian
pigeon, le pigeon, squab
pigeonneau, le squab
pilaf, le rice cooked in bouillon
pile, la battery
pilote, le pilot, driver
pilule, la pill
piment, le green pepper, hot pepper,
  pimiento
pince à épiler, la tweezers
pinces à linge, les *f* clothes pins
pintade, la guinea fowl
pintadeau, le guinea fowl
pipe, la pipe
piperade, la Spanish omelet,
  scrambled eggs with onion, sweet
  pepper, tomato

piquant(e) sharp (flavor)
piscine, la swimming pool
pissenlits au lard, le dandelion
  greens with bacon
pistache, la pistachio
piste, la runway, dance floor
  piste cyclable, la bicycle path
place, la public square, place, seat
  place de stationnement parking
  space
plafond, le ceiling
plage, la beach
  plage de nudistes nudist beach
plainte, la complaint
plaire to please
plaisir, le pleasure
plaît, il/elle me I like it
plaît, s'il vous please (= if you
  please)
plan, le plan, layout
  plan de la ville city map
plancher, le floor
plaque de chocolat, la (large)
  chocolate bar
plaque d'immatriculation, la license
  plate
plastique, le plastic
plat, le dish (of food), course
  au plat fried (e.g., egg)
  plat du jour daily special (meal)
  plat principal main course
plat(e) flat, non-carbonated, still
  (mineral water)
plateau, le tray
plein(e) full (objects)
pleuvoir to rain
plomb, le lead
  sans plomb unleaded
plouc, le hick, redneck
pluie, la rain
plume, la pen
plus (de) more
  plus que more than
  plus tard later
  plus vite, le fastest
plusieurs several
pluvieuse rainy
pneu, le tire
poche, la pocket
poché(e) poached

poêlé pan-fried
   à la poêle in a frying pan
poids, le weight
poignet, le wrist
point, à medium rare (meat)
point Internet, le Internet café,
   Internet point
pointure, la shoe size
poire, la pear
   Belle-Hélène poire cooked pear
   with vanilla ice cream and chocolate
   sauce
poireau, le leek
pois, le pea
   à pois polka-dotted
   pois chiches, les m chickpeas
poisson, le fish
   poisson d'eau douce freshwater
   fish
   poisson de mer ocean fish
poitrine, la chest
poivrade, la pepper sauce
poivre, le pepper
poivron, le bell pepper
polenta, la like cornmeal mush
poli(e) polite
police, la police
pommade, la salve
pomme, la apple
   pomme de terre potato
pommes, les f indicates potato dish
   pommes allumettes thin French
   fries
   pommes (de terre) en robe des
   champs potatoes in their skins
   pommes de terre sautées
   sautéed (fried) potatoes
   pommes frites French fries
   pommes mousseline puréed
   potatoes
   pommes nature boiled potatoes
   pommes nouvelles new potatoes
   pommes vapeur steamed
   potatoes
   purée de pommes de terre, la
   puréed/mashed potatoes
pompiers, les m fire department, fire
   fighters
pont, le bridge
porc, le pork

port, le port, harbor
portable, le cell phone, laptop
   computer
porte, la door
portefeuille, le wallet
porte-monnaie, le wallet, coin purse
porter to wear, to carry
porteur, le porter
portière, la vehicle door
portillon, le entry turnstile/gate
portion, la portion
porto with port wine
possible possible
poste, la computer terminal, post
   office
poste frontière, le border crossing
potable drinkable
   non potable non-drinkable
potage, le thick soup
   potage à l'ail garlic soup
   potage au cresson watercress
   soup
   potage bonne femme soup with
   potato, leek, maybe bacon
   potage de légumes vegetable
   soup
   potage Parmentier potato soup
pot-au-feu, le beef vegetable stew
poteau, le post
poterie, la pottery
potiron, le pumpkin
poubelle, la trash/rubbish can
pouce, le thumb
poudre, la powder
poule, la stewing fowl
poulet, le chicken
   poulet rôti roast chicken
poulpe, le octopus
poumon, le lung
pour for (e.g., number of people,
   time of showing or departure,
   length of use or stay), in order to
   Pour aller au ___? How do you
   get to ___?
   pour ce soir for this evening
   pour demain soir for tomorrow
   evening
   pour (deux) personnes for (two)
   people
pourboire, le tip

pourcentage, le percentage
pourquoi why
Pourrais-je ___? Could I ___?
pousser to push
poussin, le chick, tender young
  chicken
pouvoir to be able to, can
praire, la clam
premier/première first
prends ___, Je I'll take/have ___
prendre to take
prenez (you) take
  Prenez-vous ___? Do you take
  ___? Will you have___?
prénom, le first name
prèparer to prepare
prés close
  prés d'ici close to here
présenter to present, to introduce
préservatif, le condom
presque almost
pressé(e) freshly squeezed (juice); in
  a hurry
pressing, le dry cleaners, dry cleaning
pression, la draft beer
prêt(e) ready
  prêt-à-expédier ready to ship
  prêt-à-porter ready-to-wear
prêtre, le priest
printanier/printanière with a variety
  of vegetables
printemps, le spring
prioritaire priority (e.g., mail)
priorité, la priority, right-of-way
  priorité à droite yield to the right
prise, la electrical outlet
privé(e) private
prix, le price
problème, le problem
prochain(e) next
proche near
produits laitiers, les *m* dairy products
profession, la profession
profiterole, la cream puff with
  chocolate sauce
promenade, la walk
propre clean
propriétaire, le owner
protection solaire, la sunscreen
protège-slips, les *m* panty liners

provençale, (à la) a garnish or sauce
  with tomatoes, onion or garlic,
  possibly olives or anchovies
provisoirement temporarily
prune, la plum
pruneau, le prune
Puis-je ___? May I ___?
pull, le pullover
pull-over, le pullover
purée, la puree
  purée de pommes de terre
  mashed potatoes
pyjama, le pajamas
quai, le platform
qualité, la quality
quand when
quantité, la quantity
quarante forty
  quarante-cinq forty-five
  quarante-deux forty-two
  quarante et un forty-one
  quarante-huit forty-eight
  quarante-neuf forty-nine
  quarante-quatre forty-four
  quarante-sept forty-seven
  quarante-six forty-six
  quarante-trois forty-three
quart, un one quarter, one fourth
quatorze fourteen
  quatorze juillet, le July 14 (French
  national holiday)
quatre four
quatre-quatre four-wheel drive
quatre-vingt-cinq eighty-five
quatre-vingt-deux eighty-two
quatre-vingt-dix ninety
quatre-vingt-dix-huit ninety-
  eight
quatre-vingt-dix-neuf ninety-
  nine
quatre-vingt-dix-sept ninety-
  seven
quatre-vingt-douze ninety-two
quatre-vingt-huit eighty-eight
quatre-vingt-neuf eighty-nine
quatre-vingt onze ninety-one
quatre-vingt-quatorze ninety-
  four
quatre-vingt-quatre eighty-four
quatre-vingt-quinze ninety-five

quatre-vingts eighty
quatre-vingt-seize ninety-six
quatre-vingt-sept eighty-seven
quatre-vingt-six eighty-six
quatre-vingt-treize ninety-three
quatre-vingt-trois eighty-three
quatre-vingt-un eighty-one
que what?, that, than
　Qu'est ce que ___? What ___?
　Qu'est ce que c'est? What is it?
　Que voulez-vous? What would
　you like? What do you want?
quel(le) which, what
　à quelle heure at what time?
quelque chose anything, something
quelquefois sometimes
quelques some (plural)
quenelle, la light fish or meat
　dumpling
　quenelle de brochet pike
　dumpling
Qu'est ce que ___? What ___?
　Qu'est ce que c'est? What is it?
question, la question
queue, la line
　faire la queue wait in line
Que voulez-vous? What would you
　like?
qui who
quiche egg custard tart
　quiche lorraine bacon and egg pie
quincaillerie, la hardware store
quinze fifteen
quoi what?
quotidien, le daily newspaper
rabais, le reduction, discount
raccrochez hang up phone receiver
raclette, la melted specialty cheese
　served over potatoes
radar de contrôle de la vitesse, le
　radar for monitoring speed
radio, la radio
radis, le radish
rafraîchissement, le refreshment
ragoût, le meat stew
raifort, le horseradish
raisin, le grape
　raisin sec raisin
raison, la reason
ralentir to slow down

ralentir/ralentissez slow
rallonge, la extension cord
râpé(e) grated
rapide fast, rapid
rare rare (not for meat)
rascasse, la scorpionfish
rasoir, le razor
　rasoir électrique electric razor
ratatouille niçoise, la mixed
　vegetables: eggplant, peppers,
　tomatoes, zucchini
reblochon, le soft, creamy, mild
　cow's milk cheese
recevoir to receive
recharger to add credit to a pre-paid
　SIM, reload
rechargeur, le recharger
réchauffer to warm up, to reheat
recommander to recommend
reçu, le receipt
redémarrer to restart, to take off
　again
réduction, la discount
　réduction enfants children's
　discount
réfléchir to think about, to reflect on
réfrigérateur, le refigerator
refuser to refuse
regarder to look (at)
région, la region
régler to pay, to settle, to adjust
regretter to regret
réhausseur, le child's booster seat
rein, le kidney
reine, la queen
religion, la religion
rembourser to refund
remise, la discount
　remise des clés key return
rémoulade, la mayonnaise, mustard,
　and herb sauce
remplacer to replace
remplir to fill out (a form), to fill up
rencontrer to meet
rendez-vous, le appointment
renseignement, le information
renvoyer to send back
réparer to repair
repas, le meal
repasser to iron

répéter to repeat
répondre (à) to answer, respond (to)
repos, le relaxation, rest
reposer (se) to rest
requin, le shark
réservation, la reservation
réservé aux piétons pedestrians only
réserve du patron, la house wine
réserver to reserve, to book
réservoir, le gas tank
responable responsible
restaurant, le restaurant
rester to stay
restoroute, le rest area
résultat, le result
retard, le delay
retirer de l'argent to withdraw
  money
retouche, la alteration, touch-up
retour, le return
retourner to return
retraité(e) retired
réveil, le alarm clock
réveillon, le Christmas Eve/New
  Year's
revenir (à) to return (to), to come
  back
revoir to see again
rez-de-chaussée, le ground floor
rhubarbe, la rhubarb
rhum, le rum
rhume, le cold (illness)
  rhume des foins hay fever
riche rich
rien nothing
  de rien you're welcome
rillettes, les f spreadable pork mixture
ris de veau, le calves' sweetbreads
rissolé browned
rivage, le seashore
rive, la shore
rivière, la (medium-sized) river
riz, le rice
robe, la dress
  robe de chambre bathrobe
  robe de soir evening gown
robinet, le faucet
rognons, les m kidneys (food)
roi, le king
roman, le novel

romarin, le rosemary
rond(e) round
roquefort soft, moldy, pungent
  sheep's cheese
roquette, la arugula
rosbif, le roast beef
rose pink
rôti(e) roasted, broiled
roue, la wheel
rouge red
  rouge à lèvres, le lipstick
rouget, le red mullet, goatfish
rouillé(e) rusty
rouilleuse white wine/blood sauce
route, la road, street, route
  route barrée road closed
rue, la street
ruelle, la alley
sa his, her, its (fem.)
sable, le sand
sablé au beurre, le shortbread
sac, le bag
  sac à dos backpack
  sac-à-main purse, handbag
sachet de thé, le teabag
safran, le saffron
saignant rare (meat)
saigner to bleed
Saint-Paulin smooth, mild cow's
  milk cheese
Saint-Sylvestre, la New Year's Eve
Saint-Valentin, la Valentine's Day
saison, la season
salade, la salad
  salade Auvergnate ham/cheese
  salad
  salade composée mixed salad
  salade de museau de boeuf salad
  with marinated beef brains
  salade de thon tuna salad
  salade landaise ham, foie gras,
  gizzard salad
  salade niçoise green salad with
  egg, tomatoes, tuna, olives,
  anchovies, possibly rice or beans
  salade russe vegetable salad in
  mayo
  salade verte green salad
salami, le salami
sale dirty

salle, la hall, room
   salle à manger dining room
   salle d'attente waiting room
   salle de bains bathroom
salon, le living room
   salon de beauté beauty salon
   salon de coiffure hair stylist's
salut hi/goodbye (informal)
samedi Saturday
sandale, la sandal
sandwich, le sandwich
   sandwich au fromage cheese
   sandwich
   sandwich au jambon ham
   sandwich
sang, le blood
sanglier, le wild boar
sans without
   sans alcool non-alcoholic
   sans fil wireless
   sans glaçon without ice (straight)
   sans plomb unleaded
santé! to your health! cheers!
sardine, la sardine
sarriette, la savory
sauce, la sauce
   sauce bleue blue cheese
   vinaigrette
   sauce diable a type of hot sauce
saucisse, la sausage
   saucisse de Francfort hot dog
saucisson, le sausage (cold)
sauf except, but
   sauf riverains local access only
sauge, la sage
saumon, le salmon
   saumon fumé smoked salmon
sauna, le sauna
sauté de ____ sautéed ____
sauvage wild
savarin, le sponge cake with rum,
   rum baba
savoir to know (facts)
savon, le soap
scallopini thin, flour-coated cutlets
   either sauteed or fried
scampi, les *m* large shrimp
scooter, le motor scooter
sculpture, la sculpture
sec/sèche dry

sèche-cheveux, le hair dryer
second(e) second
seconde, la second (time)
secours, le help
secrétaire, le/la secretary
sécurité, la safety
seiche, la cuttlefish
seize sixteen
séjour, le stay
séjourner to stay
sel, le salt
self-service, le self service
selle, la seat (bicycle), saddle
semaine, la week
sens direction, way
   sens interdit wrong way
   sens unique one-way
sensibilité, la film speed, sensitivity
sentier, le path
sentir to feel, to smell
séparé(e) separated
sept seven
septembre September
serpent, le snake
serré(e) tight
serrer à droite/gauche merge
   right/left
serrez à gauche/à droite keep
   left/right
serrure, la door lock
serveur, le waiter
   serveur en ligne, le on-line service
serveuse, la waitress
service, le service
   service de dépannage
   emergency/towing assistance
serviette, la napkin, towel
   serviette de bains, bath towel
   serviette de toilette hand towel
   serviette en papier paper towel
   serviette hygiénique, la sanitary
   napkin
servir to serve
ses his, her, its (plural)
seulement only
shampooing, le shampoo
short, le pair of shorts
show, le show
si if, whether, yes (as a contradiction)
siècle, le century

siège, le seat, place
  siège-enfants child seat
signature, la signature
signer to sign
s'il vous plaît please (= if you please)
sirop, le syrup
  sirop contre la toux cough syrup
situation, la situation
  situation de famille marital status
six six
slip, le pair of underwear
SMS, le text message
soeur, la sister
soie, la silk
soin, le care
soir, le evening, night
soirée, la evening
soixante sixty
soixante-cinq sixty-five
soixante-deux sixty-two
soixante-dix seventy
soixante-dix-huit seventy-eight
soixante-dix-neuf seventy-nine
soixante-dix-sept seventy-seven
soixante-douze seventy-two
soixante et onze seventy-one
soixante et un sixty-one
soixante-huit sixty-eight
soixante-neuf sixty-nine
soixante-quatorze seventy-four
soixante-quatre sixty-four
soixante-quinze seventy-five
soixante-seize seventy-six
soixante-sept sixty-seven
soixante-six sixty-six
soixante-treize seventy-three
soixante-trois sixty-three
soldes, les *m* sales, bargains
sole, la sole
  sole meunière sole in butter sauce
soleil, le sun
sombre dark
somme, la sum, amount
sommelier, le wine waiter
somnifère, le sleeping pill
son his, her, its (masc.)
sorbet, le sherbet
sorte (de), la type, sort, kind (of)
sortie, la exit
  sortie d'autoroute freeway exit

sortir to go out, to leave
soubise, la **sauce** onion and cream sauce
souci, le problem, care
  pas de souci no problem
soucoupe, la saucer
soufflé, le fluffy egg dish browned in oven
soûl(e) drunk
soupe, la soup
  soupe à l'oignon onion soup
  soupe aux choux cabbage soup
  soupe de poisson fish soup
  soupe du jour soup of the day
souper, le supper (Canada)
souris, la mouse, knuckle of lamb
sous under
  sous-titre, le subtitle
  sous-vêtements, les *m* underwear
  sous vide vacuum packed
soutien-gorge, le bra
souvenir, le souvenir
souvent often
sparadrap, le adhesive bandage
spécialité, la specialty
spectacle, le show, performance
splendide splendid
sport, le sport
stade, le stadium
station, la station
  station de métro metro station
  station de taxis taxi stand
  station-service, la gas station
stationnement, le parking
  stationnement autorisé parking permitted
  stationnement interdit no parking
  stationnement payant paid parking
stationner to park
station-service, la gas/service station
statue, la statue
steak, le beef steak
  steak au poivre pepper steak
  steak-frites steak and French fries
  steak tartare steak tartare (ground, raw steak with seasonings)
steward de l'air, le flight attendant, airline steward
strapontin, le folding seat

stylo, le   pen
sucre, le   sugar
   sucre artifiel   artificial sweetener
sucrettes, les *f* artificial sweetener
sud, le   south
suis   (I) am
Suisse, la   Switzerland
Suisse, le   Swiss man
Suissesse, la   Swiss woman
suivant(e)   next
suivre   to follow
super   great
superbe   wonderful, superb
supermarché, le   supermarket
supplément, le   extra charge
suppositoires, les *m* suppositories
suspendu(e)   suspended
sur   on
   sur commande   made to order
sûr(e)   sure
sûrement   surely
surnom, le   nickname
surtout   especially
surveiller   to supervise
sympa(thique)   nice
synagogue, la   synagogue
syndicat d'initiative, le   tourist office
ta   your (inf., sing., fem)
tabac, le   tobacconist's shop, tobacco
table, la   table
   vin de table, le   table wine
tableau, le   painting, picture
tâché   stained
taille, la   clothes size, waist
tailleur, le   tailor, woman's suit
talon, le   heel
tampon, le   tampon, stamp (e.g.,
   passport)
tapis, le   rug
tard   late
   plus tard   later
tarif, le   charge, fee, rate, fare
tartare de boeuf   raw beef with
   seasoning
tarte, la   tart, one-crust fruit pie
   tarte au citron meringuée   lemon
      meringue pie
   tarte au fromage   cheese tart
   tarte aux fraises   strawberry tart
   tarte aux pommes   apple tart

tarte frangipane   almond cream
tart
tarte Tatin   upside-down apple tart
   with caramel
tartelette, la   small tart
tartine, la   cut baguette with butter
   and jam or honey; bread and butter
   slice
tasse, la   cup
taux de change/d'échange, le
   exchange rate
taxe, la   charge
taxi, le   taxi
   borne de taxi, la   taxi stand
te   you (direct and indirect object)
teinturerie, la   dry cleaner's
télécarte, la   local phone card
télécharger   to download
télégramme, le   telegram
téléphérique, le   suspended cable car
téléphone, le   telephone
   téléphone de secours   emergency
   phone
téléphoner (à)   to telephone, place a
   call (to)
téléphoniste, la   operator
téléski, le   ski lift
téléviseur, le   television (set)
télévision, la   television
température, la   temperature, fever
tempête, la   storm
temple, le   (Protestant) church
temps, le   time, weather
tendre   tender
tenez la gauche/la droite   keep
   left/right
tenir   to hold (to have)
tennis, les *f* tennis shoes
tente, la   tent
terminer   to finish, terminate
terrain de camping, le   campground
terrasse, la   terrace
   en terrasse   on the terrace
terre, la   earth, ground, soil
   par terre   on the ground
terrine, la   spreadable pâté
      terrine de canard   duck pâté
      terrine de saumon   salmon pâté
tête, la   head
texto, le   text message

thé, le   tea
  thé à la menthe   mint tea
  thé au lait   tea with milk
  thé citron   tea with lemon
  thé glacé   iced tea
  thé nature   plain tea
  thé noir   black tea
  thé sucré   tea with sugar
théâtre, le   theater
thermomètre, le   thermometer
thon, le   tuna
thym, le   thyme
tibia, le   shin
ticket, le   ticket, parking lot ticket,
  receipt (at gas station)
  ticket à l'unité   single-use public
  transportation ticket
tiers, un   one-third
timbre, le   stamp
  timbres-postes, des   postal stamps
tire-bouchon, le   corkscrew
tirer   to pull
tisane, la   herbal tea
titre, le   title
tlj   (= tous les jours) every day
toast, le   toast
toi   you (after preposition)
toile, la   linen
toilettes, les f   toilet, restroom
tomate, la   tomato
  tomates farcies   stuffed tomatoes
tombe, la   grave
ton   your (inf., sing., masc.)
tongs, des f   flip-flops, thongs
tonnerre, le   thunder
torchon, le   cloth, rag
tôt   early
toucher   to touch
toujours   always
tour, la   tower
tour, le   turn, tour
touriste, le/la   tourist
tournedos, les m   small beef fillets
tourner   to turn
tournez!   turn! (you, formal)
tourniquet, le   turnstile
tourte, la   meat pie
tous   all, everyone
  tous les jours   every day
Toussaint, la   All Saints' Day

tousser   to cough
tout(e)   (adj.) all, every
  toutes directions   all (other)
  destinations
  toutes les heures   every hour
tout   (adv.) quite, completely
  tout à l'heure   in a little while
  tout de suite   right away
  tout droit   straight ahead
  tout près   very near
  tout proche   very near, close
tout   (noun) all, everything
  Tout va bien?   Everything OK?
toux, la   cough
traduire   to translate
train, le   train
  train de banlieue   suburban train
trajet, le   train/bus route
  trajet direct   direct train/bus
tram, le   tram, streetcar
tranche, la   slice
  tranches de charcuterie, les   cold
  cuts
  tranches de viande froide, les   cold
  cuts
tranquillisant, le   tranquillizer
transports, le **mal des**   motion
  sickness
travail, le   work
  fête du travail, la   Labor Day
travailler   to work
travaux, les m   construction
travers, à   across
treize   thirteen
trench, le   trench coat
trente   thirty
  trente-cinq   thirty-five
  trente-deux   thirty-two
  trente et un   thirty-one
  trente-huit   thirty-eight
  trente-neuf   thirty-nine
  trente-quatre   thirty-four
  trente-sept   thirty-seven
  trente-six   thirty-six
  trente-trois   thirty-three
très   very
  très bien, merci   Very well, thanks
  très bon   very good
tripe, la   tripe
triple sec, le   orange liqueur

trois three
  trois cents three hundred
troisième third
trop (de) too, too much/many (of)
trottoir, le sidewalk
troubles, les *m* trouble, problems
  troubles cardiaques heart trouble
  troubles de la circulation
  circulatory trouble
  troubles digestifs digestive
  trouble
  troubles respiratoires respiratory
  trouble
trouver to find
truffe, la truffle
truite, la trout
T-shirt, le T-shirt
tu you (sing., informal)
tunnel, le tunnel
turquoise turquoise
TVA, la VAT tax
un(e) one, a
unique unique
uniquement only, uniquely
université, l' *f* university
un peu a little
urgence, l' *f* emergency
urgent(e) urgent
urinoir, l' *m* urinal
usage, l' *m* custom
usine, l' *f* factory
utile useful
utiliser to use
vacances, les *f* vacation
vaccination, la vaccination
vais (I) go
valable valid
Valentin, la **Saint-** Valentine's Day
valeur, la value
valider to validate
valise, la suitcase
vallée, la valley
vanille, la vanilla
vapeur, à la steamed
varié(e) varied
veau, le veal
végétarien(ne) vegetarian
veille de Noël, la Christmas Eve
vélo, le bicycle
velours, le velvet

velouté, le cream of
  velouté d'asperges cream of
  asparagus soup
  velouté de champignons cream
  of mushroom
  velouté de tomate cream of
  tomato
  velouté de volaille cream of
  chicken
vendange, la grape harvest
vendeur/vendeuse, le/la salesman/-
  woman
vendre to sell
vendredi Friday
  vendredi saint, le Good Friday
venez! (you) come!
venir (de) to come (from)
vent, le wind
  vent fort strong wind
vente, la sale
ventilateur, le fan, ventilator
ventre, le stomach
verglas, le surface ice, frost
vérifier to check, verify
vernis à ongles, le nail polish
verre, le glass
vers around, about, circa, toward
vert(e) green
verte parsley mayonnaise
vertige, le dizziness
veste, la jacket
vestiaire, le coat check
veston, le jacket
vêtements, les *m* clothing
veuf, le widower
veuve, la widow
viande, la meat
  viande hachée hamburger
  pas de viande no meat
vide empty
vie, la life
vieil(le) old
  vieille ville, la old city
viens (I) come
vieux old
vigne, la vineyard
village, le village
ville, la city
vin, le wine
  vin blanc white wine

vin de la maison   house wine
vin de table   table wine
vin du pays   local wine
vin mousseux   sparkling wine
vin ordinaire   table wine
vin rosé   rosé wine
vin rouge   red wine
vinaigre, le   vinegar
vinaigrette, la   vinegar and oil
  dressing
vingt   twenty
  vingt-cinq   twenty-five
  vingt-deux   twenty-two
  vingt et un   twenty-one
  vingt-huit   twenty-eight
  vingt-neuf   twenty-nine
  vingt-quatre   twenty-four
  vingt-sept   twenty-seven
  vingt-six   twenty-six
  vingt-trois   twenty-three
violet(te)   purple
virage, le   curve, turn
virus, le   virus
visa, le   visa
visage, le   face
visibilité, la   visibility
visite, la   visit, tour
visiter   to visit (place)
vitamine, la   vitamin
vite   fast
  le/la plus vite   fastest
vitesse, la   speed, gear
vivre   to live
voici   here is, here are
voie, la   track (train), route, path
  voie de dégagement   private
  entrance
voilà   there is, there are ___ (when
  pointing)
voir   to see
  vois   (I) see
voiture, la   car, automobile

voiture-bar, la   buffet car
vol, le   flight
volaille, le   poultry
volant, le   steering wheel
vol-au-vent, le   creamed meat in puff
  pastry shell
voleur, le   thief
votre   your (formal, plural)
  À la vôtre!   to you! cheers!
voudrais ___, Je   I would like ___
vouloir   to wish, to want
vous   you (formal or plural)
  Vous êtes prêt?   Are you ready?
  Vous (me) permettez?   May I?
voyage, le   trip
voyager   to travel
voyageur, le   traveler
  voyez!   (you) see!
vrai(e)   true
vraiment   really
vue, la   view
wagon, le   railroad car
  wagon-lit   sleeping car
  wagon-restaurant   restaurant car
WC, les *m*   toilet
Wi-Fi, le   Wi-Fi
xérès, le   sherry
y   there
yeux, les (m pl)   eyes
yoga, le   yoga
yoghourt, le   yogurt
zappeur, le   TV remote control
zéro   zero
zone, la   zone
  zone bleue   blue zone (= 1½
  hours free parking with disk)
  zone piétonne   pedestrian zone
zoo, le   zoo

English-French Dictionary

How to use this dictionary

The purpose of this dictionary is to help you find and pronounce the French words you will most likely need to communicate as a visitor in France.

English words are listed in bold. Most French verbs are listed in infinitive form; you will need to change them to get the *je* and *vous* forms. Some irregular verb forms are included, however.

a (letter) a *(ah)*

abbey abbaye, l' *f (ah-bay-ee)*

able to, to be pouvoir *(poo-vwahR)* + infinitive verb

  I am able to je peux *(zhuh puh)*

  we are able to nous pouvons *(noo poo-voh^n)*

  you are able to vous pouvez *(voo poo-vay)*

accept, to accepter *(ahk-sehp-tay)*

  Do you accept __? Acceptez-vous ___? *(ahk-sehp-tay voo ___?)*

accountant comptable, le *(koh^n-tah-bluh)*

admission entrée, l' *f (ah^n-tRay)*

  admission charge prix d'entrée, le *(pRee dah^n-tRay)*

  free admission entrée gratuite/libre *(ah^n-tRay gRah-tweet/lee-bRuh)*

admittance ticket billet, le *(bee-yay)*

adult adulte, l' *m/f (ah-dew^{p}lt)*

after après *(ah-pReh)*

afternoon après-midi, l' *m (ah-pReh mee-dee)*

  in the afternoon de l'après-midi *(duh lah-pReh mee-dee)*

aftershave, some de la lotion après-rasage *(duh lah loh-syoh^n ah-pReh Rah-zahzh)*

against contre *(koh^n-tRuh)*

ahead of avant *(ah-vah^n)*

air conditioning climatisation, la *(klee-mah-tee-zah-syoh^n)*

airmail, by par avion *(pahR ah-vyoh^n)*

airplane avion, l' *m (ah-vyoh^n)*

airport aéroport, l' *m (ah-ay-Roh-puhR)*

all, That's C'est tout. *(say too)*

allergic (to) allergique à *(ah-lehR-zheek ah)*

almond amande, l' *f (ah-mah^{n}d)*

alphabet alphabet, l' *m (ahl-fah-beh)*

also aussi *(oh-see)*

always toujours *(too-zhooR)*

am, I je suis *(zhuh swee)*

ambulance ambulance, l' *f (ah^n-bew^p-lah^{n}s)*

America Amérique, l' *f (ah-mayR-eek)*

anchovy anchois, l' *m (ah^n-shwah)*

and et *(ay)*

answer, to répondre *(Ray-poh^n-dRuh)*

  I answer je réponds *(zhuh Ray-poh^n)*

  you answer vous répondez *(voo Ray-poh^n-day)*

antacid alcalin, l' *m (ahl-kah-læ^n)*

antihistamine antihistaminique, l' *m (ah^n-tee-ee-stah-mee-neek)*

appetite appétit, l' *m (ah-pay-tee)*

  Good appetite! (=enjoy your meal) Bon appétit! *(buhn ah-pay-tee)*

appetizer hors-d'oeuvre, les *m (uhR-duh-vRuh)*

apple pomme, la *(puhm)*

  apple juice jus de pomme, le *(zhew^p duh puhm)*

April avril *(ah-vReel)*

architect architecte, l' *m/f (ahR-shee-tehkt)*

Are there __? Il y a __? *(eel yah __?)*

are, we nous sommes *(noo suhm)*

are, you vous êtes *(voo (z)eht)*

arm bras, le *(bRah)*
arrival arrivée, l' *f (ah-Ree-vay)*
arrive, to arriver *(ah-Ree-vay)*
　I arrive j'arrive *(zhah-Reev)*
　you arrive vous arrivez *(voo (z)ah-Ree-vay)*
artichoke artichaut, l' *m (ahR-tee-shoh)*
artist artiste, l' *m/f (ahR-teest)*
ashtray cendrier, le *(sah^n-dRee-ay)*
asparagus asperges, les *f (lay (z)ahs-pehRzh)*
aspirin, some de l'aspirine *f (duh lah-spee-Reen)*
asthma asthme, l' *m (ahsm)*
ATM distributeur (automatique/de billets), le *(dee-stRee-bew^p-tuhR [uh-tuh-mah-teek/duh bee-yay])*
ATM card carte de retrait, la *(kahRt duh Ruh-tRay)*
attention! Attention! *(ah-tah^n-syoh^n!)*
August août *(oot or oo)*
aunt tante, la *(tah^{n}t)*
　my aunt ma tante *(mah tah^{n}t)*
Australia Australie l' *f (oh-stRah-lee)*
　from Australia d'Australie *(doh-stRah-lee)*
Austria Autriche, l' *f (oh-tReesh)*
automatic transmission transmission automatique, la *(tRah^{n}s-mees-yoh^n uh-tuh-mah-teek)*
available libre *(lee-bRuh)*, disponible *(dees-puh-nee-bluh)*
　available rooms des chambres libres *(day shah^n-bRuh lee-bRuh)*
away, far loin *(lwæ^n)*; lointain *(lwæ^n-tæ^n)*
b b *(bay)*
baby bébé, le *(bay-bay)*
back dos, le *(doh)*
bacon lard, le *(lahR)*
bad mauvais *(moh-vay)*
bag sac, le *(sahk)*
bakery boulangerie, la *(boo-lah^n-zhRee)*
ballpoint pen stylo, le *(stee-loh)*
banana banane, la *(bah-nahn)*
Band-Aid ® pansement adhésif, le *(pah^{n}s-mah^n ah-day-seef)*
B and B chambre d'hôte, la *(shah^n-bRuh doht)*; gîte, la *(zheet)*
bank banque, la *(bah^{n}k)*
bar bar, le *(bahR)*

barber coiffeur, le *(kwah-fuhR)*
basketball shoes baskets, les *m (bahs-keht)*
bath bain, le *(bæ^n)*
bathing suit maillot de bain, le *(mah-yoh duh bæ^n)*
bathing trunks maillot de bain, le *(mah-yoh duh bæ^n)*; (Speedo-style) slip de bain, le *(sleep duh bæ^n)*
bathroom (public toilet) toilettes, les *f (twah-leht)*; (private) salle de bains, la *(sahl duh bæ^n)*
battery (elec.) pile, la *(peel)*; (car) batterie, la *(bah-tRee)*
be, to être *(eh-tRuh)*
　I am je suis *(zhuh swee)*
　we are nous sommes *(noo suhm)*
　you are vous êtes *(voo (z)eht)*
beans haricots, les *m (ah-Ree-koh)*
　broad beans fève, la *(fehv)*
　dried beans haricot sec, le *(ah-Ree-koh sehk)*
　green beans haricots verts, les *m (ah-Ree-koh vehR)*
bed lit, le *(lee)*
　double bed lit à deux places, le *(lee ah duh plahs)*
　an extra bed un lit supplémentaire *(æ^n lee sew^p-play-mah^n-tehR)*
　twin bed lit à une place, le *(lee ah ew^n plahs)*
beef boeuf, le *(buhf)*
　beef broth bouillon de boeuf, le *(boo-yoh^n duh buhf)*
beer bière, la *(byehR)*
　draft beer bière pression *(byehR pReh-syoh^n)*
before avant *(ah-vah^n)*
begin, to commencer *(kuh-mah^n-say)*
beige beige *(behzh)*
Belgium Belgique, la *(behl-zheek)*
better meilleur(e) *(may-yuhR)*
between entre *(ah^n-tRuh)*
bicycle bicyclette, la *(bee-see-kleht)*, vélo, le *(vay-loh)*
big grand(e) *(gRah^n / gRah^{n}d)*
bigger plus grand(e) *(plew^p gRah^n / gRah^{n}d)*
bike bicyclette, la *(bee-see-kleht)*; vélo, le *(vay-low)*
bird oiseau, l' *m (wah-zoh)*

birthday anniversaire, l' *m* (ah-nee-vehR-sehR)

bitter amer/amère (ah-mehR); aigre (food) (eh-gRuh)

black noir(e) (nwahR)

blood pressure, high hypertension l' *f* (ee-pehR-tah^n-syoh^n)

blouse chemisier, le (shuh-meez-yay)

blue bleu(e) (bluh)

boat trip promenade en bateau, la (pRuhm-nahd ah^n bah-toh)

book livre, le (lee-vRuh)

  bookstore librairie, la (lee-bReh-Ree)

bottle bouteille, la (boo-tehy)

  a bottle of une bouteille de __ (ew^{o}n boo-tehy duh __)

  a half-bottle of une demi-bouteille de __ (ew^{o}n duh-mee boo-tehy duh __)

boy garçon, le (gahR-soh^n)

  boyfriend petit ami, le (puh-tee (t)ah-mee)

bra soutien-gorge, le (soot-yæ^n-guhRzh)

bread pain, le (pæ^n)

  loaf of French bread baguette, la (bah-geht)

breakdown en panne (ah^n pahn)

breakfast petit déjeuner, le (puh-tee day-zhuh-nay)

bridge pont, le (poh^n)

broken cassé(e) (kah-say)

broth bouillon, le (boo-yoh^n)

brother frère, le (fRehR)

  my brother mon frère (moh^n fRehR)

brown (of objects) marron(ne) (mah-Roh^n); (of hair/eyes) brun(e) (bRuh^n/ bRew^{o}n)

burger hamburger, le (ah^n-booR-gehR)

burned brûlé(e) (bRew^o-lay)

bus bus, le (bew^{o}s)

businessman homme d'affaires, l' *m* (uhm dah-fehR)

businesswoman femme d'affaires, la (fahm dah-fehR)

but mais (meh)

butter beurre, le (buhR)

buy, to acheter (ahsh-tay)

'bye au revoir (oh Ruh-vwahR); à bientôt (ah byæ^n-toh)

c c (say)

cab taxi, le (tahk-see)

cabbage chou, le (shoo)

café café, le (kah-fay)

cake gâteau, le (gah-toh)

call, to appeler (ah-play)

  call__! Appelez __! (ah-play __!)

camera appareil photo, l' *m* (ah-pah-Rehy fuh-toh)

  camera shop magasin de photos, le (mah-gah-zæ^n duh fuh-toh)

can (= be able to) pouvoir (poo-vwahR) + infinitive verb

  Can I? Puis-je <u>verb infinitive</u>? (pweezh __?); Je peux <u>verb infinitive</u>? (zhuh puh __?)

  Can you? Pouvez-vous <u>verb infinitive</u> ? (poo-vay voo __?)

  I can Je peux <u>verb infinitive</u> (zhuh puh __)

  you can Vous pouvez <u>verb infinitive</u> (voo poo-vay __)

Canada Canada, le (kah-nah-dah)

  from Canada du Canada (dew^o kah-nah-dah)

candy, some des bonbons (day boh^n-boh^n)

cappuccino cappuccino, le (kah-poo-chee-noh)

car voiture, la (vwah-tew^{o}R)

carafe carafe, la (kah-Rahf)

  a carafe of __ une carafe de __ (ew^{o}n kah-Rahf duh __)

carbonated *f* gazeuse (gah-zuhz)

  non-carbonated *f* plate (plaht)

careful! Attention! (ah-tah^n-syoh^n!)

carpenter charpentier, le (shahR-pah^n-tyay)

carrot carotte, la (kah-Ruht)

cash du liquide (dew^o lee-keed); en espèces (ah^n (n)eh-pehs)

  in cash en liquide (ah^n lee-keed)

  cash card carte de retrait, la (kahRt duh Ruh-tReh)

  cash register caisse, la (kehs)

cashier caissier, le/cassière, la (keh-syay/key-syehR)

castle château, le (shah-toh)

cat chat, le (shah)

cathedral cathédrale, la (kah-tay-dRahl)

cauliflower chou-fleur, le (shoo-fluhR)

ceiling plafond, le (plah-foh^n)

center of town centre ville, le (sah^n-tRuh veel)

certainly bien sûr (byæ^n sew^{o}R)

chair chaise, la *(shehz)*
cheap bon marché *(boh^n mahR-shay)*
check, please! L'addition, s'il vous plaît. *(lah-dee-syoh^n, see voo play)*
checkout caisse, la *(kehs)*
checkroom vestiaire, le *(vest-yehR)*
Cheers! Santé! *(sah^n-tay)*
cheese fromage, le *(fRuh-mahzh)*
cherish, to chérir *(shay-ReeR)*
cherry cerise, la *(suh-Reez)*
chest poitrine, la *(pwah-tReen)*
chestnut marron, le *(mah-Roh^n)*
chicken poulet, le *(poo-lay)*
  chicken broth bouillon de poulet, le *(boo-yoh^n duh poo-lay)*
child enfant, l' *m/f (ah^n-fah^n)*
  my children mes enfants *(may (z)ah^n-fah^n)*
chocolate chocolat, le *(shuh-kuh-lah)*
choose, to choisir *(shwah-zeeR)*
Christmas Noël *m (nuh-ehl)*
church église, l' *f (ay-gleez)*
cider, alcoholic cidre, le *(see-dRuh)*
cigarettes, a pack of un paquet de cigarettes *(æ^n pah-kay duh see-gah-Reht)*
city ville, la *(veel)*
clean propre *(pRuh-pRuh)*
clear clair *(klehR)*
cloakroom vestiaire, le *(vest-yehR)*
clock horloge, l' *f (uhR-luhzh)*
close (location) près *(pReh)*
  close to here près d'ici *(pReh dee-see)*
closed fermé(e) *(fehR-may)*
clothes vêtements, les *(lay veht-mah^n)*; habits, les *m (lay (z)ah-bee)*
clothing store magasin de vêtements, le *(mah-gah-zæ^n duh vet-mah^n)*
cloudy, It's Il y a des nuages *(eel yah day nwahz)*
coat manteau, le *(mah^n-toh)*
coffee café, le *(kah-fay)*
  a coffee with cream un café-crème *(æ^n kah-fay kRehm)*
  a coffee with milk un café au lait *(æ^n kah-fay oh lay)*
  an iced coffee un café glacé *(æ^n kah-fay glah-say)*
  a strong, black coffee un café noir *(æ^n kah-fay nwahR)*

cola coca, le *(koh-kah)*
cold (temp.) froid(e) *(fRwah/fRwahd)*; (illness) un rhume *(æ^n Rew^o m)*
  cold cuts charcuterie, de la *(shahR-kew^o-tree)*; assiette anglaise, une *(ahs-yeht ah^n-glehz)*
color couleur, la *(koo-luhR)*
combined (as in the bill) ensemble *(ah^n-sah^n-bluh)*
come, to venir *(vuh-neeR)*
  I come Je viens *(zhuh vyæ^n)*
  we come nous venons *(noo vuh-noh^n)*
  you come vous venez *(voo vuh-nay)*
computer programmer programmeur/-euse, le/la *(pRuh-gRah-muhR/-muhz)*
computer scientist informaticien(ne), l' *m/f (æ^n-fuhR-mah-tees-yæ^n/-yehn)*
condom préservatif, le *(pRay-zehR-vah-teef)*
connection correspondance, la *(kuh-Ruh-spah^n-dah^ns)*
constipation constipation, la *(koh^n-stee-pah-syoh^n)*
cooked cuit(e) *(kwee/kweet)*
cookie biscuit, le *(bees-kwee)*
cool (temp.) frais *(fReh)*
corkscrew tire-bouchon, le *(teeR-boo-shoh^n)*
corn mäis, le *(mah-ees)*
corner coin, le *(kwæ^n)*
  around the corner après le coin *(ah-pReh luh kwæ^n)*
  on the corner au coin *(oh kwæ^n)*
cost, to coûter *(koo-tay)*
  How much does it cost? Combien ça coûte? *(koh^n-byæ^n sah koot?)*
cough drop pastille pour la toux, la *(pah-steey pooR lah too)*
cough syrup, some du syrop pour la toux *m (dew^o see-Roh pooR lah too)*; du sirop antitussif *m (dew^o see-Roh ah^n-tee-tew^o-seef)*
course (food) plat, le *(plah)*
cousin cousin/cousine, le/la *(koo-zæ^n/koo-zeen)*
  my cousin (masc.) mon cousin *(moh^n koo-zæ^n)*; (fem.) ma cousine *(mah koo-zeen)*
crab crabe, le *(kRahb)*
cream crème, la *(kRehm)*

cream puff choux à la crème, le *(shoo ah lah kRehm)*

cream puff dessert with ice cream and chocolate sauce profiteroles, des *(pRuh-fee-tRohl)*

credit card cartes de crédit, la *(kahRt duh kRay-dee)*

  with a credit card avec une carte de crédit *(ah-vehk ew°n kahRt duh kRay-dee)*

crêpe crêpe, la *(kRehp)*

croissant croissant, le *(kRwah-sah^n)*

Cross! Traversez! *(tRah-vehR-say)*

crossroads carrefour, le *(kahR-fooR)*

crudités (raw vegetables) crudités, des *f (kRew^o-dee-tay)*

cucumber concombre, le *(koh^n-koh^n-bRuh)*

cup tasse, la *(tahs)*

  a cup of __ une tasse de __ *(ew°n tahs duh __)*

currency devises, les *f (duh-veez)*

  currency exchange office bureau de change, le *(bew^o-Roh duh shah^{n}zh)*

customs douane, la *(dwahn)*

d d *(day)*

dance, to danser *(dah^n-say)*

danger! danger! *(dah^n-zhay)*

dark (color) foncé(e) *(foh^n-say)*

date (calendar) date, la *(daht)*

daughter fille, la *(feey)*

  my daughter ma fille *(mah feey)*

day jour, le *(zhooR)*

decaffeinated décaféiné(e) *(day-kah-fay-ee-nay)*

December décembre *(day-sah^n-bRuh)*

declare, to déclarer *(day-klah-Ray)*

  nothing to declare rien à déclarer *(Ryæ^n (n)ah day-klah-Ray)*

  goods to declare marchandises/ articles à déclarer *(mahR-shah^n-deez/ ahR-teek-luh ah day-Klah-Ray)*

decongestant décongestionnant, le *(day-koh^n-zhehs-tyoh-nah^n)*; décongestif, le *(day-koh^n-zhehs-teef)*

delay retard, le *(Ruh-tahR)*

deodorant déodorant, le *(day-uh-duh-Rah^n)*

department store grand magasin, le *(gRah^n mah-gah-zæ^n)*

departure départ, le *(day-pahR)*

descend, to descendre *(day-sah^n-dRuh)*

desire désirer *(day-zee-Ray)*

  You want? Vous désirez? *(voo day-zee-Ray)*

dessert dessert, le *(day-sehR)*

detour déviation, la *(day-vyah-syoh^n)*

diabetic diabétique *(dyah-bay-teek)*

diarrhea diarrhée, la *(dyah-Ray)*

diesel gas gasoil, le *(gahz-uhy/gahz-wahl)*; gazole, le *(gah-zuhl)*

direction of, in the en direction de __ *(ah^n dee-Rehk-syoh^n duh __)*

dirty sale *(sahl)*

dish (kind of food) plat, le *(plah)*

divorced divorcé(e) *(dee-vuhR-say)*

do, to faire *(fehR)*

  I do je fais *(zhuh feh)*

  you do vous faites *(voo feht)*

  we do nous faisons *(noo fuh-zoh^n)*

doctor médecin, le *(mehd-sæ^n)*

dog chien, le *(shyæ^n)*

door porte, la *(puhRt)*

double bed lit à deux places, le *(lee ah duh plahs)*

double room chambre à deux lits, la *(shah^n-bRuh ah duh lee)*

down, downstairs en bas *(ah^n bah)*

downtown centre ville, le *(sah^n-tRuh veel)*

dress robe, la *(Ruhb)*

drink, to boire *(bwahR)*

  not safe to drink non potable *(noh^n puh-tah-bluh)*

  safe to drink potable *(puh-tah-bluh)*

drink boisson, la *(bwah-soh^n)*

drive, to conduire *(koh^n-dweeR)*

driver's license permis de conduire, le *(pehR-mee duh koh^n-dweeR)*

drugstore (medicine) pharmacie, la *(fahR-mah-see)*; (sundry items) droguerie, la *(dRuh-gRee)*

duck canard, le *(kah-nahR)*

dumpling boulette de pâte, la *(boo-leht duh paht)*

e e *(uh)*

ear oreille, l' *f (uh-Rehy)*

early tôt *(toh)*

east (of), (to the) à l'est (de) *(ah lehst [duh])*

Easter Pâques *m (pahk)*

  on/at Easter à Pâques *(ah pahk)*

eat, to manger *(mah^n-zhay)*

egg oeuf, l' *m (uhf)* (les oeufs) *[lay [z]uh]*

eight huit *(weet)*

   eight hundred huit cents *(wee sah^n)*

eighteen dix-huit *(dee-zweet)*

eighty quatre-vingts *(kah-tRuh-væ^n)*

elbow coude, le *(kood)*

elevator ascenseur, l' *m (ah-sah^n-suhR)*

eleven onze *(oh^{n}z)*

email email, l' *m (ee-mehl)*

engineer ingénieur, l' *m (æ^n-zhay-nyuhR)*

England Angleterre, l' *f (ah^n-gluh-tehR)*

   from England d'Angleterre *(dah^n-gluh-tehR)*

English anglais *(ah^n-gleh)*

   Do you speak English? Parlez-vous anglais? *(pahR-lay-voo ah^n-gleh?)*

enjoy, to aimer *(eh-may)*

enough (of) assez (de) *(ah-say [duh])*

   not enough (of) pas assez (de) *(pah (z)ah-say [duh])*

entrance entrée, l' *f (ah^n-tRay)*

entrée (=Am. main course) plat principal *(plah præ^n-see-pahl)*

entry entrée, l' *f (ah^n-tRay)*

error erreur, l' *f (eh-RuhR)*

escalator escalier (mécanique/roulant), l' *m (ehs-kahl-yay [may-kah-neek/Roo-lah^n])*

espresso café-express, le *(kah-fay ehks-pRehs)*

euro cent centime, le *(sah^n-teem)*

euro dollar euro, l' *m (uhR-oh)*

evening soir, le *(swahR)*

   during the evening pendant la soirée *(pah^n-dah^n lah swah-Ray)*

   in the evening soir, le *(swahR)*

everything tout *(too)*

exchange, to échanger *(ay-shah^n-zhay)*

exchange office bureau de change, le *(bew^o-Roh duh shah^{n}zh)*

exchange rate cours de change, le *(kooR duh shah^{n}zh)*

excursion excursion, l' *f (ehks-kew^{o}R-syoh^n)*

excuse me excusez-moi *(ehks-kew~zay mwah)*; (="May I get past" or to get attention) Pardon! *(pahR-doh^n)*

exit sortie, la *(suhR-tee)*

expensive cher/chère *(shehR)*

express highway autoroute, l' *f (uh-tuh-Root)*

extra supplémentaire *(sew^o-play-mah^n-tehR)*

eye oeil, l' *m (uhy)* (les yeux—*yuh*)

   eyeglasses, some des lunettes *f (day lew^o-neht)*

f f *(ehf)*

face figure, la *(fee-gew^{o}R)*

facial tissue mouchoir en papier, le *(moosh-wahR ah^n pah-pyay)*

family famille, la *(fah-meey)*

   my family ma famille *(mah fah-meey)*

far(away) loin *(lwæ^n)*; lointain *(lwæ^n-tæ^n)*

   far away, how à quelle distance? *(ah kehl dees-tah^{n}s?)*

farmer fermier/-ière *(fehR-myay/-myehR)*

father père, le *(pehR)*

   my father mon père *(moh^n pehR)*

   Father's Day fête des pères, la *(feht day pehR)*

February février *(fay-vRee-yay)*

ferry ferry, le *(fay-Ree)*

fever fièvre, la *(fyeh-vRuh)*

fewer moins (de) *(mwæ^n [duh])*

fifteen quinze *(kæ^{n}z)*

fifty cinquante *(seh^n-kah^{n}t)*

fill up the tank Le plein, s'il vous plaît. *(luh plæ^n, see voo play)*

film, roll of pellicule, la *(peh-lee-kew^{o}l)*

fine (=OK) bien *(byæ^n)*

   Everything's fine Ça va *(sah vah)*

finger doigt, le *(dwah)*

finish, to finir *(fee-neeR)*

fire! Au feu! *(oh fuh!)*

   fire department pompiers, les *m (lay poh^n-pyay)*

first course entrée, l' *f (ah^n-tRay)*

first floor rez-de-chaussée, le *(Rayd-shoh-say)*

fish poisson, le *(pwah-soh^n)*

five cinq *(sæ^{n}k)*

   five hundred cinq cents *(sæ^n sah^n)*

fixed-price meal menu prix-fixe, le *(muh-new^o pRee feeks)*

flat plat(e) *(plah[t])*

flavor parfum, le *(pahR-fæ^n)*

flight vol, le *(vuhl)*

floor (of room) plancher, le *(plah^n-shay)*; (story of building) étage, l' *m (ay-tahzh)*
  first/ground floor rez-de-chaussée, le *(Rayd-shoh-say)*
  fourth floor troisième étage, le *(tRwah-zyehm ay-tahzh)*
  second floor premier étage, le *(pRuh-myeh [R]ay-tahzh)*
  third floor deuxième étage, le *(duh-zyehm ay-tahzh)*
foggy, It's Il y a du brouillard *(eel yah dew^p bRoo-yahR)*
food aliments, les *m ([z]ah-lee-mah^n)*
foot pied, le *(pyay)*
for pour *(pooR)*
forbidden défense de __ *(day-fah^ns duh __)*; __ interdite *(__ æ^n-tehR-deet)*
foreign étranger/ étrangerère *(ay-tRah^n-zhay/ ay-tRah^n-zhehR)*
fork fourchette, la *(fooR-shet)*
fortress forteresse, la *(fuhR-tRehs)*
forty quarante *(kah-Rah^nt)*
fountain fontaine, la *(foh^n-tehn)*
four quatre *(kah-tRuh)*
  four hundred quatre cents *(kah-tRuh sah^n)*
fourteen quatorze *(kah-tuhRz)*
fowl volaille, la *(vuh-lahy)*
France France, la *(fRah^ns)*
free (no cost) gratuit(e) *(gRah-twee[t])*; (available) libre *(lee-bRuh)*
freeway autoroute, l' *f (uh-tuh-Root)*
French fries frites, les *f (fReet)*
fresh frais/fraîche *(fReh/fRæsh)*
Friday vendredi *(vah^n-dRuh-dee)*
friend (male) ami *(ah-mee)*; (female) amie *(ah-mee)*
  my friend (female) mon amie *(moh^n [n]ah-mee)*
  my friend (male) mon ami *(moh^n [n]ah-mee)*
frog's legs cuisses de grenouille, les *f (kwees duh gRuh-nooy)*
from de *(duh)*
  from Australia d'Australie *(doh-stRah-lee)*
  from Canada du Canada *(dew^p kah-nah-dah)*
  from England d'Angleterre *(dah^n-gluh-tehR)*
  from the U.S. des États-Unis *(day [z]ay-tah [z]ew^p-nee)*

from. . . until de. . . à *(duh. . . ah)*
fruit fruit, le *(fRwee)*
  fruit juice jus de fruits, le *(zhew^p duh fRwee)*
full complet/complète *(koh^n-play/koh^n-pleht)*
g g *(zhay)*
game, wild gibier, le *(zhee-byay)*
garden jardin, le *(zhahR-dæ^n)*
gasoline essence, l' *f (ay-sah^ns)*
gas station station-service, la *(stah-syoh^n-sehR-vees)*
Germany Allemagne, l' *f (ahl-mah-nyuh)*
get off, to (bus, train) descendre du *(day-sah^n-dRuh dew^p)*
gift shop magasin de cadeaux, le *(mah-gah-zæ^n duh kah-doh)*
girl fille, la *(feey)*
  (my) girlfriend (ma) petite amie *([mah] puh-teet ah-mee)*
glass verre, le *(vehR)*
  a glass of __ un verre de __ *(æ^n vehR duh __)*
glasses (eye) des lunettes, *f (day lew^p-neht)*
glove gant, le *(gah^n)*
go, to aller *(ah-lay)*
  I go je vais *(zhuh veh)*
  we go nous allons *(noo [z]ah-loh^n)*
  you go vous allez *(voo [z]ah-lay)*
go! Allez! *(ah-lay)*
  go down! Descendez! *(day-sah^n-day)*
  go away! Allez-vous-en! *(ahl-ay-voo-zah^n!)*
God Dieu *m (dyuh)*
golden (color) doré(e) *(duh-Ray)*
good bon(ne) *(boh^n/buhn)*
goodbye au revoir *(oh Ruh-vwahR)*
good day! bonjour *(boh^n-zhooR)*
  Have a good day! bonne journée *(buhn zhooR-nay)*
good evening! bonsoir *(boh^n-swahR)*
  Have a good evening! bonne soirée *(buhn swah-Ray)*
good morning! bonjour *(boh^n-zhooR)*
good night! bonne nuit *(buhn nwee)*
goose oie, l' *f (wah)*
grandchild petit-enfant, le/la *(puh-tee-[t]ah^n-fah^n)*
  grandchildren petits-enfants, les *(puh-tee-zah^n-fah^n)*

my grandchildren　mes petits-enfants *(may puh-tee-zah^n-fah^n)*

granddaughter　petite-fille, la *(puh-teet-feey)*

my granddaughter　ma petite-fille *(mah puh-teet-feey)*

granddaughters　petites-filles, les *(puh-teet-feey)*

grandfather　grand-père, le *(gRah^n-pehR)*

my grandfather　mon grand-père *(moh^n gRah^n-pehR)*

grandmother　grand-mère, la *(gRah^n-mehR)*

my grandmother　ma grand-mère *(mah gRah^n-mehR)*

grandparent　grand-parent, le *(gRah^n-pah-Rah^n)*

grandparents　grands-parents, les *(gRah^n-pah-Rah^n)*

my grandparents　mes grands-parents *(may gRah^n-pah-Rah^n)*

grandson　petit-fils, le *(puh-tee-fees)*

my grandson　mon petit-fils *(moh^n puh-tee-fees)*

grandsons　petits-fils, les *(puh-tee-fees)*

grape　raisin, le *(Reh-zæ^n)*

grapefruit　pamplemousse, le *(pah^n-pluh-moos)*

gray　gris(e) *(gRee/gReez)*

green　vert(e) *(vehR/vehRt)*

green bean　haricot vert, le *(ah-Ree-koh vehR)*

green beans　haricots verts, les *(ah-Ree-koh vehR)*

green pepper　poivron vert, le *(pwah-vRoh^n vehR)*

grocery store　épicerie, l' *f (ay-pees-Ree)*

ground floor　rez-de-chaussée, le *(Rayd-shoh-say)*

guesthouse　pension, la *(pah^n-syoh^n)*

h　h *(ahsh)*

hairdresser　coiffeur, le/coiffeuse, la *(kwah-fuhR/kwah-fuhz)*

hair dryer　sèche-cheveux, le *(sehsh-shuh-vuh)*

half　demi(e) *(duh-mee)*

a/one half　un demi/une demie *(æ^n duh-mee/ew^n duh-mee)*

and a half　et demi/demie *(ay duh-mee)*

ham　jambon, le *(zhah^n-boh^n)*

toasted ham/cheese sandwich　croque-monsieur, le *(kRuhk muh-syuh)*

hand　main, la *(mæ^n)*

handbag　sac à main, le *(sahk ah mæ^n)*

has　a *(ah)*

hat　chapeau, le *(shah-poh)*

have, to　avoir *(ah-vwahR)*; (as in, to take) prendre *(pRah^n-dRuh)*

Do you have?　Avez-vous __? *(ah-vay-voo __?)*

I have　J'ai *(zhay)*

I don't have　Je n'ai pas de *(zhuh nay pah duh)*

we have　nous avons *(noo [z]ah-voh^n)*

you have　vous avez *(voo [z]ah-vay)*

I'll have　je prends *(zhuh pRah^n)*

you'll have　vous prenez *(voo pRuh-nay)*

have, Does it　Il y a __? *(eel yah __?)*

have to, to　devoir *(duh-vwahR)* + infinitive verb

I have to　je dois *(zhuh dwah)*

you have to　vous devez *(voo duh-vay)*

hazelnut　noisette, la *(nwah-zeht)*

he　il *(eel)*

head　tête, la *(teht)*

headache, a　mal de tête, un *(æ^n mahl duh teht)*

hear, to　entendre *(ah^n-tah^n-dRuh)*

I hear　j'entends *(zhah^n-tah^n)*

you hear　vous entendez *(voo [z]ah^n-tah^n-day)*

heart　cœur, le *(kuhR)*

I have a heart condition.　Je souffre du cœur. *(zhuh soo-fRuh dew^o kuhR)*

heating　chauffage, le *(shoh-fahzh)*

hello　bonjour *(boh^n-zhooR)*

help, to　aider *(eh-day)*

help!　Au secours! *(oh suh-kooR!)*

her　son/sa *(soh^n/sah)*

here　ici *(ee-see)*

here is　Voici __. *(vwah-see __)*

hi　salut *(sah-lew^o)*

high　haut(e) *(oh[t])*

high blood pressure　hypertension, l' *f (ee-pehR-tah^n-syoh^n)*

highway　autoroute, l' *f (uh-tuh-Root)*

his　son/sa *(soh^n/sah)*

honey miel, le *(myehl)*
hospital hôpital, l' *m (oh-pee-tahl)*
hot chaud(e) *(shoh[d])*
  hot chocolate chocolat (chaud), le *(shuh-kuh-lah [shoh])*
hotel hôtel, l' *m (oh-tehl)*
hour heure, l' *f (uhR)*
house maison, la *(meh-zoh^n)*
  housewife femme au foyer, la *(fahm oh fwah-yay)*
  house specialty spécialité de la maison, la *(spay-syah-lee-tay duh lah meh-zoh^n)*
  house wine vin ordinaire, le *(væ^n uhR-dee-nehR)*
how comment? *(kuh-mah^n?)*
  How are you? Comment allez-vous? *(kuh-mah^n [t]ah-lay voo?)*
  How's it going? Ça va? *(sah vah?)*
how far away à quelle distance? *(ah kehl dees-tah^{n}s?)*
how long (=duration) Depuis combien de temps? *(duh-pwee koh^n-byæ^n duh tah^n?)*; (=since what point in time?) depuis quand? *(duh-pwee kah^n?)*
how many combien (de)? *(koh^n-byæ^n [duh])*
how much combien (de)? *(koh^n-byæ^n [duh])*
  How much does it cost? Combien ça coûte? *(koh^n-byæ^n sah koot?)*
hundred, (a/one) cent *(sah^n)*
hurt, to (someone/something) faire mal (à) *(fehR mahl [ah])*; (=to have a pain) avoir mal *(ah-vwahR mahl)*
  It hurts here. J'ai mal ici. *(zhay mahl ee-see)*
husband mari, le *(mah-Ree)*
  my husband mon mari *(moh^n mah-Ree)*
i i *(ee)*
I je *(zhuh)*
ice glace, la *(glahs)*
  ice cream glace, la *(glahs)*
  ice cube glaçon, le *(glah-soh^n)*
  iced tea thé glacé, le *(tay glah-say)*
identity card carte/pièce d'identité, la *(kahRt/pyehs dee-dah^n-tee-tay)*
immediately immédiatement *(ee-may-dyaht-mah^n)*
in (month) en *(ah^n)*; (=inside) dans *(dah^n)*

included compris(e) *(koh^n-pree[z])*
information renseignements, les *m (Rah^n-sehng-mah^n)*
inn auberge, l' *f (oh-behRzh)*
inside, on the intérieur, l' *m (æ^n-tayR-yuhR)*
insurance assurance, l' *f (ah-sew^p-Rah^{n}s)*
interior, on the à l'intérieur, l' *m (ah læ^n-tayR-yuhR)*
Ireland Ireland, l' *f (eeR-lah^{n}d)*
is est *(ay)*
  it's C'est *(say)*
  Is there? Il y a __? *(eel yah __?)*
Italy Italie, l' *f (ee-tah-lee)*
it's C'est *(say)*
j j *(zhee)*
jacket veste, la *(vehst)*
jam confiture, la *(koh^n-fee-tew^{p}R)*
January janvier *(zhah^n-vyay)*
Japan Japon, le *(zhah-poh^n)*
jeans jean, le *(jeen)*
journalist journaliste, le/la *(zhuR-nahl-eest)*
juice jus, le *(zhew^p)*
  fruit juice jus de fruits, le *(zhew^p duh fRwee)*
  orange juice jus d'orange, le *(zhew^p duh-Rah^{n}zh)*
July juillet *(zhwee-yeh)*
June juin *(zhwæ^n)*
just a moment un moment *(æ^n muh-mah^n)*
k k *(kah)*
ketchup ketchup, le *(keh-tschup)*
key clé, la *(klay)*
kiss bise, la *(bees)*
Kleenex® mouchoir en papier, le *(moosh-wahR ah^n pah-pyay)*
knee genou, le *(zhuh-noo)*
knife couteau, le *(koo-toh)*
know (people and places), to/to know (how) (+ infinitive) savoir *(sahv-wahR)*
  I know (how) je sais *(zhuh say)*
  you know (how) vous savez *(voo sah-vay)*
l l *(ehl)*
laborer ouvrier/ouvière, l' *m/f (oo-vRee-yay/oo-vRee -yehR)*
lady dame, la *(dahm)*
lamb agneau, l' *m (ah-nyoh)*
lamp lampe, la *(lah^{n}p)*
late tard *(tahR)*

lawyer avocat(e), l' *m/f (ah-voh-kah/ah-voh-kaht)*

leaded, high-octane gasoline
supercarburant, le *(sewᵖ-pehR-kahR-bewᵖ-Rahⁿ)*

leave, to partir *(pahR—teeR)*
I leave je pars *(zhuh pahR)*
we leave nous partons *(noo pahR-tohⁿ)*
you leave vous partez *(voo pahR-tay)*

leek poireau, le *(pwah-Roh)*

left gauche *(gohsh)*
to/on the left à gauche *(ah gohsh)*

leg jambe, la *(zhahⁿb)*

lemon citron, le *(see-tRohⁿ)*
lemonade citronnade, la *(see-tRuh-nahd)*

less moins *(mwæⁿ)*
less ___ mois de *(mwæⁿ duh ___)*

letter lettre, la *(leht-Ruh)*

lettuce laitue, la *(leh-tewᵖ)*

light lumière, la *(lewᵖ-myehR)*
light colored clair(e) *(klehR)*

lighter (for a cigarette) briquet, le *(bRee-keh)*

like, to aimer (bien) *(eh-may [byæⁿ])*
I (don't) like it. Je (ne) l'aime (pas). *(zhuh [nuh] lehm [pah])*
I would like je voudrais *(zhuh voo-dReh)*
we would like nous voudrions *(noo voo-dRee-yohⁿ)*
you (would) like vous voulez *(voo voo-lay)*
What would you like? Vous désirez? *(voo day-see-Ray?)*

liqueur digestif, le *(dee-jehs-teef)*

liquor store marchand de vin, le *(mahR-shahⁿ duh væⁿ)*

liter litre, le *(lee-tRuh)*

little petit(e) *(puh-tee[t])*
a little (of) peu (de) *(puh [duh])*

live in, to habiter *(ah-bee-tay)*

liver foie, le *(fwah)*

loaf of French bread baguette, la *(bah-geht)*

lobster homard, le *(uh-mahR)*

locker, luggage consigne automatique, la *(kohⁿ-seen-yuh uh-tuh-mah-teek)*

long long(ue) *(lohⁿ/lohⁿg)*

long? how (duration) combien de temps? *(kohⁿ-byæⁿ duh tahⁿ?)*; (since when) depuis quand? *(duh-pwee kahⁿ?)*

long way, a loin *(lwæⁿ)*

look! Regardez! *(Ruh-gahR-day!)*

look (at), to regarder *(Ruh-gahR-day)*
I look (at) je regarde *(zhuh Ruh-gahRd)*
we look (at) nous regardons *(noo Ruh-gahR-dohⁿ)*
you look (at) vous regardez *(voo Ruh-gahR-day)*

look for, to chercher *(shehR-shay)*
I look/am looking for je cherche *(zhuh shehRsh)*
we look/are looking for nous cherchons *(noo shehR-shohⁿ)*
you look/are looking for vous cherchez *(voo shehR-shay)*

looking
I'm just looking. Je regarde seulement. *(zhuh Ruh-gahRd suhl-mahⁿ)*

lot, a beaucoup *(boh-koo)*

loud/loudly fort *(fuhR)*; (noisy) bruyant(e) *(bRwee-yahⁿ([t])*

louder/more loudly plus fort *(plewᵖ fuhR)*

luggage bagages, les *m (bah-gahzh)*
luggage checkroom consigne, la *(kohⁿ-seen-yuh)*
luggage locker consigne automatique, la *(kohⁿ-seen-yuh uh-tuh-mah-teek)*

lunch déjeuner, le *(day-zhuh-nay)*

m m *(ehm)*

magazine magazine, le *(mah-gah-zeen)*

mailbox boîte aux lettres, la *(bwaht oh leht-Ruh)*

main square place principale, la *(plahs pRæⁿ-see-pahl)*

make, to faire *(fehR)*
I make je fais *(zhuh feh)*
we make nous faisons *(noo fuh-zohⁿ)*
you make vous faites *(voo feht)*

man homme, l' *m (uhm)*

manager directeur/-trice *(dee-Rehk-tuhR/-tRees)*

map carte, la *(kahRt)*
a city map plan de ville, le *(plahⁿ duh veel)*
a road map carte routière, la *(kahRt Roo-tyehR)*

March mars *(mahRs)*

market marché, le *(mahR-shay)*
married marié(e) *(mahR-yay)*
match(stick) allumette, l' *f (ah-lew^o-meht)*
may (=be able to)
  may I? Puis-je __? *(pweezh __?)*
  may you/you may __ vous
  pouvez __ *(voo poo-vay)*
  may we/we may __ nous
  pouvons __ *(noo poo-voh^n)*
May mai *(may)*
maybe peut-être *(puh-teh-tRuh)*
mayonnaise mayonnaise, la *(mah-yoh-nehz)*
meal repas, le *(Ruh-pah)*
meat viande, la *(vyah^nd)*
  meatball boulette, la *(boo-let)*
  meat dish plat de viande, le *(plah duh vyah^nd)*
mechanic mécanicien(ne) *(may-kah-nee-syæ^n/-syehn)*
medication médicaments, les *m (may-dee-kah-mah^n)*
medicine (for) médicament (pour), le *(may-dee-kah-mah^n [poor])*
medium moyen (size) *(mwah-yæ^n)*
  medium rare à point *(ah pwæ^n)*
men's room hommes, les *m (lay [z]uhm)*
menu carte, la *(kahRt)*
  daily special plat du jour, le *(plah dew^o zhooR)*
  fixed-price menu menu prix-fixe, le *(muh-new^o pRee feeks)*
middle, in the au milieu *(oh meel-yuh)*
midnight minuit *m (meen-wee)*
mild (cheese) maigre *(meh-gRuh)*
milk lait, le *(lay)*
  milkshake frappé, le *(fRah-pay)*
million, a un million *(æ^n meel-yoh^n)*
mineral water eau minérale, l' *f ([l]oh mee-nay-Rahl)*
minister pasteur, le *(pahs-tuhR)*
minus moins *(mwæ^n)*
minute minute, la *(mee-new^ot)*
miss (young woman) mademoiselle, la *(mahd-mwah-zehl)*
mistake erreur, l' *f (eh-RuhR)*
moment, (just a) un moment *(æ^n muh-mah^n)*
Monday lundi *(læ^n-dee)*
money argent, l' *m (ahR-zhah^n)*

month mois, le *(mwah)*
more plus *(plew^os)*
morning matin, le *(mah-tæ^n)*
mother mère, la *(mehR)*
  my mother ma mère *(mah mehR)*
  Mother's Day fête des mères, la *(feht day mehR)*
motorcycle moto, la *(moh-toh)*
mousse mousse, la *(moos)*
mouth bouche, la *(boosh)*
much beaucoup *(boh-koo)*
museum musée, le *(mew^o-zay)*
mushroom champignon, le *(shah^n-pee-nyoh^n)*
musician musicien(ne), le/la *(mew^o-zee-syæ^n/-syehn)*
must devoir + infinitive verb *(duh-vwahR)*
  I must je dois *(zhuh dwah)*
  you must vous devez *(voo duh-vay)*
mustard moutarde, la *(moo-tahRd)*
my mon (sing., masc.) *(moh^n)*; (sing., fem.) ma *(mah)*; (pl.) mes *(may)*

n n *(ehn)*
name nom, le *(noh^n)*
  What is your name? Comment vous appelez-vous? *(kuh^n-mah^n voo [z]ah-play voo?)*
  My name is __. Je m'appelle __. *(zhuh mah-pehl __)*
napkin serviette, la *(sehR-vyeht)*
near proche *(pRuhsh)*
neck cou, le *(koo)*
  necktie cravate, la *(kRah-vaht)*
need
  I need Il me faut __. *(eel muh foh __)*
  We need Il nous faut __. *(eel noo foh __)*
nephew neveu, le *(nuh-vuh)*
newspaper journal, le *(zhooR-nahl)*
  an American newspaper journal américain, un *(æ^n zhooR-nahl ah-may-Ree-kæ^n)*
  an English newspaper journal anglais, un *(æ^n zhooR-nahl ah^n-gleh)*
newstand kiosque à journaux, le *(kyuhsk ah zhooR-noh)*
nice sympathique *(sæ^n-pah-teek)*; gentil(le) *(zhah^n-teey)*
niece nièce, la *(nyehs)*
night nuit, la *(nwee)*
nine neuf *(nuhf)*

nine hundred neuf cents *(nuhf sahⁿ)*

nineteen dix-neuf *(deez-nuhf)*

ninety quatre-vingt-dix *(kah-tRuh-væⁿ dees)*

no non *(nohⁿ)*

no __ défense de __ *(day-fahⁿs duh __)*; __ interdit(e) *(__æⁿ-tehR-dee[t])*

noisy bruyant(e) *(bRwee-yahⁿ[t])*

non-carbonated plate *(plaht)*

noon midi *(mee-dee)*

north (of), (to the) au nord (de) *(oh nuhR ([duh])*

nose nez, le *(nay)*

not ne (verb) pas *(nuh verb pah)*

November novembre *(noh-vahⁿ-bRuh)*

number numéro, le *(newᵖ-may-Roh)*

nun soeur, la *(suhR)*

nurse infirmier/infirmière, l' *m/f* *(æⁿ-feeR-myay/-myehR)*

nut noix, la *(nwah)*

o o *(oh)*

occupied occupé(e) *(uh-kewᵖ-pay)*

October octobre *(uhk-tuh-bRuh)*

of de *(duh)*

oil huile, l' *f* *(weel)*

OK d'accord *(dah-kuhR)*

  It's OK. C'est d'accord *(say dah-kuhR)*

old vieux/vieille *(vyuh/vyehy)*

  old part of town vieille ville, la *(vyehy veel)*

olive olive, l' *f* *(uh-leev)*

  olive oil huile d'olive, l' *(weel duh-leev)*

omelet omelette, l' *f* *(uhm-let)*

on sur *(sewᵖR)*

one un *(æⁿ)*

  one hundred cent *(sahⁿ)*

  one thousand mille *(meel)*

  one-way (traffic) à sens unique *(ah sahⁿs ewᵖ-neek)*; (ticket) aller simple *(ah-lay sæⁿ-pluh)*

onion oignon, l' *m* *(uh-nyohⁿ)*

only seulement *(suhl-mahⁿ)*

open (to be) ouvert(e) *(oo-vehR[t])*

opera opéra, l' *f* *(oh-pay-Rah)*

or ou *(oo)*

orange (fruit) orange, l' *f* *(uh-Rahⁿzh)*; (color) orange *(uh-Rahⁿzh)*;

  orange juice jus d'orange, le *(zhewᵖ duh-Rahⁿzh)*

order, to place an commander *(kuh-mahⁿ-day)*

our (sing.) notre *(nuh-tRuh)*; (pl) nos *(noh)*

outside extérieur, l' *m* *(ehks-tayR-yuhR)*

overcoat manteau, le *(mahⁿ-toh)*

overcooked trop cuit(e) *(tRoh kwee[t])*

oyster huître, l' *f* *(wee-tRuh)*

p p *(pay)*

palace palais, le *(pah-lay)*

pants, pair of pantalon, le *(pahⁿ-tah-lonⁿ)*

paper papier, le *(pah-pyay)*

  toilet paper papier toilette, le *(pah-pyay twah-leht)*

pardon me! (sorry!) Pardon! *(pahR-dohⁿ)*

parent parent, le *(pah-Rahⁿ)*

  my parents mes parents *(may pah-Rahⁿ)*

park parc, le *(pahRk)*

  free parking area zone bleue, la *(zohn bluh)*

  parking disk disque de stationnement, le *(deesk duh stah-syuhn-mahⁿ)*

  parking lot parking, le *(pahRk-ing)*

  parking meter parcmètre, le *(pahRk-meh-tRuh)*

passport passeport, le *(pahs-puhR)*

  passport control contrôle des passeports, le *(kuhn-tRuhl day pahs-puhR)*

pasta pâtes, les *f* *(paht)*

pastry shop pâtisserie, la *(pah-tees-Ree)*

pay, to payer *(pay-yay)*

  How will you pay? Comment payez-vous? *(kuh-mahⁿ pay-yay voo?)*

  I'll pay __. Je paie __. *(zhuh pay __)*

pay attention! Attention! *(ah-tahⁿ-syohⁿ!)*

pea pois, le (les pois) *(pwah)*

peach pêche, la *(pesh)*

peanuts cacahuète, le *(kah-kah-weht)*

pear poire, la *(pwahR)*

pen stylo, le *(stee-loh)*

penicillin pénicilline, la *(pay-nee-see-leen)*

people personnes, les *(pehR-suhn)*

pepper poivre, le *(pwah-vRuh)*

perfume parfum, le *(pahR-fæⁿ)*

perfumery parfumerie, la *(pahR-few^{o}m-Ree)*

person personne, la *(pehR-suhn)*

pharmacy pharmacie, la *(fahR-mah-see)*

pheasant faisan, le *(fuh-zah^n)*

photo shop magasin de photos, le *(mah-gah-zæ^n duh fuh-toh)*

pictures, to take prendre des photos *(pRah^n-dRuh day fuh-toh)*

pie (open-faced) tarte, la *(tahRt)*

pink rose *(Rohz)*

plate assiette, l' *f* *(ahs-yeht)*

platform (train station) quai, le *(kay)*

please s'il vous plaît *(see voo play)*

Pleased to meet you. Enchanté(e). *(ah^n-shah^n-tay)*

plumber plombier, le *(ploh^n-byay)*

plus plus *(plew^{o}s)*

p.m. de l'après-midi *(duh lah-pReh-mee-dee)*

police, the police, la *(puh-lees)*

pop soda, le *(suh-dah)*

pork porc, le *(puhR)*

postage stamp timbre, le *(tæ^n-bRuh)*

postcard carte postale, la *(kahRt puhs-tahl)*

post office poste, la *(puhst)*

potato pommes de terre, la *(puhm duh tehR)*

poultry volaille, la *(vuh-lahy)*

prawns crevettes, les *f* *(kRuh-veht)*

prescription ordonnance, l' *f* *(uhR-duh-nah^{n}s)*

preservatives des agents de conservation *(day [z]ah-zhah^n duh koh^n-sehR-vah-syoh^n)*

press, to appuyer *(ah-pwee-yay)*

pretty joli(e) *(zhuh-lee)*

priest prêtre, le *(pReh-tRuh)*

professor professeur, le *(pRuh-feh-suhR)*

prohibited défense de __ *(day-fah^{n}s duh __)*; __ interdite *(__ æ^n-tehR-dee[t])*

pudding pudding, le *(poo-ding)*

whipped pudding mousse, la *(moos)*

pull, to tirer *(tee-Ray)*

pull! tirez *(tee-Ray)*

pullover pull-over, le *(pew^o-luh-vehR)*

purple violet(te) *(vyuh-leh/-leht)*

purse sac à main, le *(sahk ah mæ^n)*

push, to pousser *(poo-say)*

push! poussez *(poo-say)*

q q *(kew^o)*

quarter quart, le *(kahR)*

quiet calme *(kahlm)*

r r *(ehR)*

rabbit lapin, le *(lah-pæ^n)*

raining, It's Il pleut. *(eel pluh)*

rare (cooked meat) saignant(e) *(seh-nyah^n[t])*

raspberry framboise, la *(fRah^n-bwahz)*

rate of exchange cours du change, le *(kooR dew^o shah^{n}zh)*

raw cru(e) *(kRew^o)*

razor blade lame de rasoir, la *(lahm duh Rah-zwahR)*

ready prêt(e) *(pReh[t])*

receipt reçu, le *(Ruh-sew^o)*; (for fuel) ticket, le *(tee-kay)*

recommend, to recommander *(Ruh-kuh-mah^n-day)*

red rouge *(roozh)*

red wine vin rouge, le *(væ^n Roozh)*

regret, to regretter *(Ruh-gReh-tay)*

remote control (TV) zappeur, le *(zah-puhR)*

rent, to louer *(lway)*

repeat, to répéter *(Ray-pay-tay)*

reservation réservation, la *(Ray-zehR-vah-syoh^n)*

respond, to répondre *(Ray-poh^n-dRuh)*

restaurant restaurant, le *(Rehs-toh-Rah^n)*

retired retraité(e) *(Ruh-tRay-tay)*

rice riz, le *(Ree)*

right, (to/on the) (à) droite *([ah] dRwaht)*

right now (=immediately) tout de suite *(toot sweet)*

road route, la *(Root)*; chemin, le *(shuh-mæ^n)*

roll (bread) petit pain, le *(puh-tee pæ^n)*

roll of film pellicule, la *(peh-lee-kew^{o}l)*

room chambre, la *(shah^n-bRuh)*

available rooms des chambres libres *(day shah^n-bRuh lee-bRuh)*

rooster coq, le *(kuhk)*

round trip (ticket) (billet) aller-retour, (le) *([bee-yay] ah-lay-ruh-tooR)*

s s *(ehs)*

salad salade, la *(sah-lahd)*

green salad salade verte *(sah-lahd vehRt)*

mixed salad salade composée *(sah-lahd koh^n-poh-zay)*

sales (=bargains) soldes, les *m (lay suhld)*
salesperson vendeur/-euse, le/la *(vah^n-duhR/-duhz)*
sales receipt/slip ticket, le *(tee-kay)*
sales representative représentant(e), le/la *(Ruh-pRay-zah^n-tah^n[t])*
sales tax TVA, la *(tay vay ah)*
salmon saumon, le *(soh-moh^n)*
salt sel, le *(sehl)*
salty salé(e) *(sah-lay)*
sandal sandale, la *(sah^n-dahl)*
Saturday samedi *(sahm-dee)*
sauce sauce, la *(sohs)*
sausage(s) saucisse, la *(soh-sees)*; andouilles, l' *f (ah^n-dooy)*
school école, l' *f (ay-kuhl)*
scientist scientifique, le/la *(syah^n-tee-feek)*
scoop (ice cream) boule, la *(bool)*
Scotland Ecosse, l' *f (lay-kuhs)*
seafood fruits de mer, les *m (fRwee duh mehR)*
second seconde, la *(suh-goh^{n}d)*
secretary secrétaire, le/la *(suh-kRay-tehR)*
see voir *(vwahR)*
  I see je vois *(zhuh vwah)*
  we see nous voyons *(noo vwah-yoh^n)*
  you see vous voyez *(voo vwah-yay)*
self-employed, I'm Je travaille à mon compte *(zhuh tRah-vahy ah moh^n koh^{n}t)*
self-service libre-service *(lee-bRuh-sehR-vees)*
sell, to vendre *(vah^n-dRuh)*
  I sell je vends *(zhuh vah^n)*
  you sell vous vendez *(voo vah^n-day)*
separate séparément *(say-pah-Ray-mah^n)*
separated séparé(e) *(say-pah-Ray)*
September septembre *(sep-tah^n-bRuh)*
service service, le *(sehR-vees)*
  service charge service, le *(sehR-vees)*
set-priced meal menu à pix fixe, le *(muh-new^o ah pRee feeks)*
seven sept *(seht)*
  seven hundred sept cents *(seht sah^n)*
seventeen dix-sept *(dee-seht)*
seventy soixante-dix *(swah-sah^{n}t dees)*

shampoo shampooing, le *(shah^n-pwæ^n)*
sharp (flavor) piquant(e) *(pee-kah^n[t])*
shaving cream crème à raser, la *(kRehm ah Rah-zay)*
shirt chemise, la *(shuh-meez)*
shoe chaussure, la *(shoh-sew^{o}R)*
shorts short, le *(shuht)*
shoulder epaule, l' *f (ay-pohl)*
shower douche, la *(doosh)*
shrimp crevette, la *(kRuh-veht)*
sick, I'm Je suis malade. *(zhuh swee mah-lahd)*
sightseeing tour visite touristique, la *(vee-zeet too-Rees-teek)*
silver (metal) argent, l' *m (ahR-zhah^n)*; (color) argenté(e) *(ahR-zhah^n-tay)*
simple simple *(sæ^n-pluh)*
single (unmarried) célibataire *(say-lee-bah-tehR)*
  single room chambre à un lit, la *(shah^n-bRuh ah æ^n lee)*
sister soeur, la *(suhR)*
  my sister ma soeur *(mah suhR)*
six six *(sees)*
  six hundred six cents *(see sah^n)*
sixteen seize *(sehz)*
sixty soixante *(swah-sah^{n}t)*
skin peau, la *(poh)*
skirt jupe, la *(zhew^{o}p)*
slice tranche, la *(tRah^{n}sh)*
slow lent(e) *(lah^n[t])*
  slower plus lent(e) *(plew^o lah^n[t]*
slowly lentement *(lah^{n}t-mah^n)*
  more slowly plus lentement *(plew^o lah^{n}t-mah^n)*
small petit(e) *(puh-tee/-tee[t])*
smoking, no non-fumeur *(noh^n few^o-muhR)*
  a no-smoking section une zone non-fumeur *(ew^{o}n zohn noh^n few^o-muhR)*
snack bar snack-bar, le *(snahk-bahR)*; bar, le *(bahR)*; café, le *(kah-fay)*
snail escargot, l' *m (ehs-kahR-goh)*
snowing, It's Il neige. *(eel nehzh)*
soap savon, le *(sah-voh^n)*
  bar of soap savonette, la *(sah-vuh-neht)*
sock chaussette, la *(shoh-set)*
soda pop soda, le *(suh-dah)*
soft (cheese) à pâte molle *(ah paht muhl)*

soft drink soda, le *(suh-dah)*
something quelque chose *(kehl-kuh shohz)*
son fils, le *(fees)*
  my son mon fils *(moh^n fees)*
Sorry! pardon *(pahR-doh^n)*
  I'm sorry (=I regret) Je regrette *(zhuh Ruh-gReht)*
soup soupe, la *(soop)*; potage, le *(puh-tahzh)*
  soup of the day soupe du jour, la *(soop dew^p zhooR)*
sour aigre *(eh-gRuh)*
south (of), (to the) au sud (de) *(oh sew^{p}d [duh])*
Spain Espagne, l' *f* *(leh-spah-nyuh)*
sparkling wine vin mousseux, le *(væ^n moo-suh)*
speak, to parler *(pahR-lay)*
  Do you speak? vous parlez *(voo pahR-lay)*
  I speak je parle *(zhuh pahRl)*
  We speak nous parlons *(noo pahR-loh^n)*
special of the day (food) plat du jour, le *(plah dew^p zhooR)*
specialty spécialité, la *(spay-syah-lee-tay)*
spicy épicé(e) *(ay-pee-say)*
spinach épinards, les *m* *([z]ay-pee-nahR)*
spoon cuiller, la *(kwee-yehR)*
square place, la *(plahs)*
  main square place principale, la *(plahs pRæ^n-see-pahl)*
stadium stade, le *(stahd)*
stairway escalier, l' *m* *(ehs-kahl-yay)*
stamp timbre, le *(tæ^n-bRuh)*
starter (food) entrée, l' *f* *(ah^n-tRay)*
steak bifteck, le *(beef-tehk)*
  steak and fries steak frites *(stehk freet)*
stew ragoût, le *(Rah-goo)*
stomach estomac, l' *m* *(eh-stuh-mah)*
  stomach ache mal à l'estomac *(mahl ah leh-stoh-mah)*
stop! arrête! *(ah-Reht)*
store/shop magasin, le *(mah-gah-zæ^n)*
straight ahead tout droit *(too dRwah)*
strawberry fraise, la *(fRehz)*
street rue, la *(Rew^p)*
  streetcar tramway, le *(tRahm-weh)*
student étudiant(e), l' *m/f* *(ay-tew^p-dyah^n/-dah^{n}t)*

subway métro, le *(may-tRoh)*
sugar sucre, le *(sew^p-kRuh)*
suitcase valise, la *(vah-leez)*
Sunday dimanche *(dee-mah^{n}sh)*
sunglasses lunettes de soleil, les *f* *(lew^p-neht duh suh-lay)*
sunny, it's Il y a du soleil. *(eel yah dew^p suh-lehy)*
suntan cream crème solaire, la *(kRehm suh-lehR)*
suntan oil huile solaire, l' *f* *(weel suh-lehR)*
sun umbrella parasol, le *(pah-Rah-suhl)*
supermarket supermarché, le *(sew^p-pehR-mahR-shay)*
supper dîner, le *(dee-nay)*
suppository suppositoire, le *(sew^p-poh-zeet-wahR)*
sweater pull, le *(pew^{p}l)*
sweatshirt sweat-shirt, le *(sweht-shuhRt)*
sweet (adj) doux/douce *(doo/doos)*; (candy) bonbon, le *(boh^n-boh^n)*
swimsuit maillot de bain, le *(mah-yoh duh bæ^n)*
swim trunks (Speedo-style) slip de bain, le *(sleep duh bæ^n)*
Switzerland Suisse, la *(swees)*
t t *(tay)*
table table, la *(tah-bluh)*
take! prenez *(pRuh-nay)*
take, to prendre *(pRah^n-dRuh)*
  I/I'll take je prends *(zhuh pRah^n)*
  I'll take it take it. Je le/la prends. *(zhuh luh/lah pRah^n)*
  we/we'll take nous prenons *(noo pRuh-noh^n)*
  you/you'll take vous prenez *(voo pRuh-nay)*
tap water eau ordinaire, l' *f* *(loh uhR-dee-nehR)*
taxi taxi, le *(tahk-see)*
tea thé, le *(tay)*
  iced tea thé glacé *(tay glah-say)*
teacher professeur, le *(pRuh-feh-suhR)*
telephone téléphone, le *(tay-lay-fuhn)*
television télévision, la *(tay-lay-vee-zyoh^n)*
ten dix *(dees)*
thank you (very much) merci (beaucoup) *(mehR-see [boh-koo])*
that (object) ça *(sah)*; cela *(suh-lah)*
that's all c'est tout *(say too)*

then ensuite *(ah^n-sweet)*
there (location) là *(lah)*
there is Voilà ___. *(vwah-lah ___)*
think, to (believe) croire *(kRwahR)*
  I think that ___ Je crois que___ *(zhuh kRwah kuh ___)*
thirteen treize *(tRehz)*
thirty trente *(tRah^{n}t)*
this (object) ceci *(suh-see)*
thousand, a mille *(meel)*
three trois *(tRwah)*
  three hundred trois cents *(tRwah sah^n)*
throat gorge, la *(guhRzh)*
Thursday jeudi *(zhuh-dee)*
ticket billet, le *(bee-yay)*
tie cravate, la *(kRah-vaht)*
tip pourboire *(pooR-bwahR)*; service, le *(sehR-vees)*
tire pneu, le *(pnuh)*
tissue, facial mouchoir en papier, le *(moosh-wahR ah^n pah-pyay)*
to à *(ah)*
toast pain grillé, le *(pæ^n gRee-yay)*
tobacconist's shop tabac, le *(tah-bah)*
today aujourd'hui *(oh-zhooR-dwee)*
together (as in the bill) ensemble *(ah^n-sah^n-bluh)*
toilet toilette, la *(twah-leht)*
  toilet paper papier toilette, le *(pah-pyay twah-leht)*
toll (on road) péage *(pay-ahzh)*
tomato tomate, la *(tuh-maht)*
tomorrow demain *(duh-mæ^n)*
  day after tomorrow après-demain *(ah-pReh-duh-mæ^n)*
tonight ce soir *(suh swahR)*
tonsils amygdales, les *f* *([z]ah-mee-dahl)*
too trop *(tRoh)*
tooth dent, la *(dah^n)*
  toothpaste dentifrice, le *(dah^n-tee-fRees)*
touch, to toucher *(too-shay)*
tough dur(e) *(dew^{o}R)*
tourist information office office du tourisme, l' *m* *(uh-fees dew^o too-Reesm)*
town hall hôtel de ville, l' *f* *(oh-tehl duh veel)*
town square place principale, la *(plahs pRæ^n-see-pahl)*

traffic jam emboutillage, l' *m* *(ah^n-boo-tay-ahzh)*
train train, le *(tRæ^n)*
  train platform quai, le *(kay)*
  train station gare, la *(gahR)*
  train ticket billet, le *(bee-yay)*
tram tramway, le *(tRahm-weh)*
transmission transmission, la *(tRah^{n}s-mees-yoh^n)*
  with automatic transmission à transmission automatique *(ah tRah^{n}s-mees-yoh^n uh-tuh-mah-teek)*
travel, to voyager *(vwah-yah-zhay)*
traveler's check chèque de voyage, le *(shehk duh vwah-yahzh)*
trip voyage, le *(vwah-yahzh)*; excursion, l' *f* *(ek-skew^{o}R-syoh^n)*
tripe sausage andouille(tte), l' *f* *(ah^n-dooy/ah^n-doo-yeht)*
trout truite, la *(tRweet)*
T-shirt tee-shirt, le *(tee-shuhRt)*
Tuesday mardi *(mahR-dee)*
tuna thon, le *(toh^n)*
turkey dinde, la *(dæ^{n}d)*
twelve douze *(dooz)*
twenty vingt *(væ^n)*
twin bed lit à une place, le *(lee ah ew^{o}n plahs)*
two deux *(duh)*
  two hundred deux cents *(duh sah^n)*
u u *(ew^o)*
umbrella parapluie, le *(pah-Rah-plwee)*
uncle oncle, l' *m* *(oh^{n}kl)*
  my uncle mon oncle *(moh^n [n]oh^{n}kl)*
under sous *(soo)*
underpants slip, le *(sleep)*
understand, to comprendre *(koh^n-pRah^n-dRuh)*
  I understand Je comprends *(zhuh koh^n-pRah^n)*
  I don't understand Je ne comprends pas *(zhuh nuh koh^n-pRah^n pah)*
underwear, pair of slip, le *(sleep)*
unemployed au chômage *(oh shoh-mahzh)*
United States, the États-Unis, les *(lay [z]ay-tah [z]ew^o-nee)*
unleaded (gas) sans plomb *(sah^n ploh^n)*; SP95
until jusqu'à *(zhew^{o}s-kah)*
up en haut *(ah^n oh)*

USA États-Unis, les *(lay [z]ay-tah [z]ew^p-nee)* *(lay [z]ay-tah*
[z]ew^p-nee)
   from the U.S. des États-Unis *(day [z]ay-tah [z]ew^p-nee)*
   to the U.S. aux États-Unis *(oh (z)ay-tah-zew^p-nee)*

v v *(vay)*

vacant libre *(lee-bRuh)*

vanilla vanille, le *(vah-neey)*

veal veau, le *(voh)*

vegetable légume, le *(lay-gew^{p}m)*

vegetarian (person) végétarien(ne) *(vay-zhay-tah-Ryæ^n/Ryehn)*

venison chevreuil, le *(shuhv-Ruhy)*; venaison, le *(vuh-neh-zoh^n)*

very très *(tReh)*
   very much beaucoup *(boh-koo)*

vinegar vinaigre, le *(vee-neh-gRuh)*

visit, to (place) visiter *(vee-zee-tay)*

vomiting vomissement, le *(vuh-mees-mah^n)*

w w *(doo-bluh-vay)*

wait for, to attendre *(ah-tah^n-dRuh)*
   I'm waiting for j'attends *(zhah-tah^n)*
   Are you waiting for? vous attendez *(voo (z)ah-tah^n-day)*

waiter/waitress serveur, le *(sehR-vuhR)*/serveuse, la *(sehR-vuhZ)*

waiter! Monsieur! *(muh-syuh!)*

waitress! Madame!/Mademoiselle! *(mah-dahm! /mahd-mwah-zehll!)*

wall mur, le *(mew^{p}R)*

walnut noix, la *(nwah)*

want, to vouloir *(vool-wahR)*
   I want je veux *(zhuh vuh)*
   you want vous voulez *(voo voo-lay)*

warm chaud(e) *(shoh[d])*

warn, to avertir *(ah-vehR-teeR)*

Watch out! Attention! *(ah-tah^n-syoh^n!)*

water eau, l' *f* *(loh)*
   some water de l'eau *(duh loh)*

we nous *(noo)*

weak faible *(feh-bluh)*

weather temps, le *(tah^n)*

Web web, le *(web)*; toile Internet, la *(twahl æ^n-tehr-neht)*

Wednesday mercredi *(mehR-kRuh-dee)*

week semaine, la *(suh-mehn)*
   weekend fin de semaine, la *(fæ^n duh suh-mehn)*; week-end, le *(wee-kehnd)*

welcome! bienvenue *(byæ^n–vuh-new^p)*
   You're welcome. de rien *(duh ryæ^n)*; il n'y a pas de quoi *(eel nyah pah duh kwah)*

well bien *(byæ^n)*
   well-done/well-cooked (cooked meat) bien cuit(e) *(byæ^n kwee[t])*

west (of), (to the) à l'ouest (de) *(ah lwehst [duh])*

wharf quai, le *(kay)*

what quel(le) *(kehl)*
   What is that? Qu'est-ce que c'est? *(kehs-kuh say?)*

wheel roue, la *(Roo)*

when quand *(kah^n)*

where où *(oo)*
   where are Où sont __? *(oo soh^n __?)*
   where is Où est __? *(oo ay __?)*
   where from d'où *(doo)*

white blanc/blanche *(blah^n[sh])*
   white wine vin blanc, le *(væ^n blah^n)*

who qui *(kee)*

why pourquoi *(pooR-kwah)*

widowed person (woman) veuve, la *(vuhv)*; (man) veuf, le *(vuhf)*

wife femme, la *(fahm)*
   my wife ma femme *(mah fahm)*

window fenêtre, la *(fuh-neh-tRuh)*

windy, It's Il y a du vent. *(eel yah dew^p vah^n)*

wine vin, le *(væ^n)*
   house wine vin ordinaire, le *(væ^n uhR-dee-nehR)*; vin maison, le *(væ^n meh-zoh^n)*
   red wine vin rouge, le *(væ^n Roozh)*
   sparkling wine vin mousseux, le *(væ^n moo-suh)*
   white wine vin blanc, le *(væ^n blah^n)*
   wine list carte des vins, la *(kahRt day væ^n)*

with avec *(ah-vehk)*

without sans *(sah^n)*

woman femme, la *(fahm)*

women's room les femmes *(lay fahm)*

work, to travailler *(tRah-vah-yay)*

would like, I je voudrais *(zhuh voo-dReh)*

would like, we nous voudrions *(noo voo-dRee-yoh^n)*

write, to écrire *(ay-kReeR)*

Can you write it down for me?
Pouvez-vous me l'écrire? *(poo-vay voo muh lay-kReeR?)*

writing paper papier à lettres, le *(pah-pyay ah leht-Ruh)*

x x *(eeks)*

y y *(ee-gRehk)*

year an, l' *m (ah^n)*

yellow jaune *(zhohn)*

yes oui *(wee)*

yesterday hier *(yehR)*

day before yesterday avant-hier *(ah-vah^n-tyehR)*

yield céder le passage *(say-day luh pah-sahzh)*

you (formal) vous *(voo)*; (inf.) tu *(tew^o)*

your (sing.) votre *(vuh-tRuh)*; (pl.) vos *(voh)*

you're welcome de rien *(duh ryæ^n)*; il n'y a pas de quoi *(eel nyah pah duh kwah)*

z z *(zehd)*

zero zéro *(zay-Roh)*

Index

Order Form

Italian Survival Guide: The Language and Culture You Need to Travel with Confidence in Italy. 192-page paperback book.

French Survival Guide: The Language and Culture You Need to Travel with Confidence in France. 216-page paperback book.

See www.worldprospect.com for the latest list of products.

Shipping Information—*Please print clearly.*

Name _____

Address _____

City/State/Zip _____

Day phone _____

Email address _____

U.S. shipping and handling: $3 first item, $1 each additional item

_____ *Italian Survival Guide*, book   x $19.95 $_____

_____ *French Survival Guide*, book   x $19.95 $_____

Subtotal: $_____

Iowa addresses add 7% sales tax $_____

__1__ Shipping, 1st item*   x $3.00 $___3.00_____

_____ Shipping, additional items   x $1.00 $_____

_____ Priority mail   add $3 per order $_____

Order Total $_____

* Allow 2-3 weeks for delivery

Send with check to:
World Prospect Press, PO Box 253, Waverly, IA 50677

Survival Summary
Part Two

Transportation

a taxi	un taxi	$æ^n$ tahk-see
from. . . to	de . . . à	duh . . . ah
I get off here.	je descends ici	zhuh day-sah^n ee-see
a city bus	un bus	$æ^n$ bew^{p}s
a charter bus	un autocar	$æ^n$ (n)uh-tuh-kah$_R$
the entrance	l'entrée (f)	lah^n-t$_R$ay
the exit	la sortie	lah suh$_R$-tee
the subway	le métro	luh may-t$_R$oh
connection(s)	la corres-pondance	lah kuh-$_R$ehs-poh^n-dah^{n}s
the train	le train	luh t$_R$æ^n
train platform	le quai	luh kay
the ticket	le billet	luh bee-yay
the car	la voiture	lah vwah-tew^p_R
I would like to rent a car.	Je voudrais louer une voiture.	zhuh voo-d$_R$eh loo-ay ew^{p}n vwah-tew^p_R
I have a reservation.	J'ai une réservation	zhay ew^{p}n $_R$ay-zeh$_R$-vah-syoh^n
from . . . to	de . . . à	duh . . . ah
driver's license	le permis de conduire	luh peh$_R$-mee duh koh^n-dwee$_R$
plane flight	le vol	luh vuhl
airport	l'aéroport(m)	lah-ay-$_R$uh-puh$_R$

Services

public toilet	les toilettes	lay twah-leht
gentlemen	les messieurs	lay may-syuh
ladies	les dames	lay dahm
available	libre	lee-b$_R$uh
occupied	occupé	uh-kew^p-pay
ATM	le distributeur automatique	luh dee-st$_R$ee-bew^p-tuh$_R$ uh-tuh-mah-teek
bank	une banque	ew^{p}n bah^{n}k
telephone	un téléphone	$æ^n$ ^{n} tay-lay-fuhn
post office	la poste	lah puhst
stamp	le timbre	luh tæ^n-b$_R$uh
to the U.S.	aux Ètats-Unis	oh (z)ay-tah-zew^p-nee
by airmail	par avion	pah$_R$ ah-vyoh^n

Temperature Conversion Guide

1. Multiply the Celsius reading by 2.
2. Add 30, for approximate Fahrenheit temperature.

Numbers

0	zéro	zay-$_R$oh
1	un	$æ^n$
2	deux	duh
3	trois	t$_R$wah
4	quatre	kah-t$_R$uh
5	cinq	sæ^{n}k
6	six	sees
7	sept	seht
8	huit	weet
9	neuf	nuhf
10	dix	dees
11	onze	oh^{n}z
12	douze	dooz
13	treize	t$_R$ehz
14	quatorze	kah-tuh$_R$z
15	quinze	kæ^{n}z
16	seize	sehz
17	dix-sept	dee-seht
18	dix-huit	dee-(z)weet
19	dix-neuf	dees-nuhf
20	vingt	væ^n
21	vingt et un	væ^n tay $æ^n$
22	vingt-deux	væ^n-duh
33	trente- trois	t$_R$ah^{n}t-t$_R$wah
44	quarante-quatre	kah-$_R$ah^{n}t kah-t$_R$uh
55	cinquante-cinq	suh^n-kah^{n}t- sæ
66	soixante- six	swah-sah^{n}t-sees
77	soixante-dix-sept	swah-sah^{n}t-de seht
88	quatre-vingt-huit	kah-t$_R$uh-væ^n-weet
99	quatre-vingt-dix-neuf	kah-t$_R$uh-væ^n-dees-nuhf
100	cent	sah^n
101	cent un	sah^n $æ^n$
102	cent deux	sah^n duh
200	deux cents	duh sah^n
300	trois cents	t$_R$wah sah^n
400	quatre cents	kah-t$_R$uh sah^n
500	cinq cents	sæ^n sah^n
600	six cents	see sah^n
700	sept cents	seht sah^n
800	huit cents	wee sah^n
900	neuf cents	nuhf sah^n
1.000	mille	meel
2.000	deux mille	duh meel